IMAGES
of America

THE COLORADO FUEL AND IRON COMPANY

ON THE COVER: Wire fencing and shipping department workers are pictured in 1926. (Courtesy of Steelworks Center of the West.)

IMAGES
of America

The Colorado Fuel and Iron Company

Victoria Miller and Christopher Schreck

ARCADIA PUBLISHING

ISBN 978-1-4671-2708-0

Published by Arcadia Publishing
Charleston, South Carolina

Printed in the United States of America

Library of Congress Control Number: 2017959245

For all general information, please contact Arcadia Publishing:
Telephone 843-853-2070
Fax 843-853-0044
E-mail sales@arcadiapublishing.com
For customer service and orders:
Toll-Free 1-888-313-2665

Visit us on the Internet at www.arcadiapublishing.com

Contents

Acknowledgments

We would like to thank those who worked diligently to make this book happen. First and foremost, a thank-you goes to the board of directors of the Steelworks Center of the West for its support in allowing us to take time from our busy schedules to research and select photographs for the creation of this book. We would also like to thank Blake Hatton and Shelby Kissell for their skills at editing text and providing scanning support. We would also like to thank the Pueblo staff of EVRAZ Steel for allowing us to photograph on their property. Thank you, to Janet Boyd and Frank Yaklich for their editing skills and checking for accuracy regarding the technical captions and more recent historical facts throughout the book. Tom Cummins, thank you for your dedication and commitment to entering 65 years of Colorado Fuel and Iron publication data into a computer for easy retrieval. Your work entering thousands of names, dates, places, and events into a database will endure for many years to come. We would also like to thank professors Jonathan Rees and Fawn-Amber Montoya of Colorado State University–Pueblo for their scholarly research, social and cultural knowledge, and additions to the collective body of Colorado Fuel and Iron and industry-related research. We would also like to recognize former Colorado Fuel and Iron archivists Jay Trask and Bev Allen, archives technicians, Pueblo Community College and Colorado State University–Pueblo students, and volunteers for their efforts to preserve and organize this vast collection.

Finally, we would also like to thank our title manager at Arcadia Press, Stacia Bannerman, for her patience, guidance, and responses to our questions as we ventured through this project.

Unless otherwise noted, all images appear courtesy of the Steelworks Center of the West.

INTRODUCTION

As the West opened with railroad opportunities in the 1870s, William Jackson Palmer, a prominent railroad entrepreneur, envisioned a line traveling from Denver along the spine of the Rocky Mountains to Mexico to build profitable north-south trade. Palmer quickly realized that to make this vision possible, a local source of steel and iron was needed. Pueblo, a trading center 120 miles south of Denver, served as the steelmaking center due to its proximity to necessary natural resources. Pueblo shifted from a small trading community to an industrial capital when its first steel rail was produced in 1882.

It took thousands of employees to operate a massive company, and for decades, Colorado Fuel and Iron Company (CF&I) served as Colorado's largest private employer. The promise of work in the mill brought immigrant groups from around the county and globe to the West. The workers brought their families, creating incredibly diverse communities.

At the CF&I Steelworks, furnaces and support mills turned out hundreds of types of products for use in mining, construction, agriculture, and transportation. In addition to mining and steel facilities, the company also owned vast amounts of water rights along the Arkansas River. With their own hospital, company stores, and entertainment opportunities, employees' needs were met. News relating to company operations was available in *Camp and Plant*, the *Industrial Bulletin*, or the *CF&I Blast*, printed at various times during the company's history.

CF&I saw a period of dramatic growth and maintained a national presence following World War II. Hit hard by the collapse of the American steel industry in the 1970s and 1980s, the company filed for bankruptcy in the autumn of 1990. More than 130 years after Palmer's initial tap of steel, CF&I's legacy remains powerful throughout Southern Colorado.

All images in this book are from the collections of the Steelworks Center of the West, located in Pueblo, Colorado. Although CF&I was a major extractor of minerals in the region, the focus of this book will be on its steelmaking, medical, and administrative facilities. The company's Southern Colorado mining influence is highlighted in *The Mining Towns of Southern Colorado*, also published by Arcadia Publishing.

One

The Early Years

Retired Civil War general William Jackson Palmer first visited Colorado in the 1860s. Inspired by the expanding railroad market moving west, he envisioned a route for a railroad along the spine of the Rocky Mountains to build north-south trade. His ultimate goal was to connect Denver, Colorado, to the rich markets of Santa Fe, New Mexico, Texas, and eventually Mexico.

Palmer filed incorporation papers creating the Central Colorado Improvement Company with the Territory of Colorado on January 11, 1872. Set up on a vertically integrated business model, it controlled all the necessary resources to make steel, including land and water rights, transportation right-of-ways, and mining interests, in addition to the steelmaking facility. Palmer chose Pueblo for the steel mill because of its key geographic location near the necessary resources provided by his many other existing subsidiary companies: the Central Colorado Improvement Company, Southern Colorado and Coal Town Company, and the Colorado Coal and Steelworks Company. In 1880, these companies consolidated to form the Colorado Coal and Iron Company. In 1892, the Colorado Coal and Iron Company merged with its chief rival Colorado Fuel Company, creating the Colorado Fuel and Iron Company.

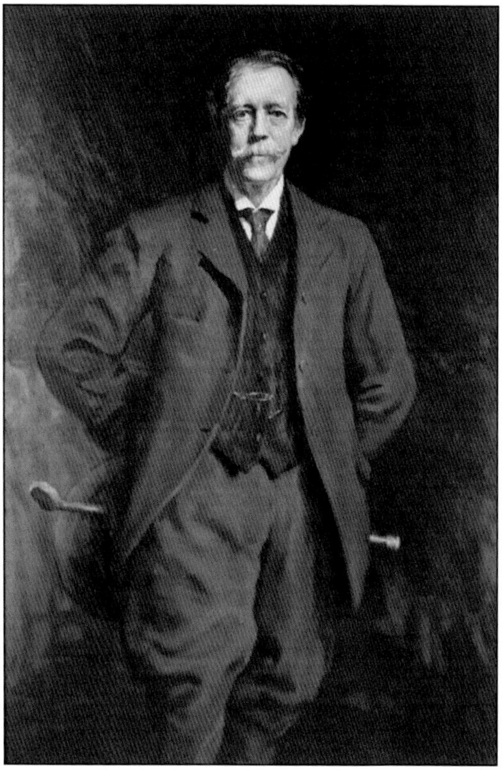

Gen. William Jackson Palmer envisioned an industrial utopia complete with facilities for producing steel rails for his Denver & Rio Grande Railroad, mining, and transportation systems to support the steelworks. In addition to his work in Pueblo, Palmer's generosity as a benefactor can be seen throughout Southern Colorado in schools, public libraries, parks, and walking trails. (From *Semi-Centennial History of the State of Colorado.*)

Eight men began excavating the first structures in 1880. As the labor force grew, clusters of makeshift homes blossomed around the construction area west of the furnace sites. Local residents named the settlement around the future steelworks in honor of the superintendent of construction, Col. W.W. Taylor. Taylorville remained the popular name until 1881, when the company insisted that the proper designation for the steel mill was Minnequa Steelworks.

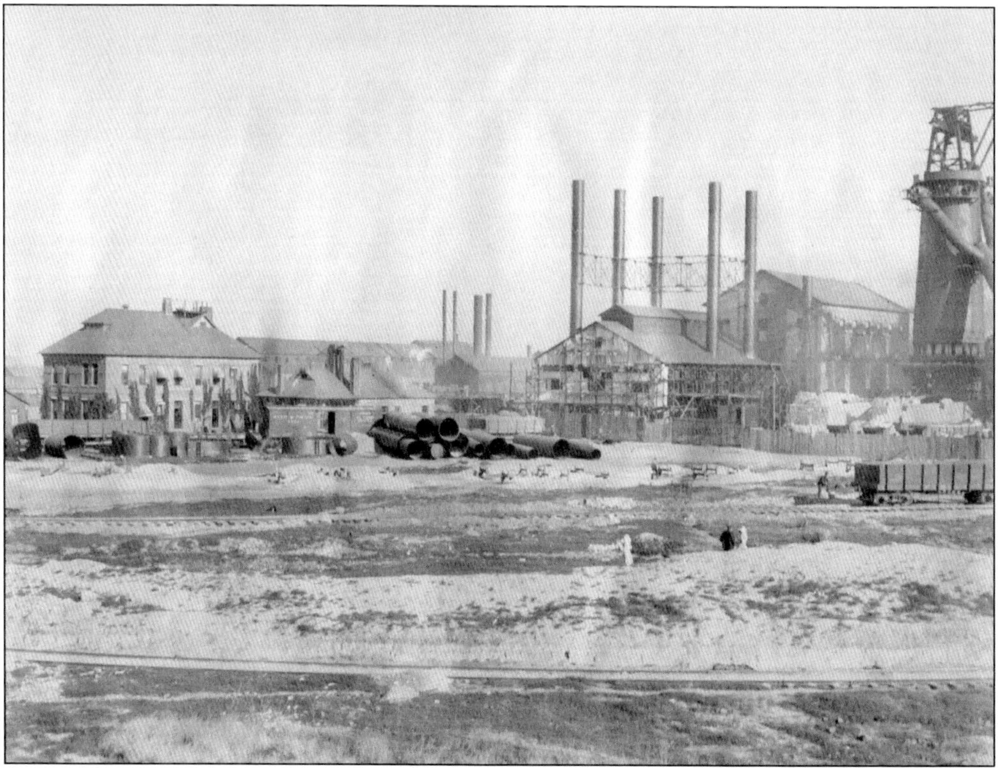

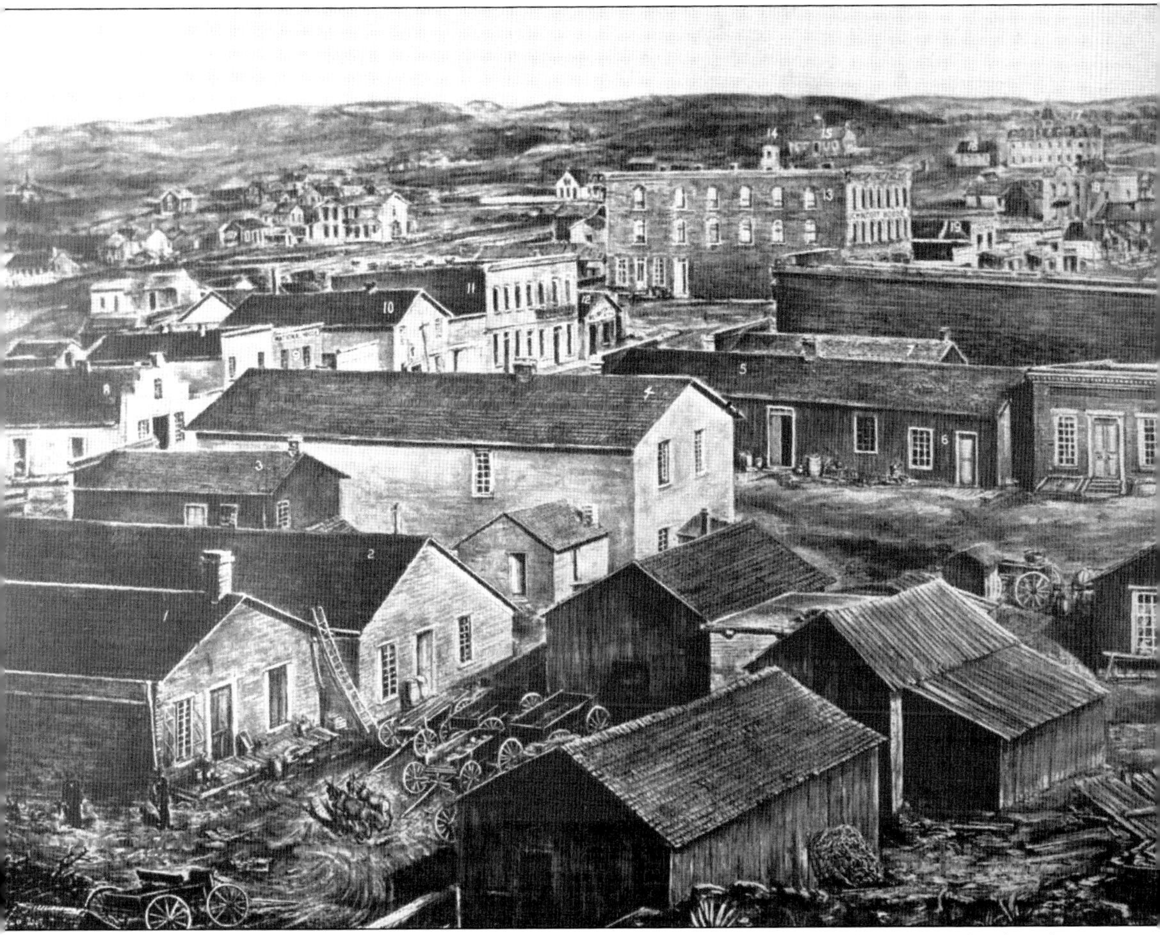

An 1872 view of Pueblo looks northwest from a hill east of Santa Fe Avenue between Third and Fourth Streets. Located in Southern Colorado, Pueblo lies at the confluence of the Arkansas River and Fountain Creek. Though first developed in 1859, Pueblo was formally incorporated in 1870, with the main industries concentrating on trade, ranching, and farming. When iron production began in 1880, Pueblo exploded from an agricultural town to a bustling industrial city. Pueblo was chosen to function as the steel empire due to its proximity to the necessary natural resources for steel production: coal mined in nearby Huerfano, Fremont, and Las Animas Counties; iron ore found 100 miles west in the San Luis Valley; limestone from about six miles south of Pueblo; and water via the St. Charles and Arkansas Rivers.

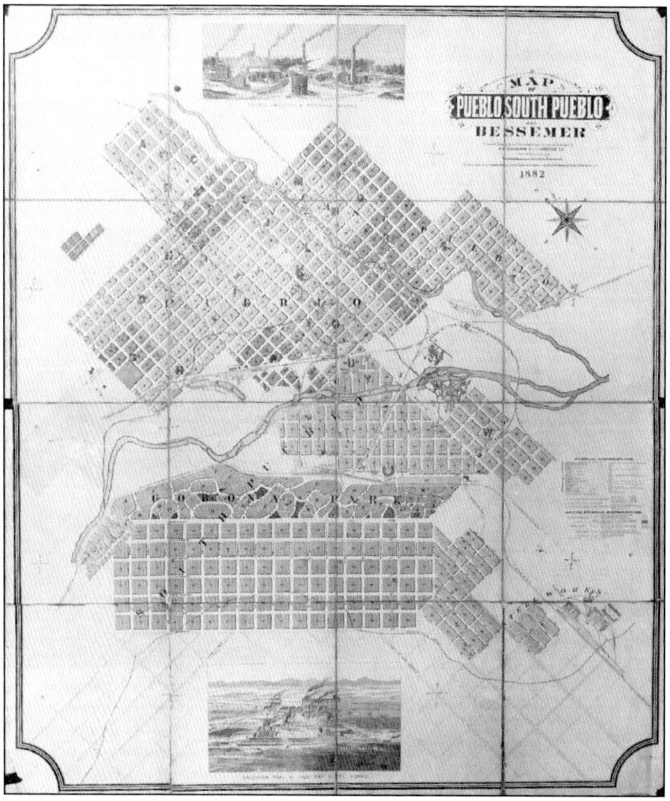

In 1886, Palmer developed the town of Bessemer, named after the steelmaking process, complete with homes for steelworkers and small businesses. Palmer, a utopian enthusiast, also plotted out the town of South Pueblo to house his Denver & Rio Grande Railroad workers. Today, these areas are part of the city of Pueblo.

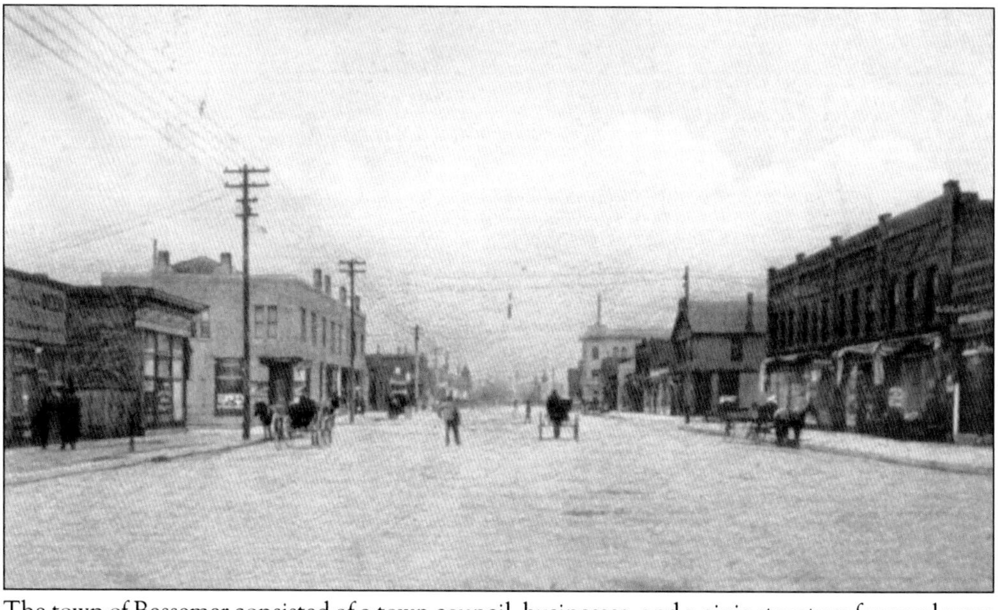

The town of Bessemer consisted of a town council, businesses, and a civic structure for employees at the steelworks. Northern Avenue still serves as a main thoroughfare. Bessemer survived independently until 1894, when it was annexed by Pueblo. Residents commonly refer to Bessemer as the business area of the neighborhood. Minnequa, from an American Indian word meaning "quiet waters," is the residential area.

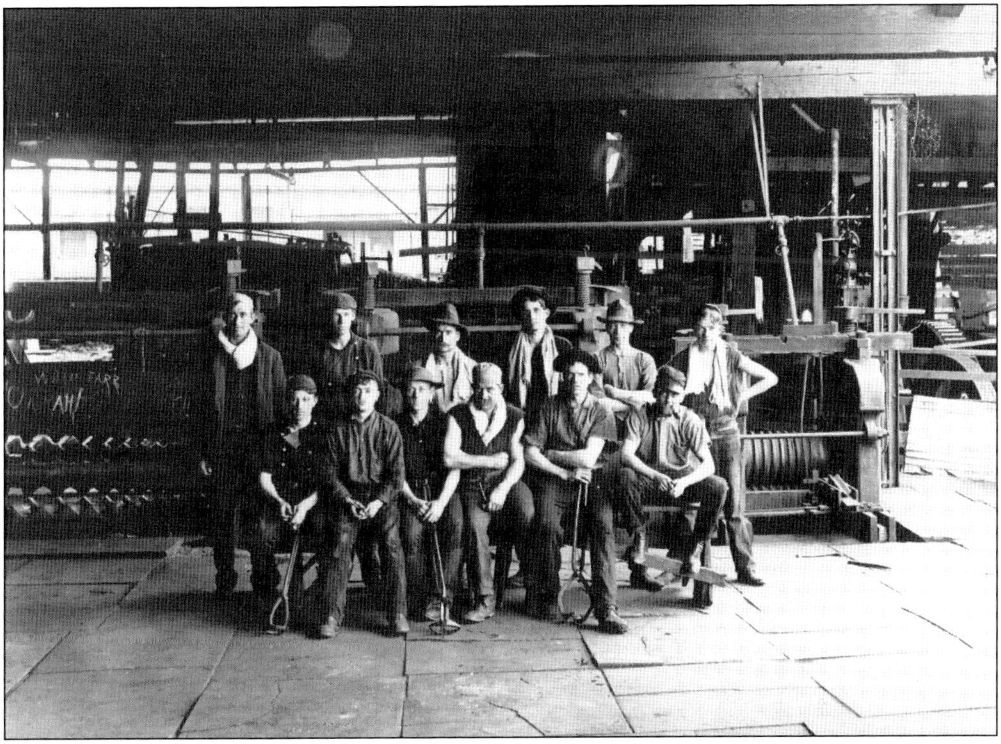

Workers pose at the rolling mill around 1890. Millions of immigrants from around the world migrated to the United States in the late 19th and early 20th centuries. In the first decade of the 20th century, company records documented more than 30 nationalities and more than 26 different languages spoken among employees. Most of the immigrants came from Mexico and southern, western, and eastern Europe.

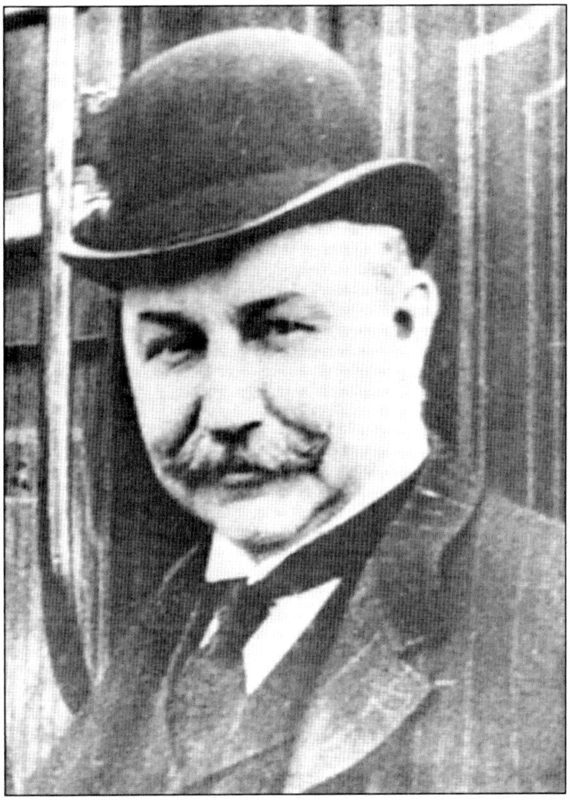

Born in Brooklyn, New York, John C. Osgood traveled to Colorado in 1882 to examine coal mines for the Chicago, Burlington & Quincy Railroad. He soon realized the potential value of Colorado's coal resources and decided to form his own company, the Colorado Fuel Company. It quickly became a major rival to Palmer's Colorado Coal and Iron Company, driving Palmer out and acquiring the assets in 1892.

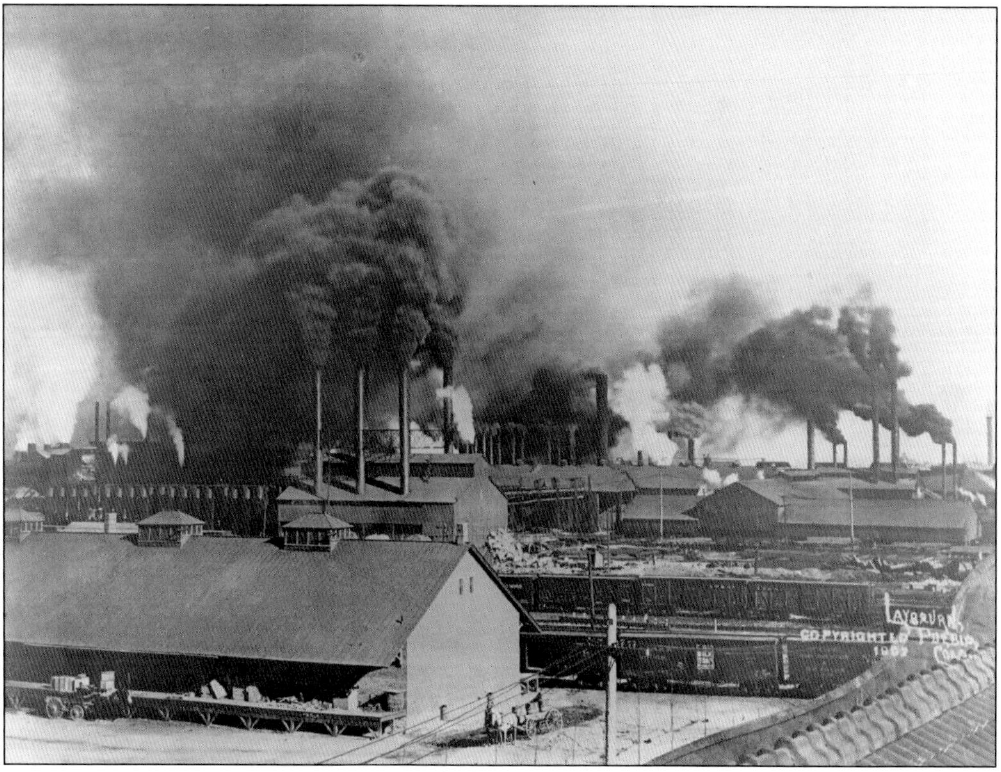

Black smoke belching from furnace stacks was a familiar sight in Pueblo during the days when soft coal was the principal source of heat. The smoke problem began to lessen with the use of natural gas in 1926 and was completely eradicated in the 1970s with the introduction of electric furnaces.

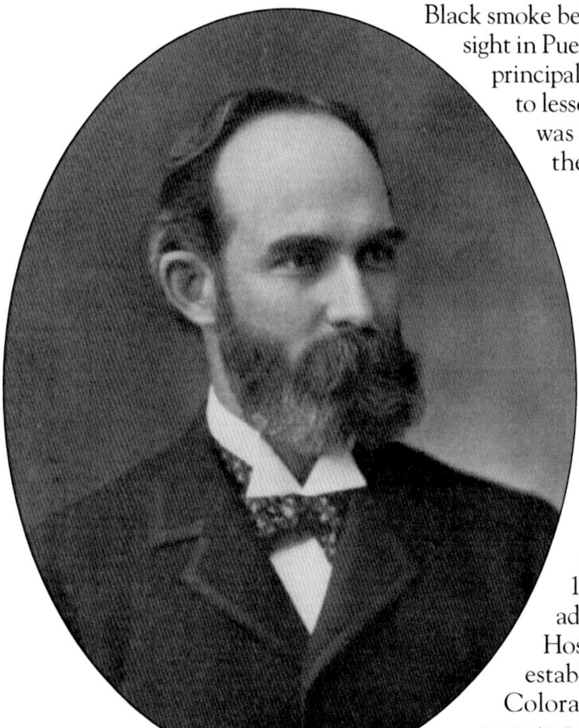

To care for its large workforce, the company hired Dr. Richard Corwin as chief surgeon in 1880, and he remained with the company until his death in 1929. He is credited with many medical advances, including establishing Minnequa Hospital and Minnequa Nursing School and establishing industrial sociology in Southern Colorado. Minnequa Hospital continues to operate today under the name St. Mary-Corwin Medical Center.

Established in 1899, the Minnequa School of Nursing educated more than 500 nurses during its 50-year existence. The three-year program instructed young women in both practical and theoretical medical principals relating to public health. Following graduation, the nurses' duties included assisting physicians with medical procedures, conducting welfare checks on employees and their families, and educating employees' wives about the benefits of exercise, clean water, and a balanced diet.

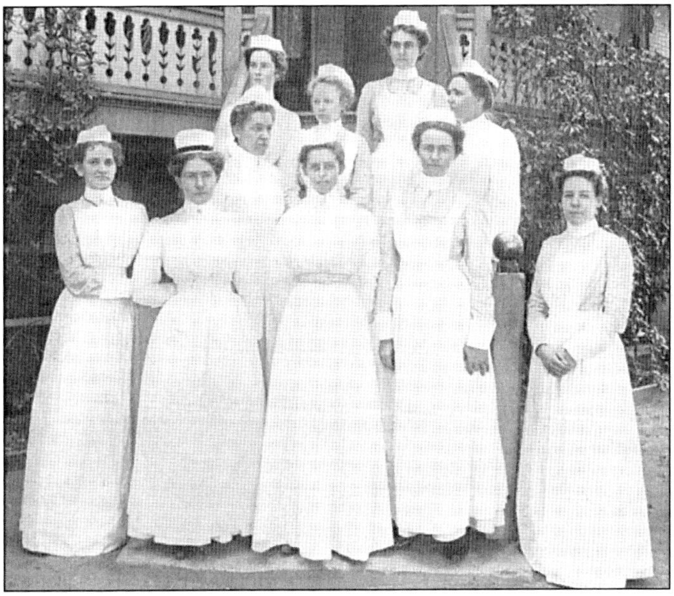

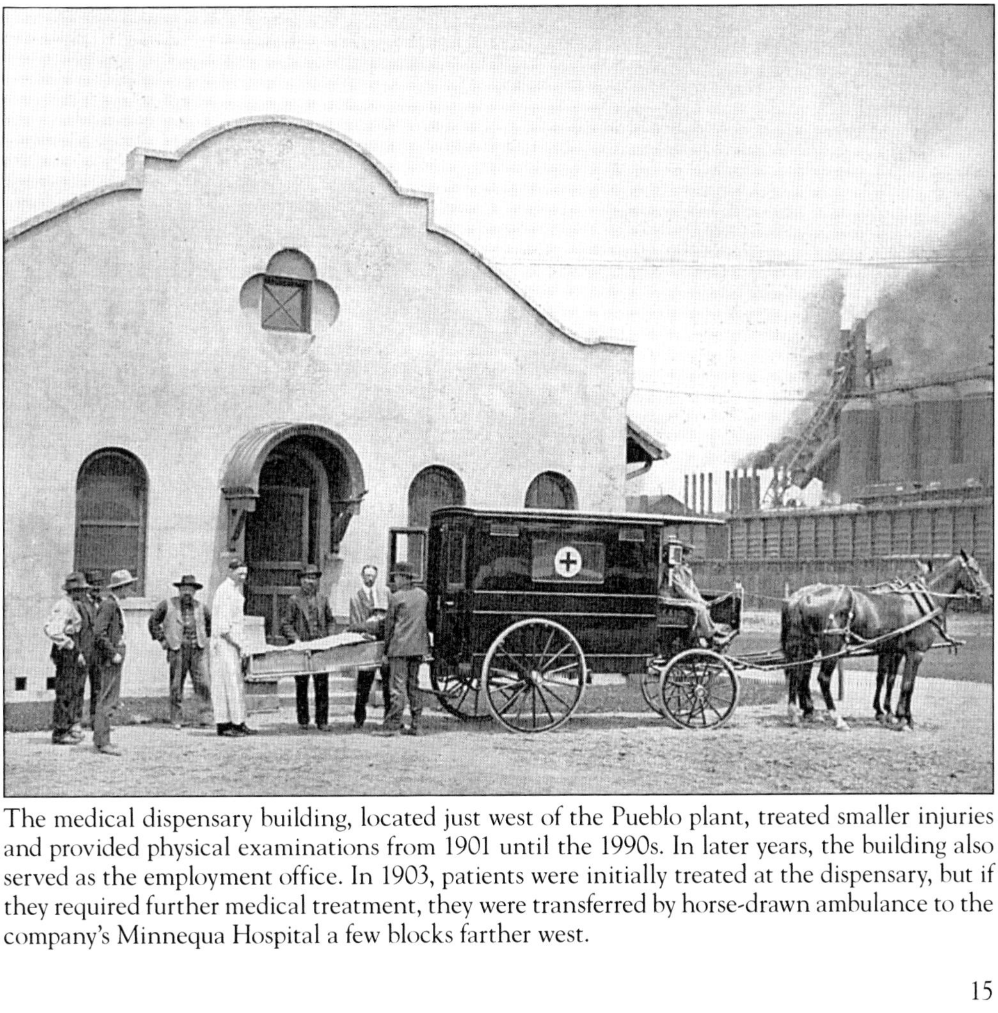

The medical dispensary building, located just west of the Pueblo plant, treated smaller injuries and provided physical examinations from 1901 until the 1990s. In later years, the building also served as the employment office. In 1903, patients were initially treated at the dispensary, but if they required further medical treatment, they were transferred by horse-drawn ambulance to the company's Minnequa Hospital a few blocks farther west.

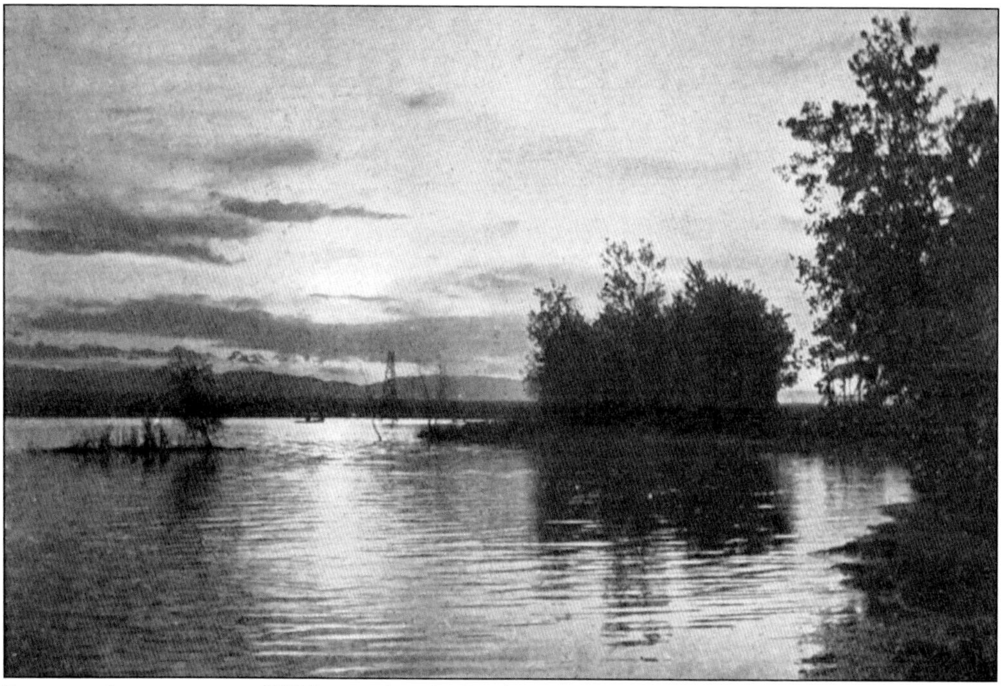

For more than a century, CF&I served as the Rocky Mountain region's largest private water rights owner. Drawn mainly from the Arkansas and St. Charles Rivers, the majority of the water was used for cooling purposes in the furnaces and various mills and for steam power in converters and condensers. In 1902, the steelworks consumed approximately 60 million gallons of water per day. Three man-made reservoirs stored water when not in use. In 1902, the Minnequa Amusement Association leased the property immediately surrounding Lake Minnequa, one of the reservoirs, and developed it into a resort and amusement park. Included in the plans were indoor and outdoor theaters, a boathouse, a dance pavilion, a roller coaster, and a carousel. Although the carousel has been moved from its original location, locals can still enjoy riding it today.

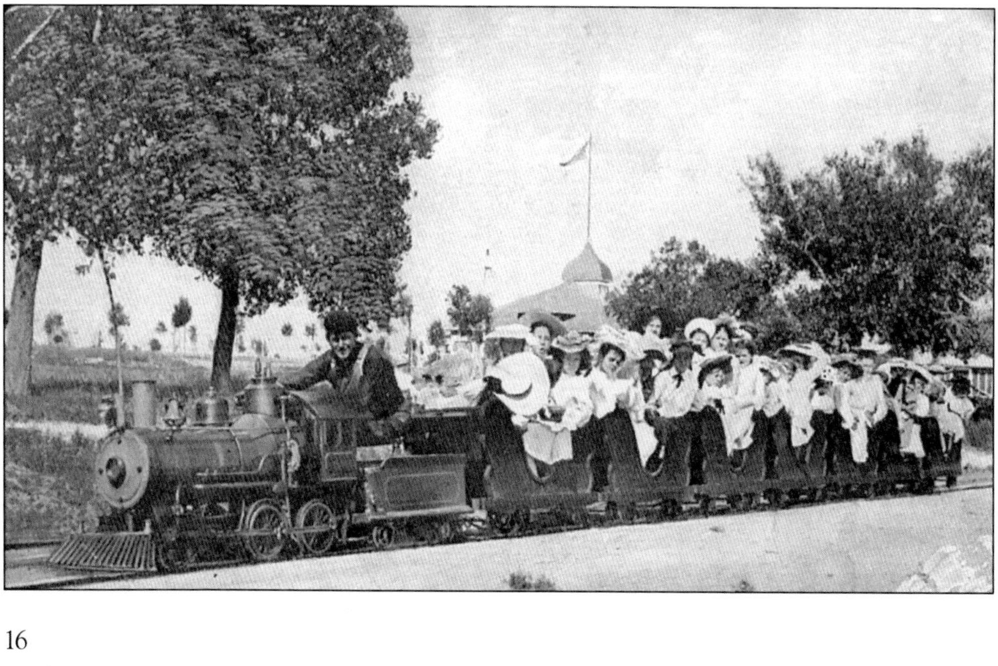

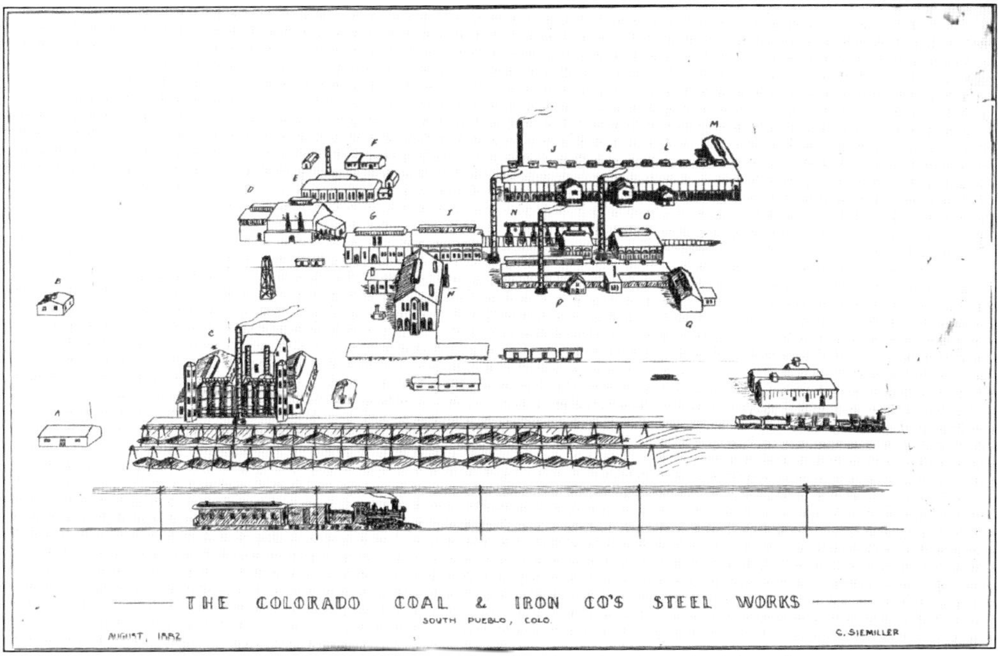

A schematic shows the buildings of the steelworks shortly after the blast furnace was put into production in 1882. Over the next century, the site would sprawl to encompass more than 600 acres.

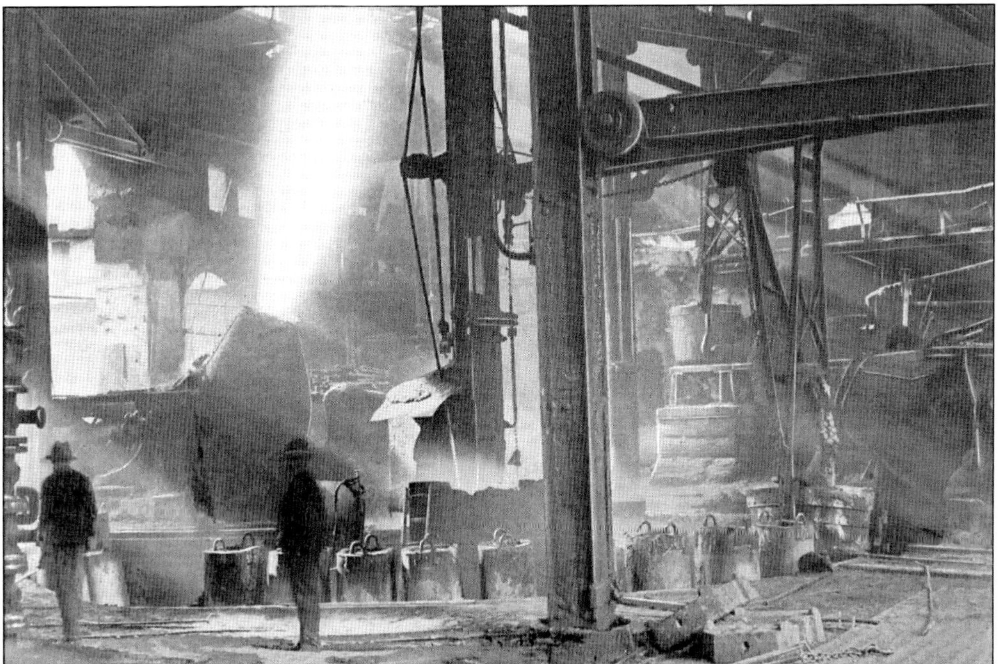

The air blast in this Bessemer converter burned off any impurities from pig iron, as shown by the flames shooting out of the top. The ingot molds into which molten steel is poured are shown in the center. This method was abandoned by the company in 1903 for a more advanced technology known as the open hearth process.

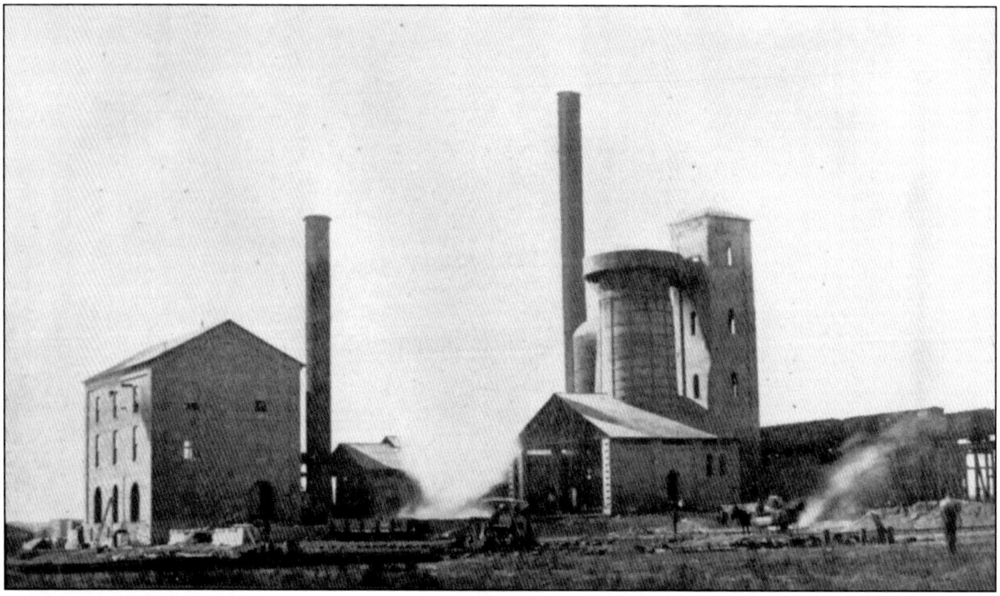

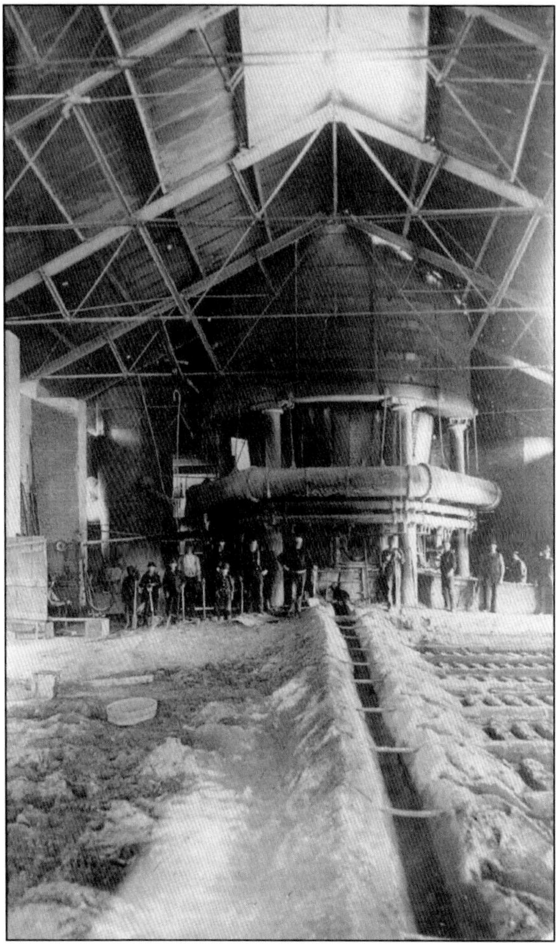

Excavation work on "Betsy," the company's first blast furnace (named after the superintendent's daughter), began in 1880, and it was "blown-in" during a formal ceremony on September 5, 1881. A blast furnace is a large furnace in which a mixture of limestone other minerals is added to melted pig iron for transformation into steel. Blasts of air are introduced into the furnace, increasing the temperature, which causes chemical reactions to occur.

A sand runner down the center of the photograph awaits the first tap of pig iron from the first blast furnace's caster house in 1881. On the right are sand molds for making pigs, or transferable blocks of iron, which were taken to another furnace to be refined into steel. Workers were both adults and children, as seen here.

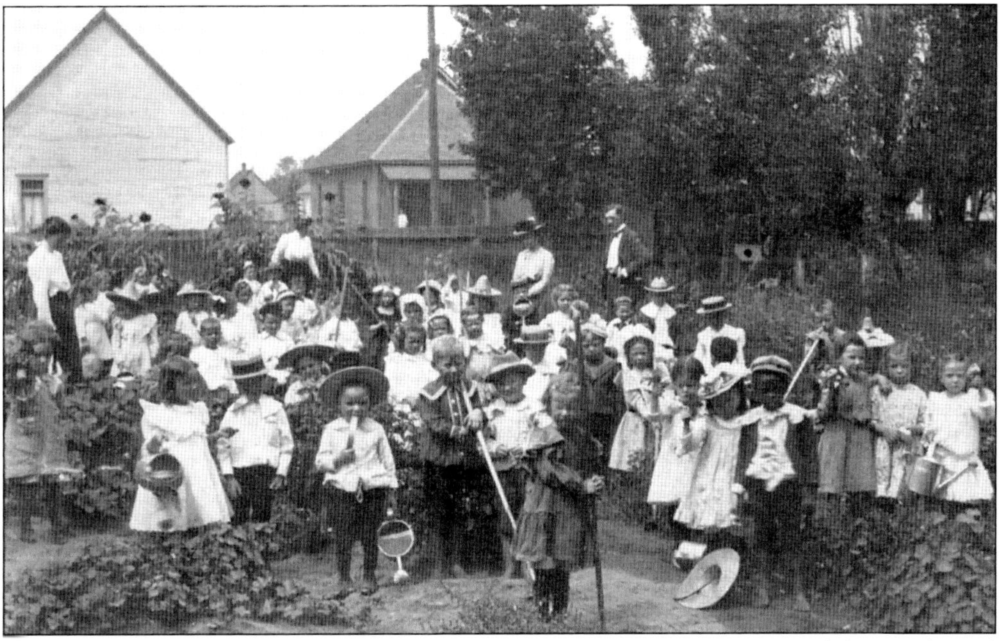

To improve the lives of employees and their families, Dr. Richard Corwin created the sociological department in 1901 to oversee the "betterment of all workers." The department launched five programs in education, social and industrial training, housing, and communications. Classes included hygiene, civics, politics, home economics, citizenship, and trades. Other activities included providing and improving company housing, entertainment and exercise opportunities, and retreats for men injured on the job. Pueblo children learned about gardening through hands-on lessons during the school day, and a company-sponsored baseball team, which took a break for a photograph in 1902.

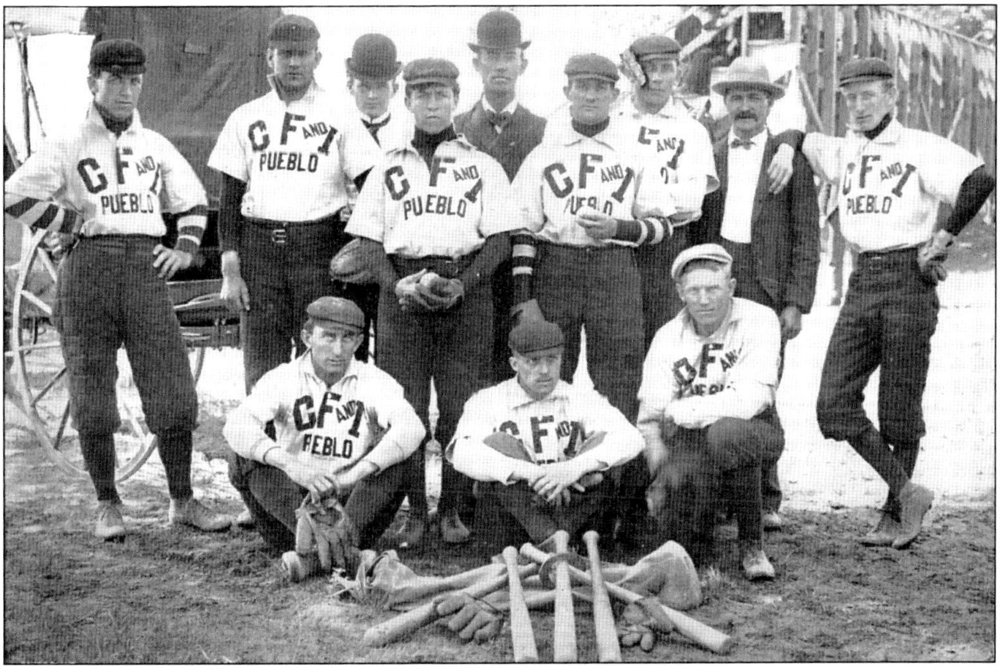

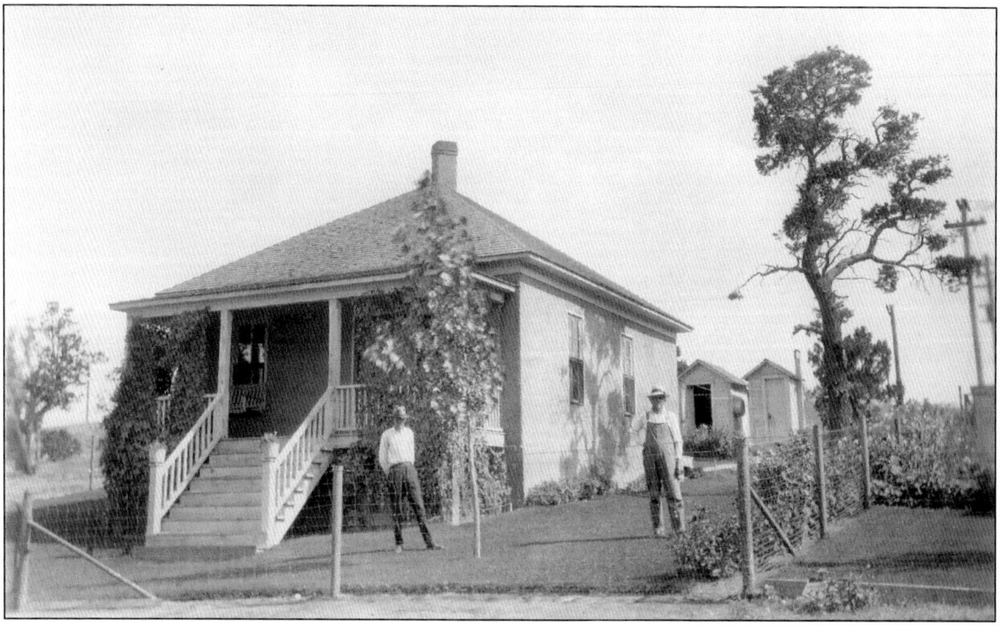

One sociological department goal was to improve the general look of the company-built homes and create model villages. Lath-and-plaster walls, wallpaper, and curtains were standard inside the homes, which rented for $2 per room per month with water furnished free in most company-dominated areas. The typical four-room home cost $700 to build. Company steelworkers and miners lived in homes built from the same floor plans.

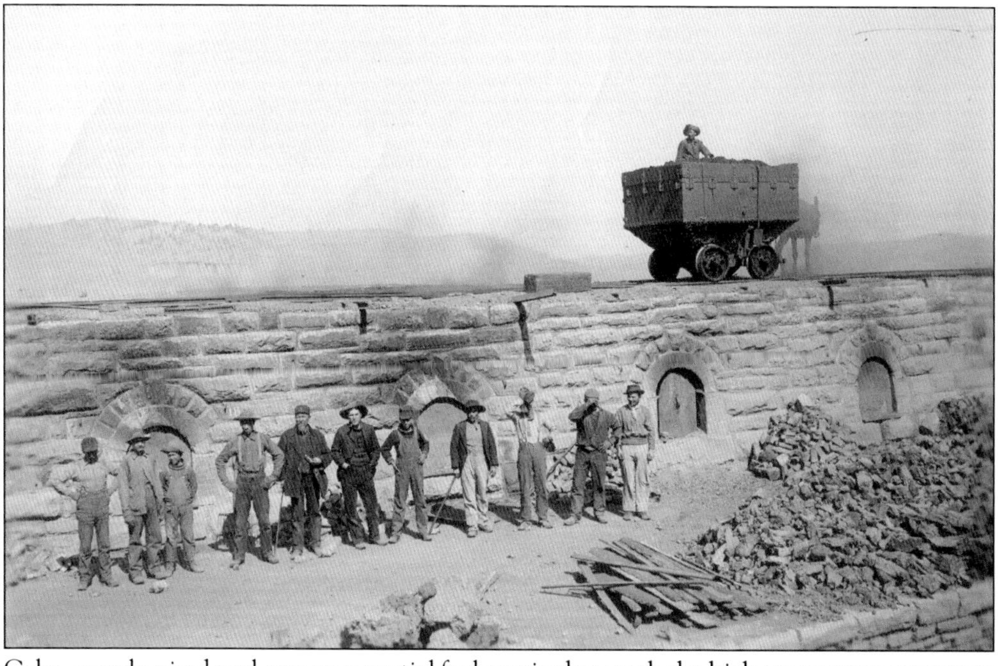

Coke, or carbonized coal, was an essential fuel required to reach the high temperature necessary in the steelmaking process. In the early years, coke was created by burning coal slowly over a period of three days in beehive coke ovens at the mining sites, as seen here in 1900. In 1917, a new coke plant was built in Pueblo, and it was used until the 1980s.

Workers and management welcomed electricity, a relatively new convenience in the steel industry at the turn of the century. In 1901, the powerhouse contained only two small generators with a combined 375 horsepower. The current was used to electrify incandescent lights in the offices. Just two years later, electric equipment in the mill included compressed-air power drills, overhead cranes, saws, fans, and ore crushers.

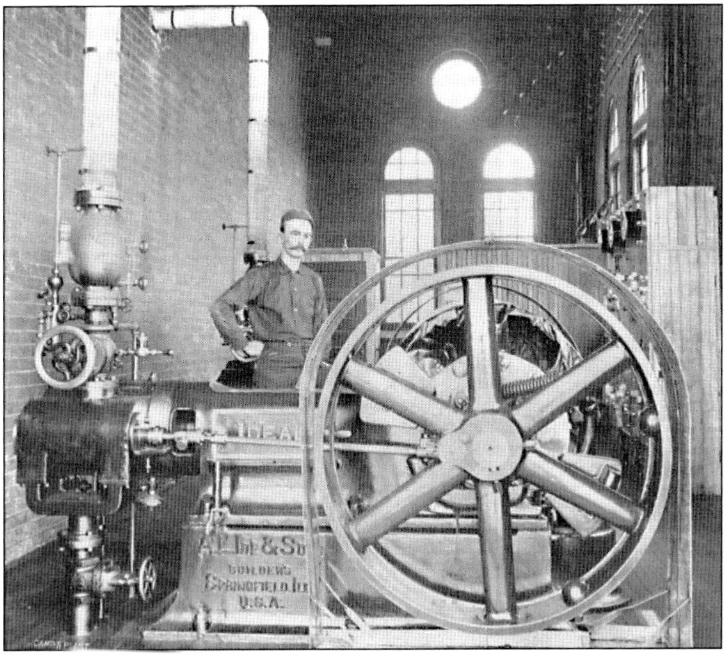

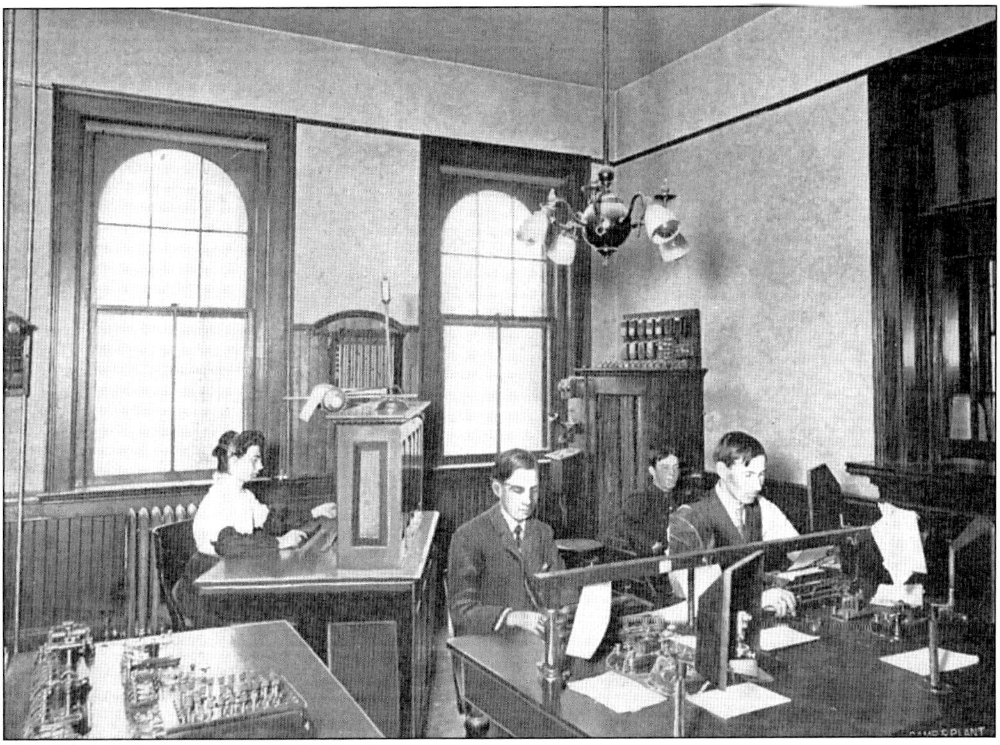

Local telephone service was first utilized at CF&I in 1901 at an operator station within the main office building. Immediate connection was available between the main office, the hospital, and various buildings at the plant site. A switchboard with 100 different lines was designed to accommodate 100 telephone units at once, rather than the traditional party-line system of the era. Operators were on duty 24 hours per day to connect callers.

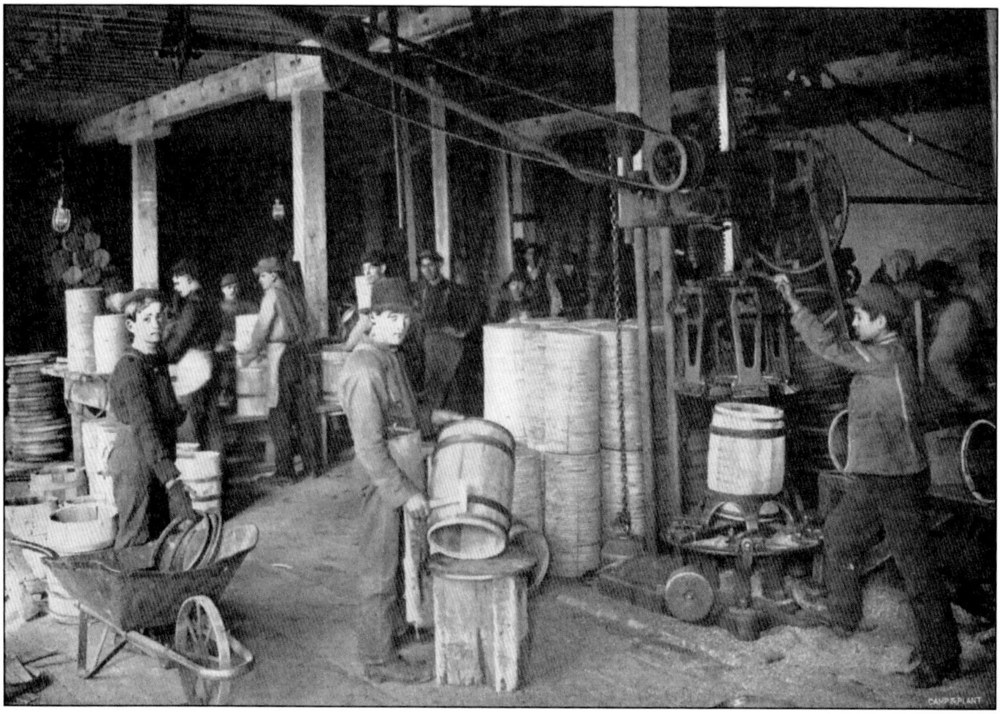

The cooperage and adjoining keg shop supplied barrels and kegs for completed nails, spikes, staples, bolts, and nuts created in other areas of the mill. In 1901, the cooperage shop's capacity was 5,000 to 8,000 kegs every 10 hours.

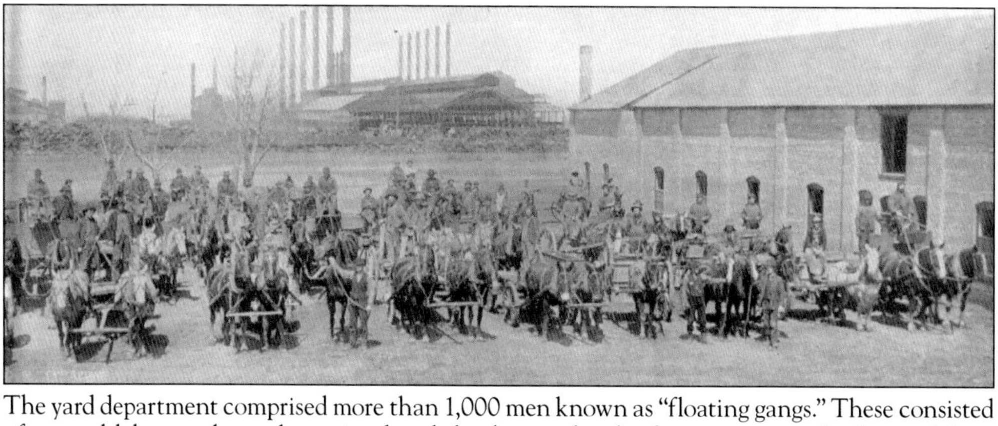

The yard department comprised more than 1,000 men known as "floating gangs." These consisted of general labor workers who assisted with loading and unloading raw minerals obtained from the mines, using large shears to cut scrap metal into manageable pieces for reuse in furnaces, and moving iron produced in the blast furnaces to the open hearth furnaces for further processing. Horses and mules were used in an era before cranes and rail transportation.

Two

The Early Rockefeller Years

Significantly lacking capital, John Osgood, president of CF&I, sought the investment power of John Rockefeller Jr. and George Gould in 1904. Although he was the primary shareholder, John Rockefeller Jr. himself had very little involvement in CF&I's operations before 1913–1914. The Colorado Coal Field Wars, a 16-month-long strike in the company's Southern Colorado mining districts, culminated in the Ludlow Massacre, one of the bloodiest events in the history of the American labor movement. This strike led the way for sweeping reforms and changes in company policy and administration. Following the strike, Rockefeller became more involved in company operations.

In 1915, in an effort to keep labor unions out of CF&I affairs, John D. Rockefeller Jr. and labor policy expert William Lyon Mackenzie King drafted an alternative to union organization, which they called the Employee Representation Plan (also known as the Rockefeller plan). Although the plan faced heavy criticism, conditions at the Pueblo mill improved. The health and safety of the workers became a greater focus of the company, an eight-hour workday was implemented, a YMCA was built near the mill for recreational purposes, and the first company newspaper in 11 years, the *Industrial Bulletin*, was published to increase communication between management and workers.

The era was also a time of unprecedented expansion at the mill. A sixth blast furnace, a seventh open hearth furnace, additional soaking pits, additions to the bolt and spike factories, a calcining plant, a continuous merchant mill, a 24-inch mill, a power plant, and two full batteries of by-product coke ovens were all constructed between 1904 and 1927.

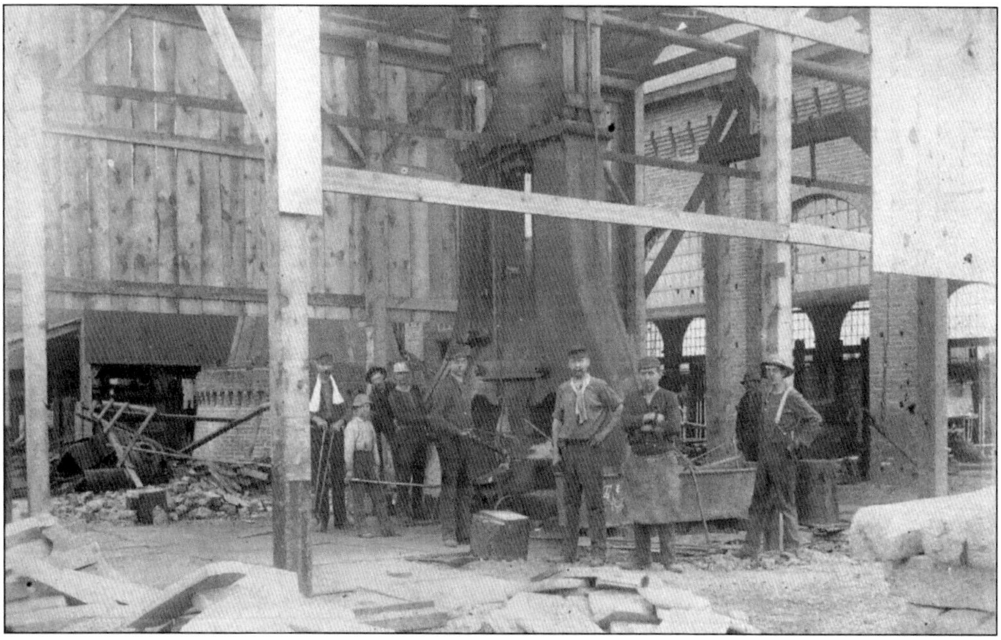

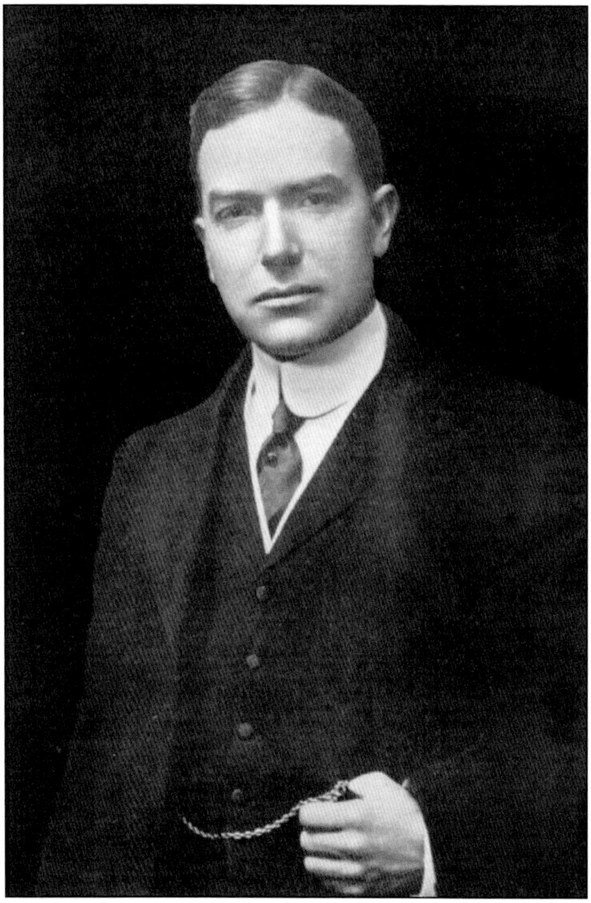

In the last years of the 19th century, CF&I management noticed the company had fallen behind technologically. A campaign began in which a new roller mill, a wire mill, two new blast furnaces, a blooming mill, an open hearth furnace, an administration building, and a hospital were built. Social programs, as well as opening new coal mines and supporting towns, eventually drained CF&I of capital and forced Osgood to seek investors George Gould and John Rockefeller Jr. to support company operations.

Rockefeller (pictured), son of Standard Oil tycoon John D. Rockefeller Sr., served as the majority stockholder of CF&I from 1904 to 1944. George Gould, the son of another industrialist, first took an interest in the enterprise and approached the Rockefellers to form a partnership. A financial panic in 1907 forced Gould to relinquish his shares, leaving Rockefeller Jr. in complete control of the company.

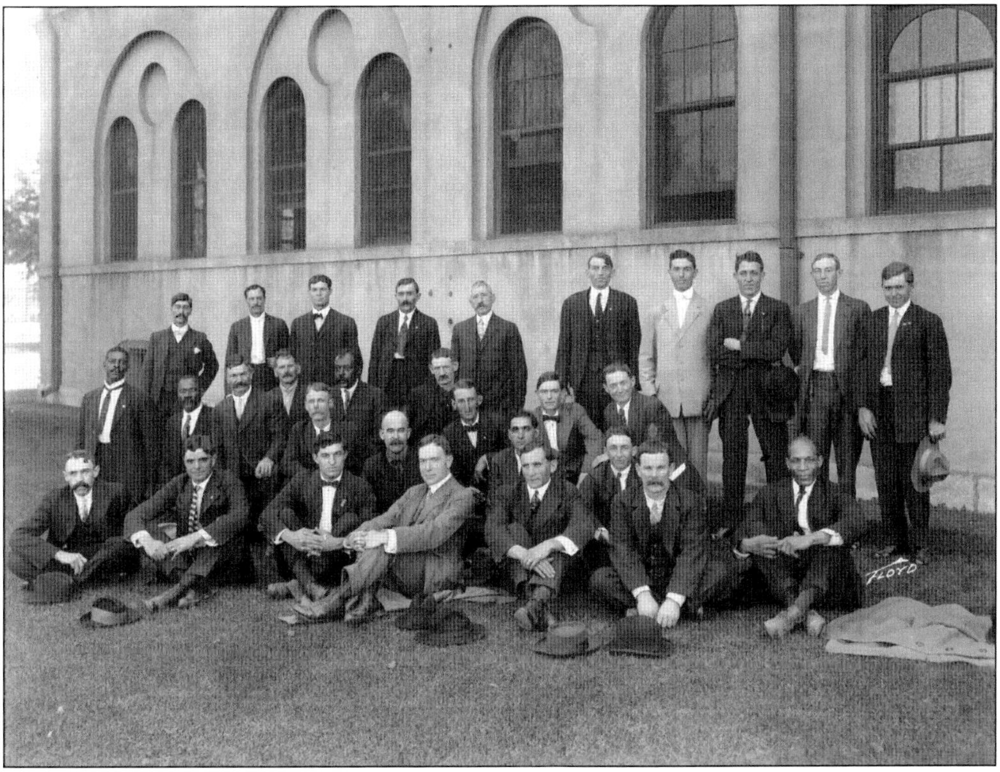

John D. Rockefeller Jr. visited Pueblo in October 1915 to introduce the groundbreaking Employee Representation Plan to CF&I managers and employees. While in Pueblo, he stated that it was "the first time that I have ever had the good fortune to meet the representatives of the employees of this great company. . . . I am proud to be here, and I shall remember this gathering as long as I live."

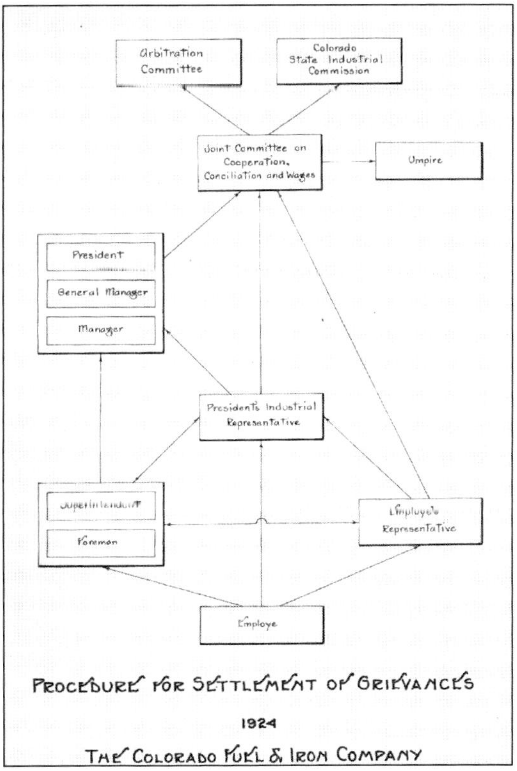

The Employee Representation Plan, the first of its kind in the nation, allowed workers to report grievances on the jobsite through a series of elected representatives. This new system allowed workers to form unions among themselves and gave them just enough voice over their working conditions so that they would not strike to gain formal union recognition. The plan continued in the steel mill until 1942, when it was invalidated by the National War Labor Board under the National Labor Relations Act of 1935 as an illegal "company union."

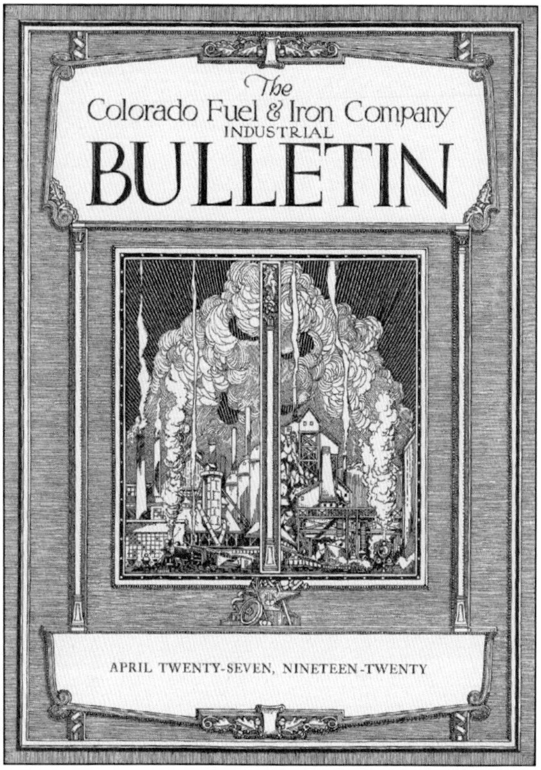

In an effort to better communicate with its workforce, CF&I published the *Industrial Bulletin* from 1915 to 1929. An introduction in the first issue in October 1915 states that "this periodical shall be used as a means of coordinating, harmonizing and furthering the social and industrial betterment work, and of informing the employees of the personnel and proceedings of conferences, boards, and committees, in which they are interested."

In 1918, Capt. George Hutchison of the London Irish Rifles, a volunteer rifle regiment with the British army, addresses Minnequa Steel Works employees, many of whom can be seen crowding the stage and perched on the rafters above. Throughout World War I, CF&I and its employees were staunch supporters of the Allied troops and the war effort in general.

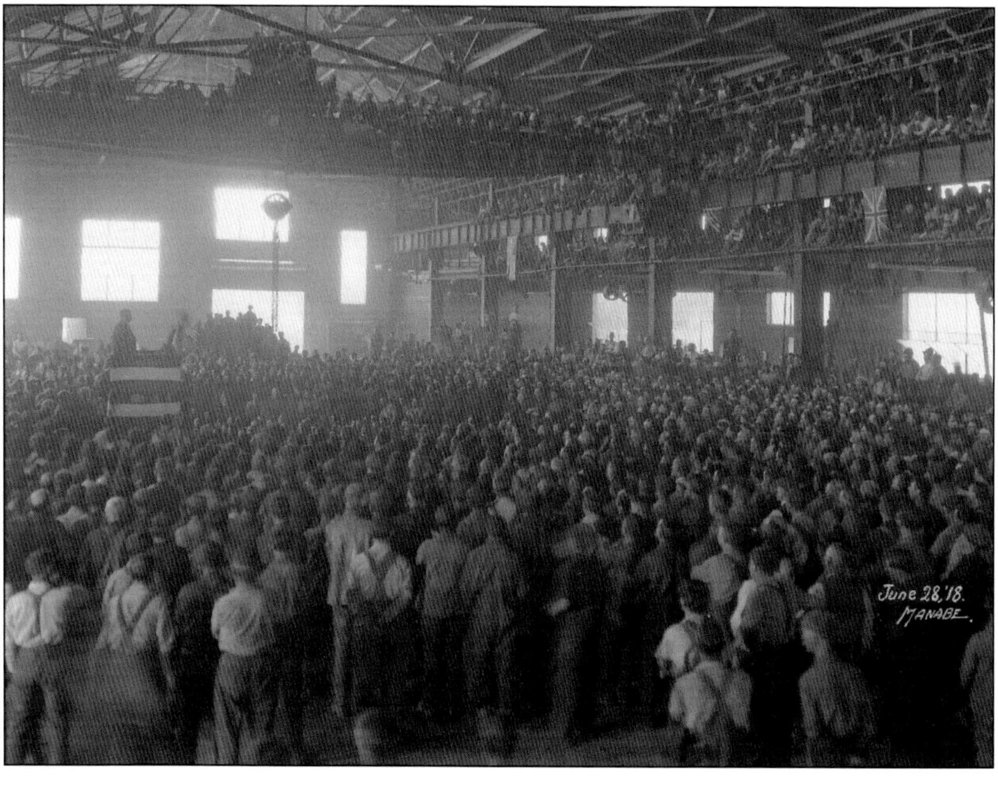

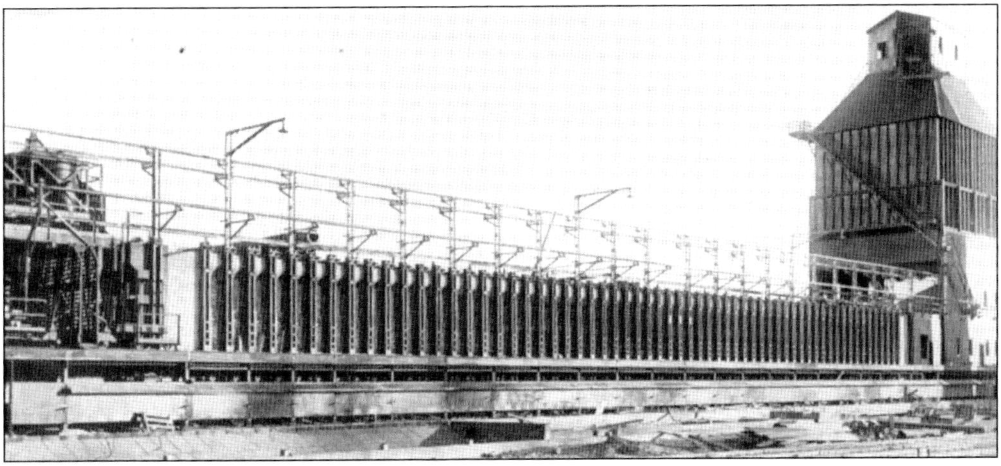

Construction of the by-product coke oven plant was completed on July 1, 1918, at a cost of $4 million. It incorporated 120 ovens producing up to 46,000 tons of coke per month. Coke, a product made from coal that has been superheated in an oxygen-free environment for up to 16 hours, was required to produce steel, as it burned much hotter than other fuels available at the time. The construction of a coke plant at the mill led to the abandonment of much less efficient beehive ovens located throughout Southern Colorado.

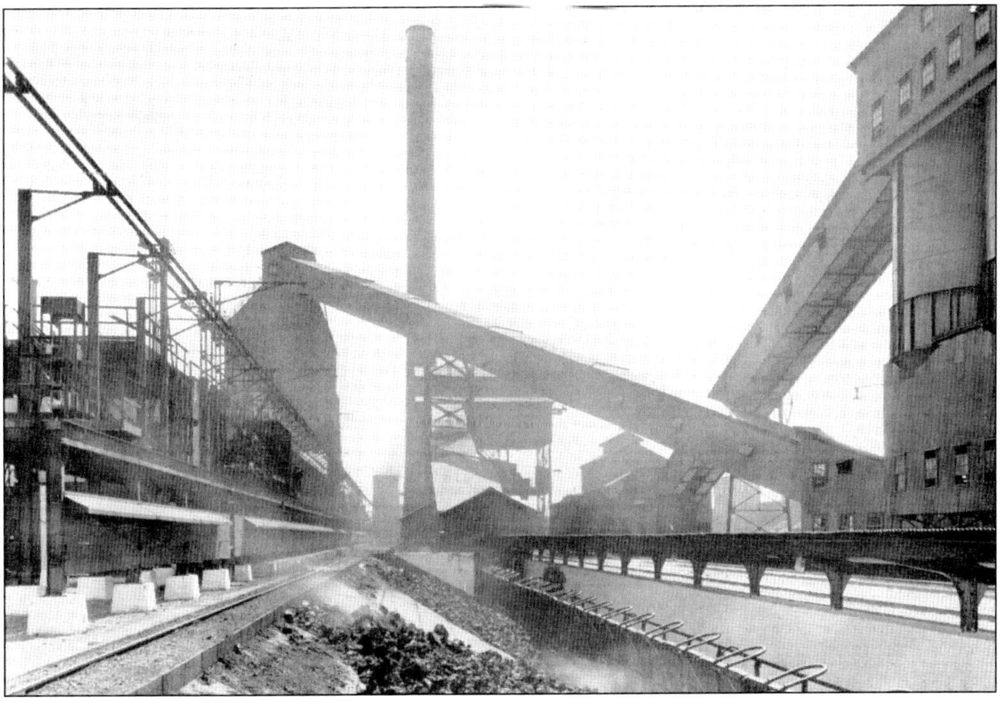

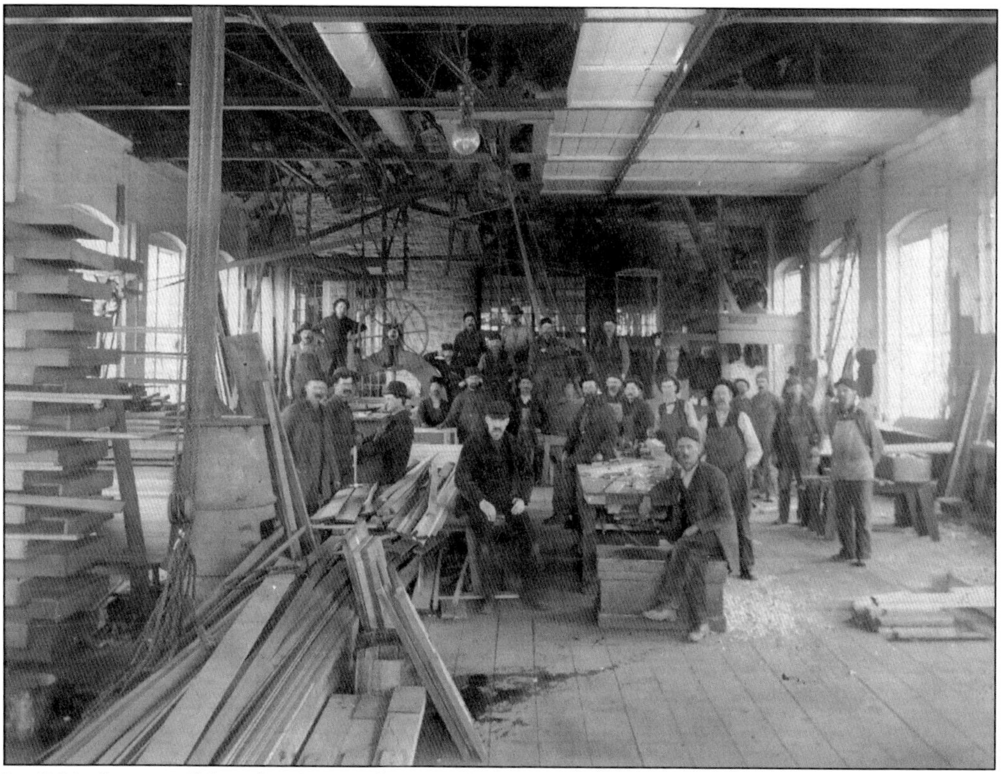

In 1900, the payroll listed 8,688 employees, which included those who worked in the mines, mill, administration, medical, and subsidiary departments. Four years later, the payroll was 15,087 workers. According to the September 22, 1906, edition of *Scientific American*, "ten per cent of Colorado's population is dependent upon wages earned by employees of the Colorado Fuel and Iron Company," making CF&I one of the largest employers in the West.

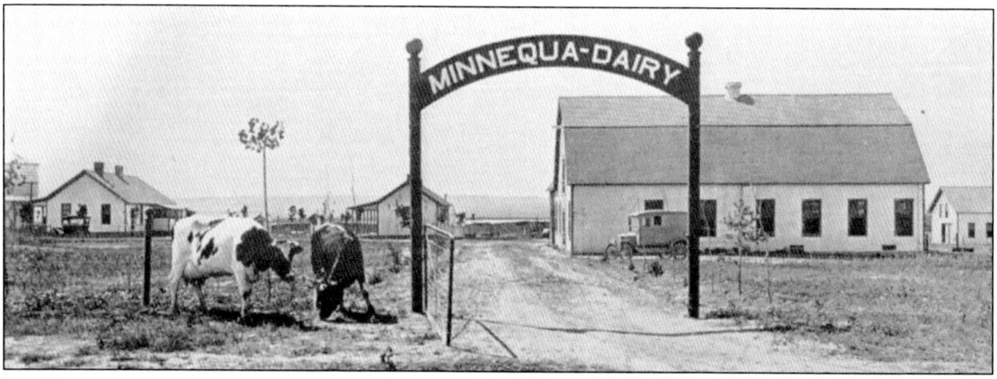

In 1917, improvements were made to the Minnequa Dairy, including new sanitary cement floors, window screens, feed bins, and a drainage system. Holstein cows were bred and kept in the dairy, located about five miles south of the Pueblo plant, to provide milk for patients within the hospital, showing the vastness of the integrated business model of the company.

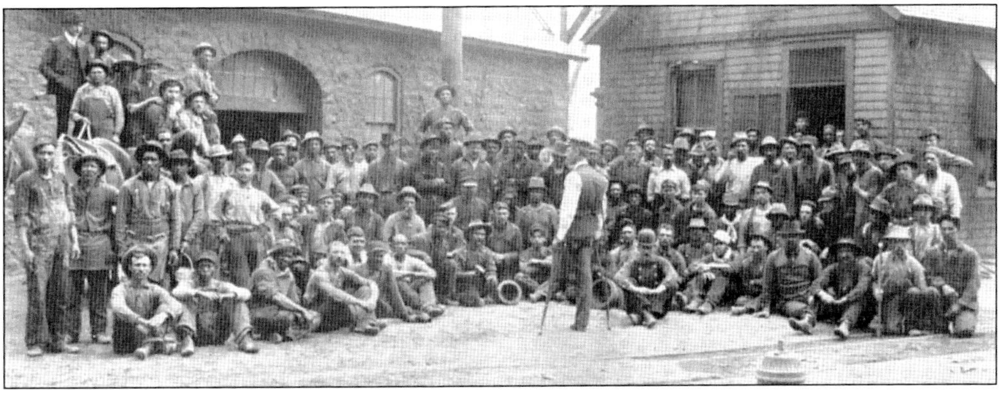

Employment at the mill was difficult and dangerous. Most workers spent up to 12 hours a day surrounded by molten steel and heavy machinery, and one defective unit or misstep by an employee could lead to a serious accident. Injuries occurred frequently, and fatal accidents were common. Though it helped to relieve stress and improve safety, the implementation of an eight-hour workday in November 1918 could not prevent a steelworkers strike in 1919. This strike was relatively short-lived, but it was evidence that the Employee Representation Plan may not have been meeting the needs of all CF&I workers.

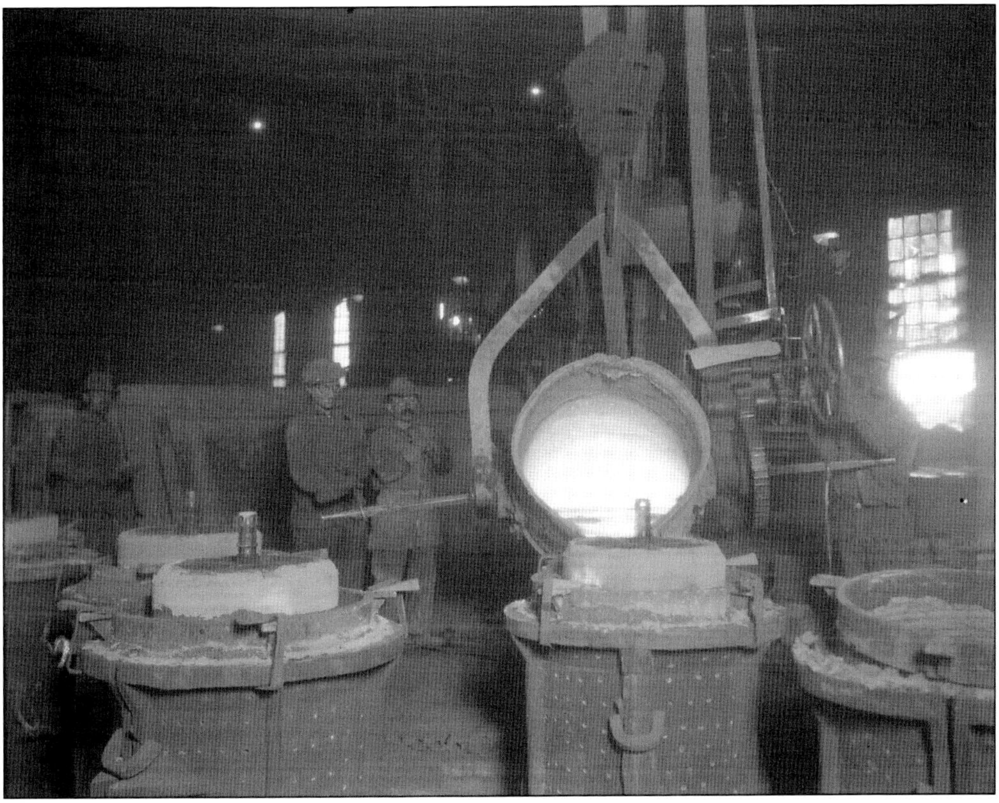

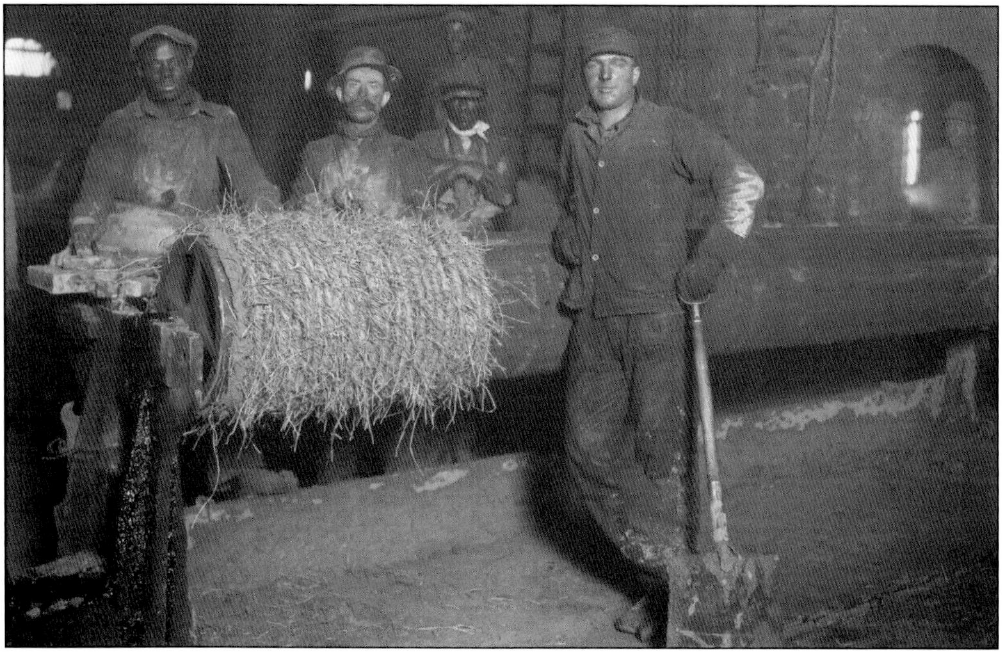

Pigs were taken from the blast furnace to the open hearth furnace for purifying. From there, the pigs were combined with other materials for steel production. This steel was then transferred to other departments to produce the majority of CF&I's products. In the early years of the company, a portion of pig iron was taken to the pipe foundry, shown below, where the metal was re-melted into a liquid and poured into a pipe-shaped mold. Hay was wrapped around the core and then layered with adobe mud and sand to assist in removing the pipe from the mold when completed. CF&I's cast-iron pipes were one of the few non-steel products the company produced on a large scale. They were sold to municipalities for underground water and sanitation needs.

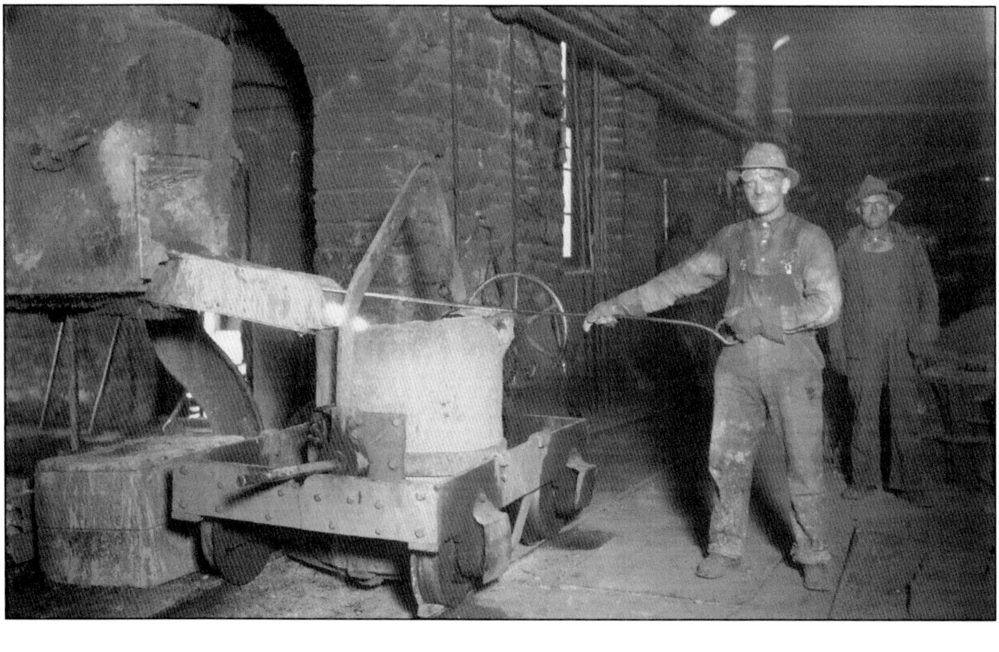

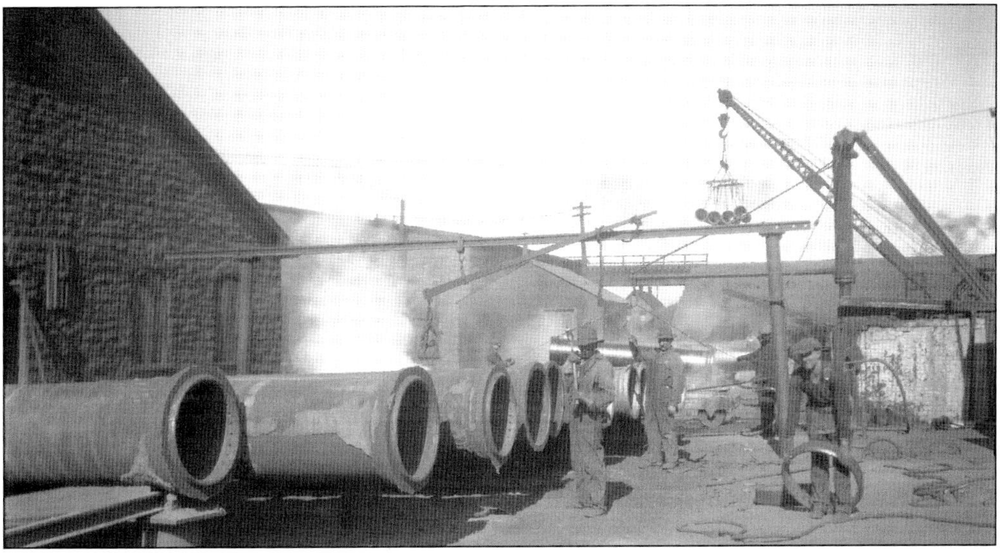

Once cast-iron pipes were completed in the manufacturing process, workers in the foundry testing yard ensured the quality through a series of rigorous tests. Pipes were given a hydrostatic pressure test and subjected to a hammer test under pressure to ensure their strength.

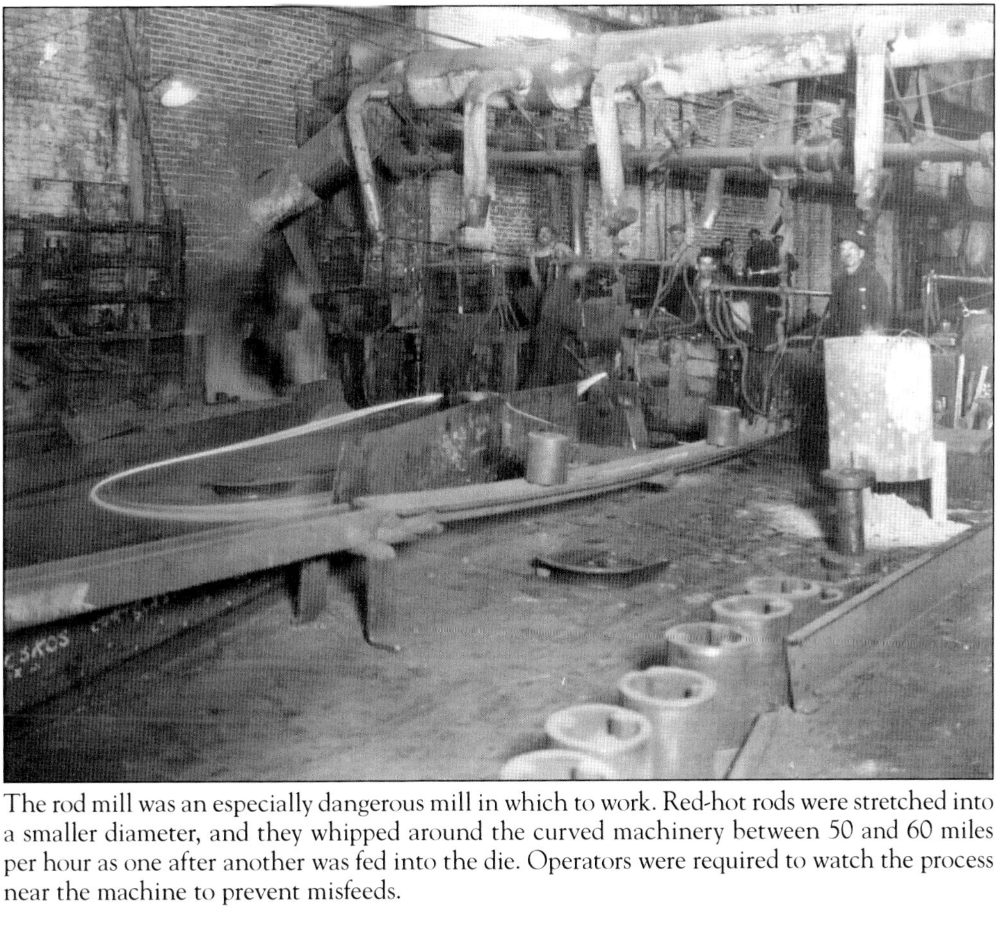

The rod mill was an especially dangerous mill in which to work. Red-hot rods were stretched into a smaller diameter, and they whipped around the curved machinery between 50 and 60 miles per hour as one after another was fed into the die. Operators were required to watch the process near the machine to prevent misfeeds.

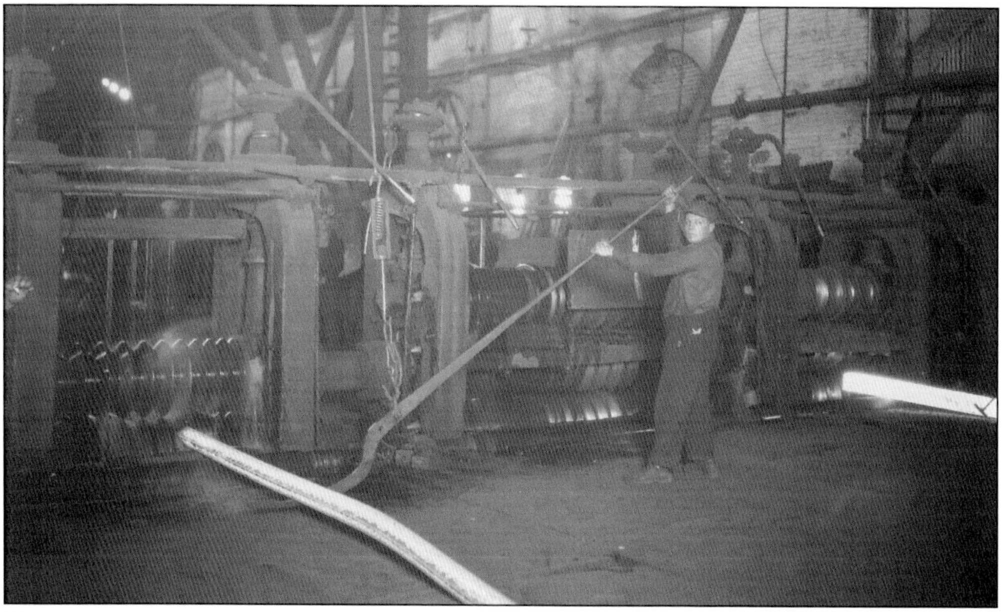

The company's original intent was to become the premier regional source for rail and rail accessories for the transportation industry, and the rail mill's first product emerged in 1882. Over the next 30 years, rail manufacturing encompassed about 60 percent of all the company's production efforts. The rail mill employed 325 to 375 workers, with a daily output of about 1,000 tons. In the 1920s, rails from the Pueblo plant were sold almost entirely to railroads running west of the Mississippi River, but some sales were on an international level, including to Asia and Mexico.

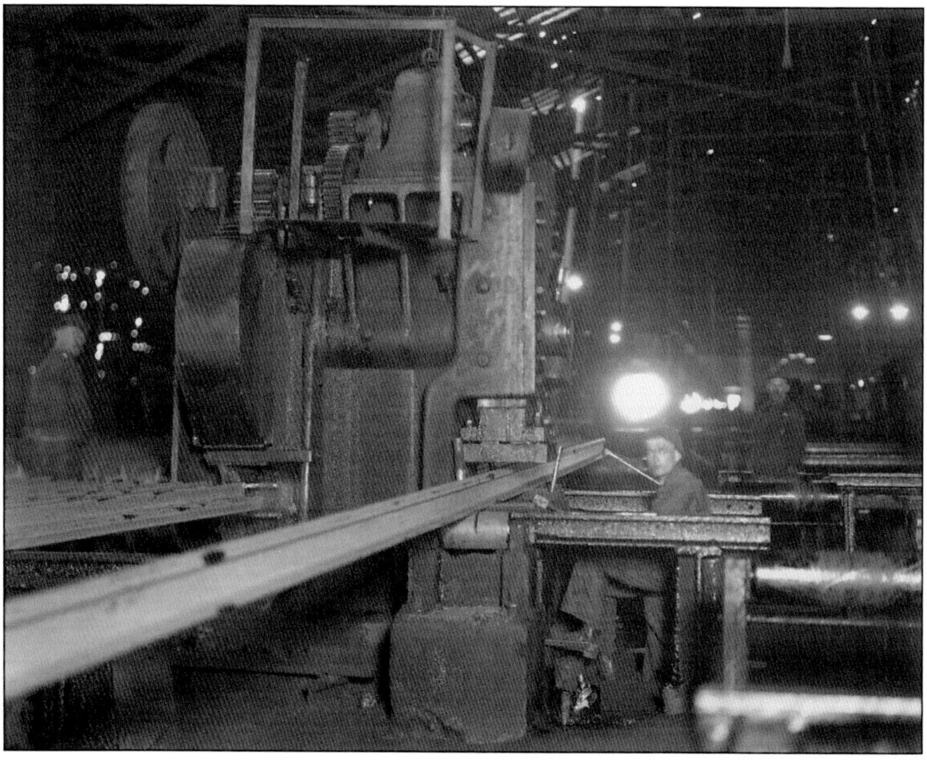

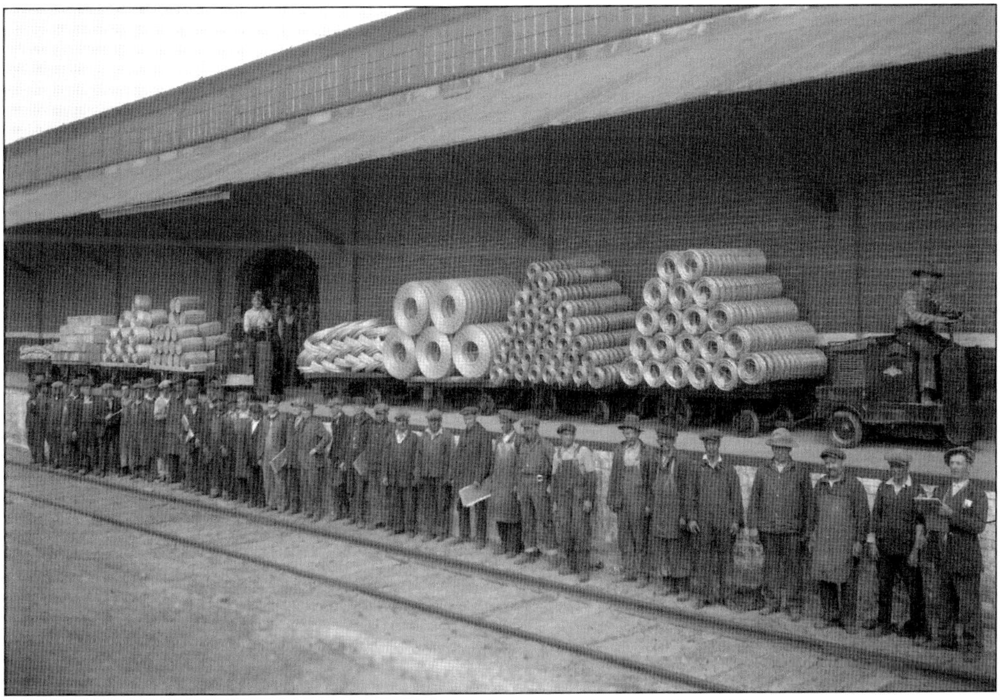

In its advertising campaigns, CF&I commonly referred to itself as "the company that fences the West" due to the thousands of miles of wire fence that was produced. During the 1910s and 1920s, the wire mill saw a number of improvements, such as the rebuilding of the boiler house, two new turbine electric generators, a new cooper shop and warehouse, and the addition of a "comfort station," a section of a building that provided showers, washstands, and toilets for about 300 men.

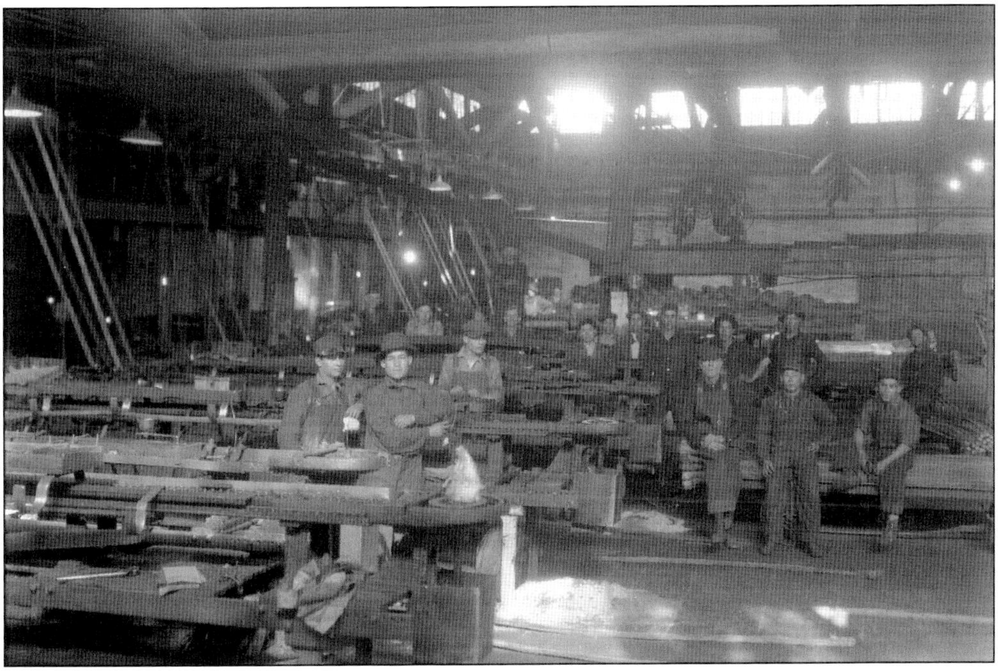

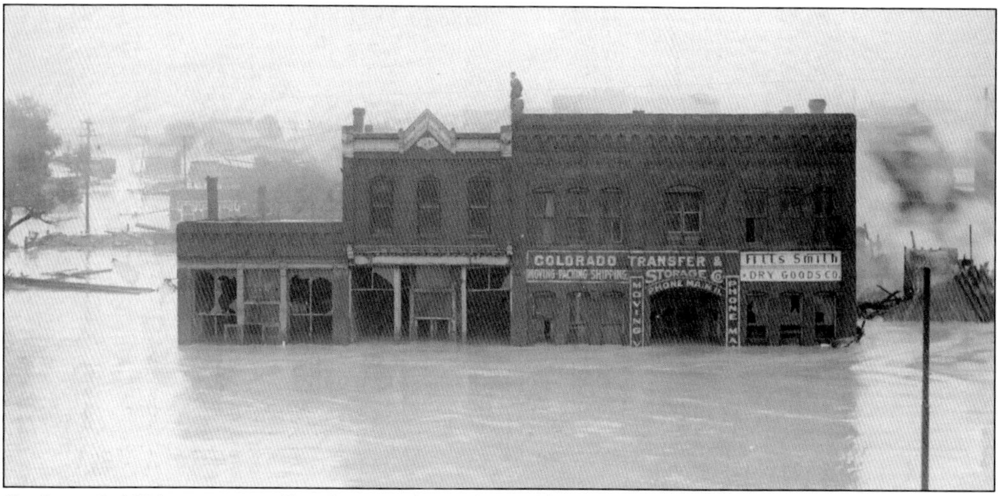

On June 3, 1921, a massive flood swept through Pueblo, killing hundreds and causing millions of dollars' worth of damage. The mill suffered no serious damage from the flood, but the company and its workers immediately set to work helping the community, providing electricity, fresh drinking water, supplies, and medical care to Pueblo's residents until the crisis had passed and the water receded.

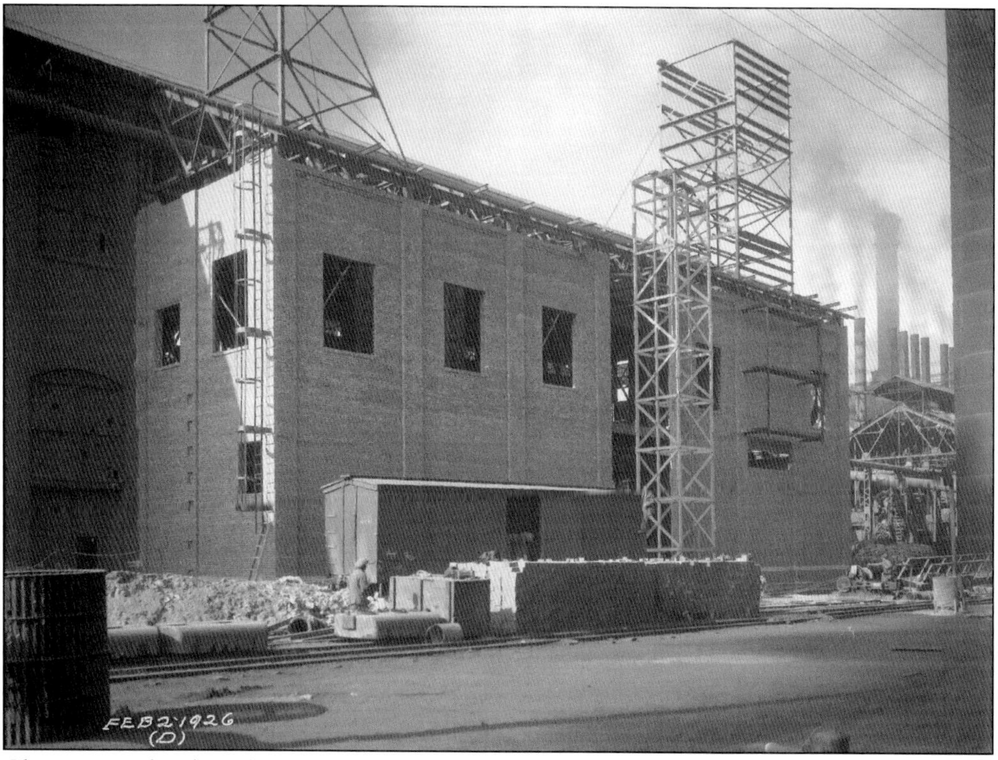

Changing technology forced the company to become more reliant on electricity. The mill's powerhouse, seen during construction, was completed in July 1926. It housed three General Electric 10,000-kilowatt turbine generators and two 1,000-kilowatt motor generators, enough to power the entire plant at that time. The powerhouse was built to replace several existing power and boiler houses and allowed CF&I to replace all of its steam engines with electric motors.

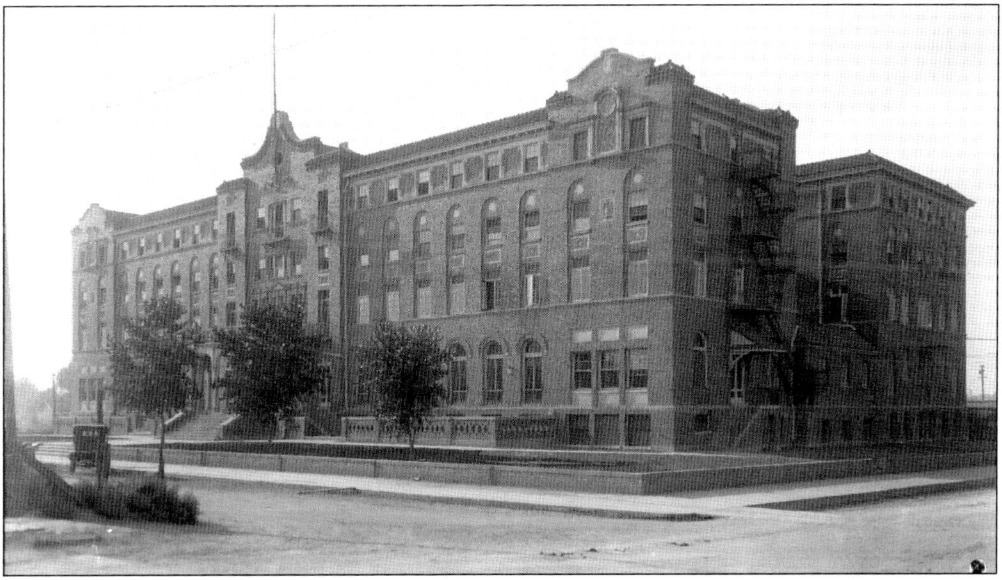

The YMCA and CF&I formed a partnership to help rebuild the company image following the Colorado Coal Field Wars. The $500,000 Steelworks YMCA opened in 1920 west of the company administration building and was largely funded by gifts from the Rockefeller family. The "Steel Y," as it came to be known, boasted a 1,200-seat auditorium, motion-picture theater, gymnasium, billiard room, bowling alley, library, ballroom, and a soda fountain. The top floor served as dormitories for single men. The Y also offered educational classes to employees and their families including accounting, arithmetic, American government and civics, chemistry, and automobile repair. Lessons for children included tap dancing, Ping-Pong, and xylophone and harmonica. Smaller YMCA buildings were also constructed and operated in CF&I's mining communities.

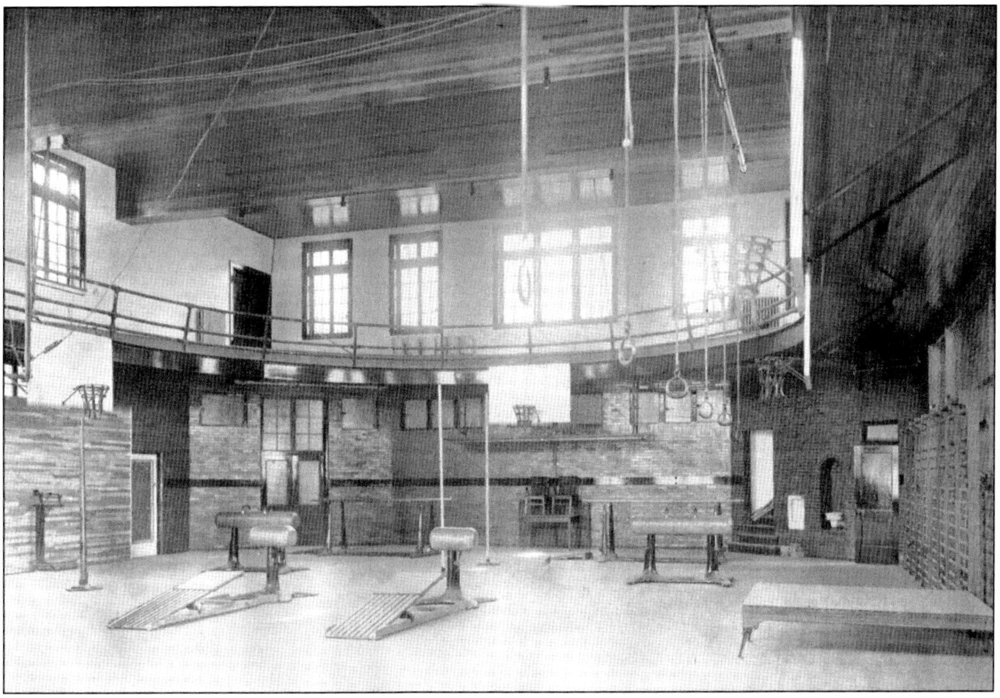

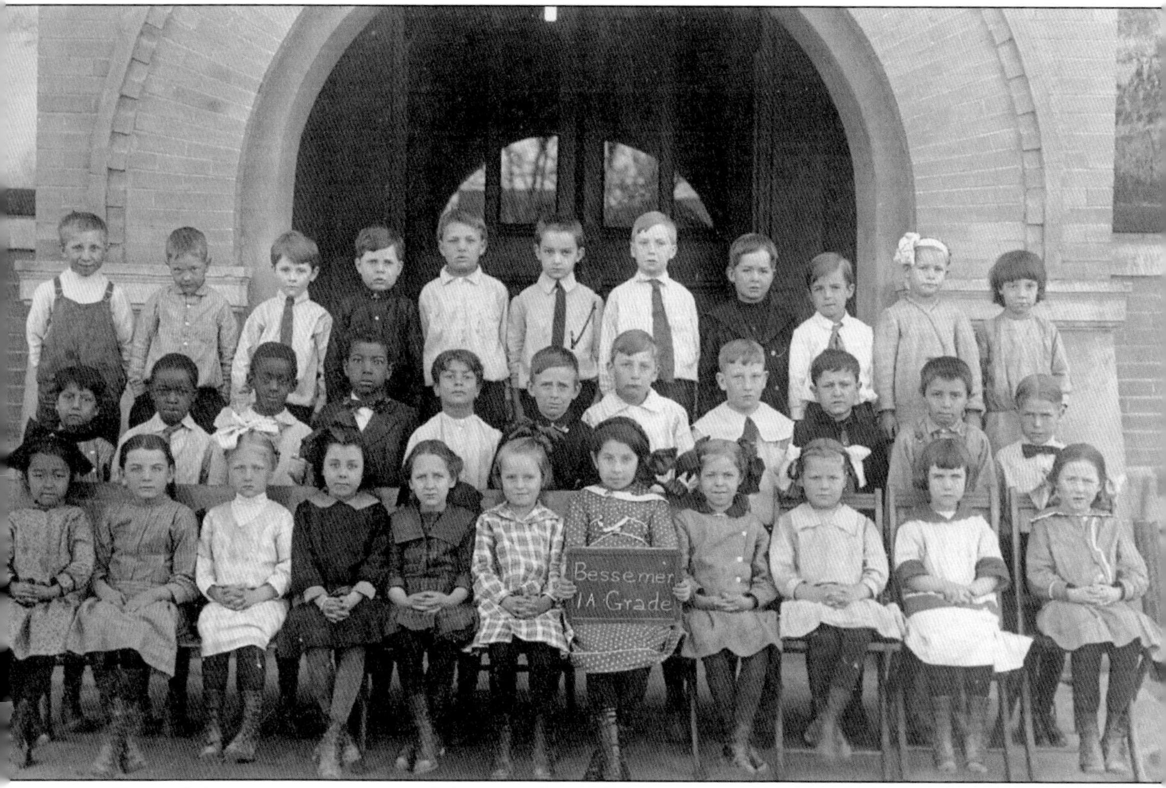

One of the most innovative of the sociological department's programs was kindergartens. As mentioned in articles written by company officials, kindergartens sought to develop strong, healthy, refined young people, primarily between the ages of three and six. The department developed classes that placed each child on an equal standing and taught sympathy, unselfishness, and an appreciation for equal rights. Schools under the guidance of the sociological department were set up as part of the state education system and not directly under the control of the company or its officials. Teachers were selected for their experience and other qualifications, and their work was under the supervision of the boards of education. The public Bessemer School continues to educate students today from kindergarten to eighth grade.

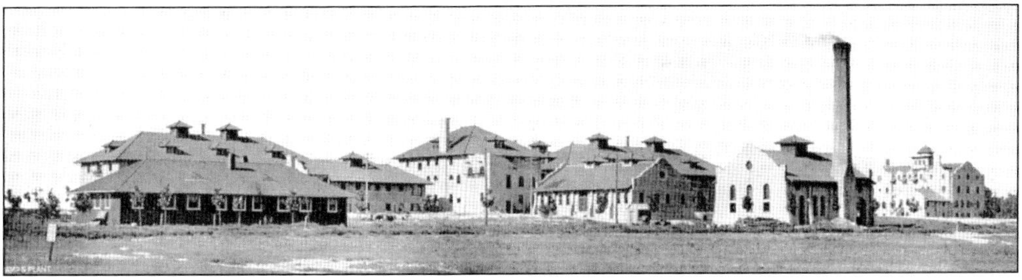

With an increase in employee numbers, demand for medical services justified building Minnequa Hospital in 1902. The new hospital consisted of multiple Spanish Mission–style buildings sprawling across 20 acres. Included on the campus was a separate ward for communicable diseases, a main building, a laundry, a chapel, a powerhouse, and a physicians' residence. An on-site dormitory for nursing staff opened in 1917. Keeping patients' needs in mind, revolutionary ideas for the time were incorporated in the design, including ramps instead of stairs to comfort those with back injuries, a lead-lined operating room floor and walls for easy cleaning, pastel paint on the walls to ease anxiety in patients, and a museum and displays to keep patients' minds active while recuperating. Garden paths and outdoor activities were also incorporated to speed up recovery time for patients.

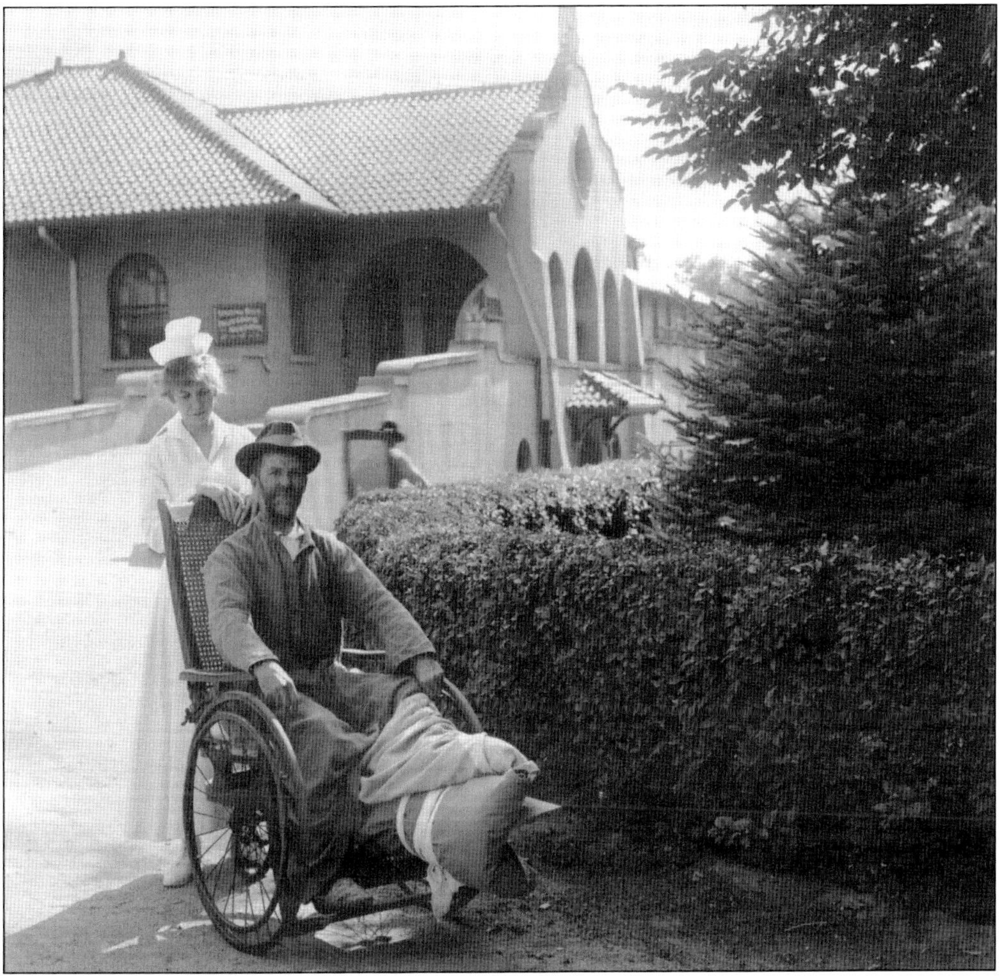

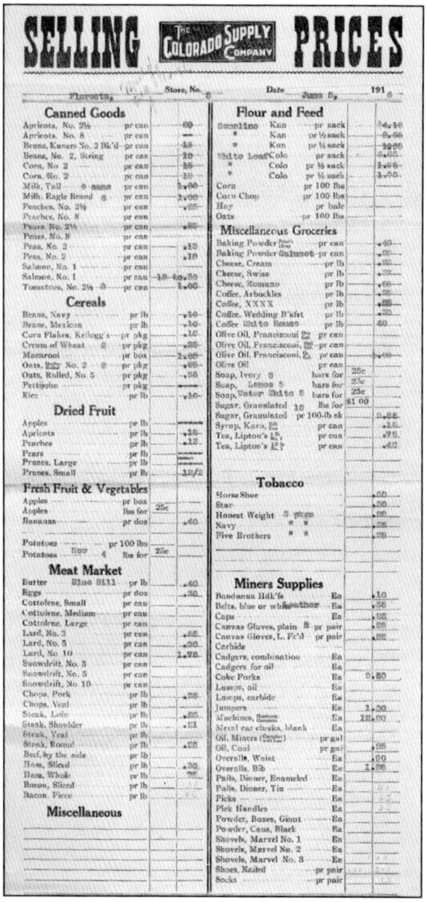

SELLING ~~The Colorado Supply Company~~ PRICES

Store, No. 5 ... Florests ... Date June 5, 1916

Canned Goods			
Apricots, No. 2½	pr can		.60
Apricots, No. 8	pr can		—
Beans, Kuners No. 2 Bk'd	pr can		.13
Beans, No. 2, String	pr can		.10
Corn, No 2	pr can		.15
Corn, No. 2	pr can		.10
Milk, Tall 9 cans	pr can		1.00
Milk, Eagle Brand 6	pr can		1.00
Peaches, No. 2½	pr can		.25
Peaches, No. 8	pr can		
Pears, No. 2½	pr can		.25
Pears, No. 8	pr can		
Peas, No. 2	pr can		.15
Peas, No. 2	pr can		.10
Salmon, No. 1	pr can		
Salmon, No. 1	pr can	15 to .30	
Tomatoes, No. 2½ 8	pr can		1.00
Cereals			
Beans, Navy	pr lb		.10
Beans, Mexican	pr lb		.10
Corn Flakes, Kellogg's	pr pkg		.10
Cream of Wheat 2	pr pkg		.35
Macaroni	pr box		1.60
Oats, [illegible] No. 2 2	pr pkg		.25
Oats, Rolled, No. 5	pr pkg		.35
Pettijohn	pr pkg		—
Rice	pr lb		.10
Dried Fruit			
Apples	pr lb		—
Apricots	pr lb		.18
Peaches	pr lb		.13
Pears	pr lb		—
Prunes, Large	pr lb		—
Prunes, Small	pr lb		12/2
Fresh Fruit & Vegetables			
Apples	pr box		
Apples	lbs for	25c	
Bananas	pr doz		.40
Potatoes	pr 100 lbs		
Potatoes New 4	lbs for	25c	
Meat Market			
Butter Blue Hill	pr lb		.40
Eggs	pr doz		.30
Cottolene, Small	pr can		
Cottolene, Medium	pr can		
Cottolene, Large	pr can		
Lard, No. 3	pr can		.55
Lard, No. 5	pr can		.90
Lard, No 10	pr can		1.75
Snowdrift, No. 3	pr can		
Snowdrift, No. 5	pr can		
Snowdrift, No 10	pr can		
Chops, Pork	pr lb		.25
Chops, Veal	pr lb		
Steak, Loin	pr lb		.25
Steak, Shoulder	pr lb		.21
Steak, Veal	pr lb		
Steak, Round	pr lb		.22
Beef, by the side	pr lb		
Ham, Sliced	pr lb		.30
Ham, Whole	pr lb		[illegible]
Bacon, Sliced	pr lb		[illegible]
Bacon, Piece	pr lb		[illegible]
Miscellaneous			

Flour and Feed			
Semolino Kan	pr sack		4.10
" Kan	pr ½ sack		2.05
" Kan	pr ¼ sack		1.00
White Leaf Colo	pr sack		5.05
" Colo	pr ½ sack		1.95
" Colo	pr ¼ sack		1.00
Corn	pr 100 lbs		
Corn Chop	pr 100 lbs		
Hay	pr bale		
Oats	pr 100 lbs		
Miscellaneous Groceries			
Baking Powder [illegible]	pr can		.40
Baking Powder Calumet	pr can		.20
Cheese, Cream	pr lb		.22
Cheese, Swiss	pr lb		.32
Cheese, Romano	pr lb		.60
Coffee, Arbuckles	pr lb		.22
Coffee, XXXX	pr lb		.25
Coffee, Wedding B'kfst	pr lb		.30
Coffee White House	pr lb		40
Olive Oil, Francisconi [illegible]	pr can		
Olive Oil, Francisconi, [illegible]	pr can		
Olive Oil, Francisconi, [illegible]	pr can		1.40
Olive Oil	pr can		
Soap, Ivory 5	bars for	25c	
Soap, Lenox 5	bars for	25c	
Soap, Water White 5	bars for	25c	
Sugar, Granulated 10	lbs for	$1 00	
Sugar, Granulated	pr 100-lb sk		8.25
Syrup, Karo, [illegible]	pr can		.15
Tea, Lipton's [illegible]	pr can		.75
Tea, Lipton's [illegible]	pr can		.40
Tobacco			
Horse Shoe			.50
Star			.50
Honest Weight 5 pkgs			.25
Navy " "			.25
Five Brothers " "			.25
Miners Supplies			
Bandanna Hdk'fs	Ea		.10
Belts, blue or white leather	Ea		.35
Caps	Ea		.25
Canvas Gloves, plain 8	pr pair		.25
Canvas Gloves, L. Fc'd	pr pair		.25
Carbide			
Cadgers, combination	Ea		
Cadgers for oil	Ea		
Coke Forks	Ea		2.50
Lamps, oil	Ea		
Lamps, carbide	Ea		
Jumpers	Ea		1.20
Machines, [illegible]	Ea		12.00
Metal car checks, blank	Ea		
Oil, Miners [illegible]	pr gal		
Oil, Coal	pr gal		.25
Overalls, Waist	Ea		.90
Overalls, Bib	Ea		1.25
Pails, Dinner, Enameled	Ea		
Pails, Dinner, Tin	Ea		[illegible]
Picks	Ea		[illegible]
Pick Handles	Ea		[illegible]
Powder, Boxes, Giant	Ea		
Powder, Cans, Black	Ea		
Shovels, Marvel No. 1	Ea		
Shovels, Marvel No. 2	Ea		
Shovels, Marvel No. 3	Ea		[illegible]
Shoes, Nailed	pr pair	[illegible]	[illegible]
Socks	pr pair		[illegible]

The Colorado Supply Company Store, which provided goods for work and home, served both the Pueblo steelworkers and outlying company mines with branch outlets. A listing of goods available in 1916 details that pricing was competitive and affordable to shoppers.

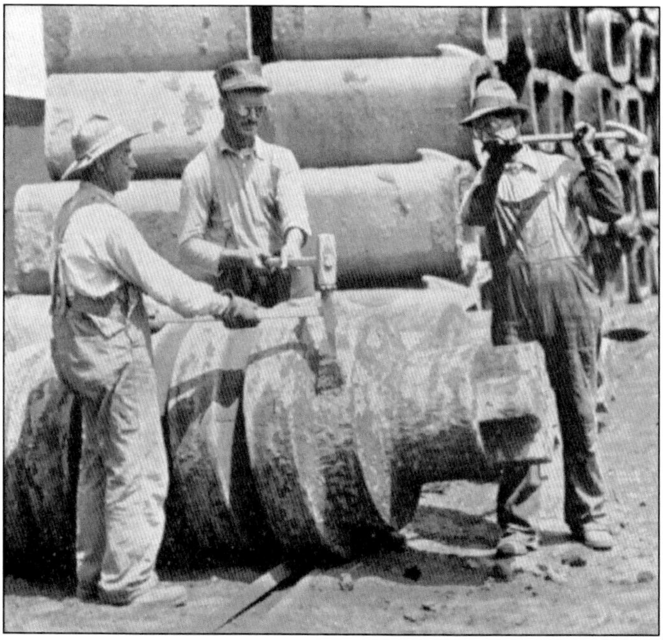

Revolutionary for the era, workplace safety was discussed on a regular basis by a committee created under the Employee Representation Plan. Suggestions ranged from addressing potential fire hazards to installing overhead lights for workers at night. New equipment and methods to make work safer were also discussed and implemented. Three steelworkers demonstrate the benefits of wearing safety goggles in 1917.

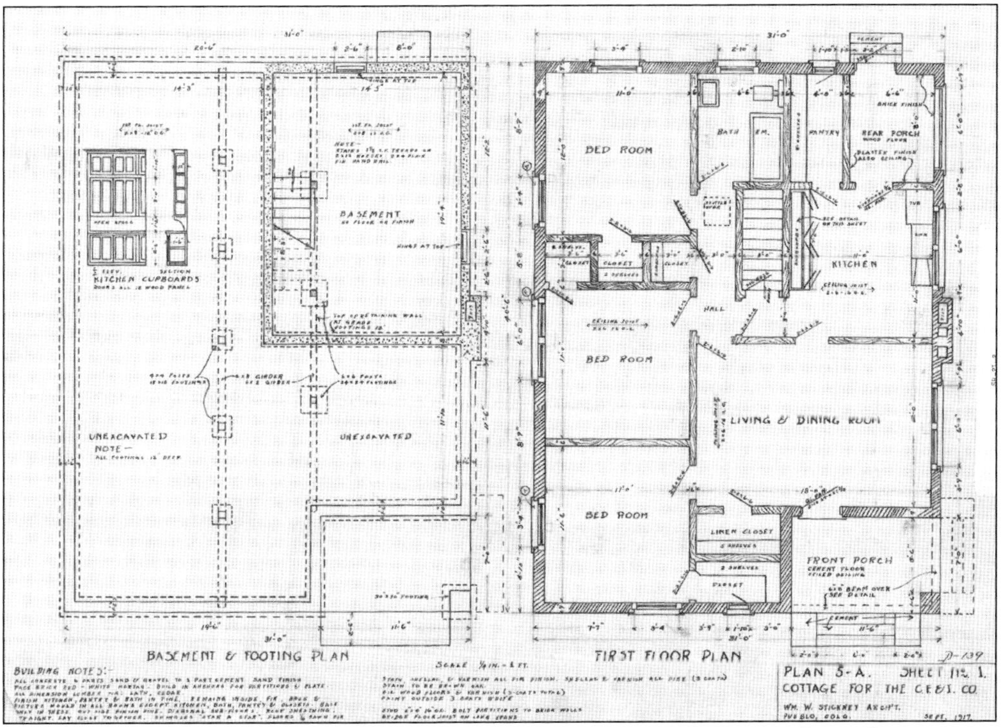

Established in 1899 as a subsidiary of CF&I, the Minnequa Town Company devoted its energies to building small cottages to the west of the steelworks for resale or rent to employees. By 1903, approximately 300 modern units, mostly consisting of four and five rooms, were built to the west of the steelworks. The standard rent at the turn of the century was $2 per room per month for three-, four-, or five-room homes. The rent did not include electric lights, heat, or indoor plumbing. In the early part of the century, the employee was charged 35¢ per month for each electrical outlet in the home and between $1.50 and $2 per ton for domestic coal for cooking and heating. Electric lights within the home were 25¢ per month per outlet.

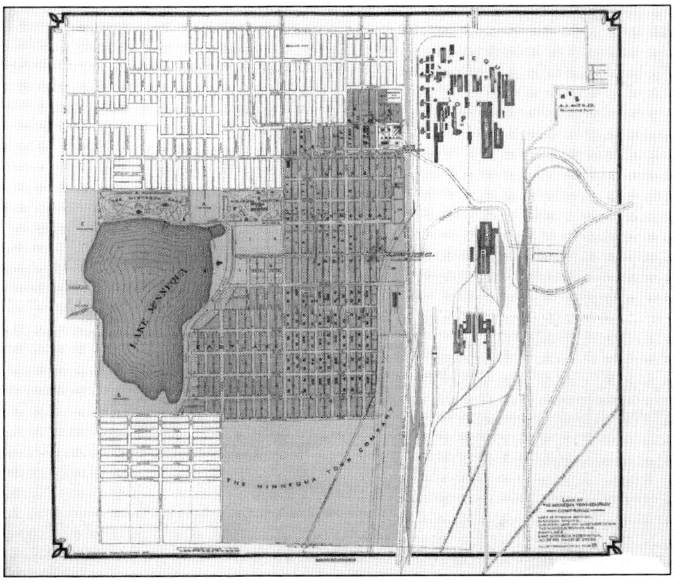

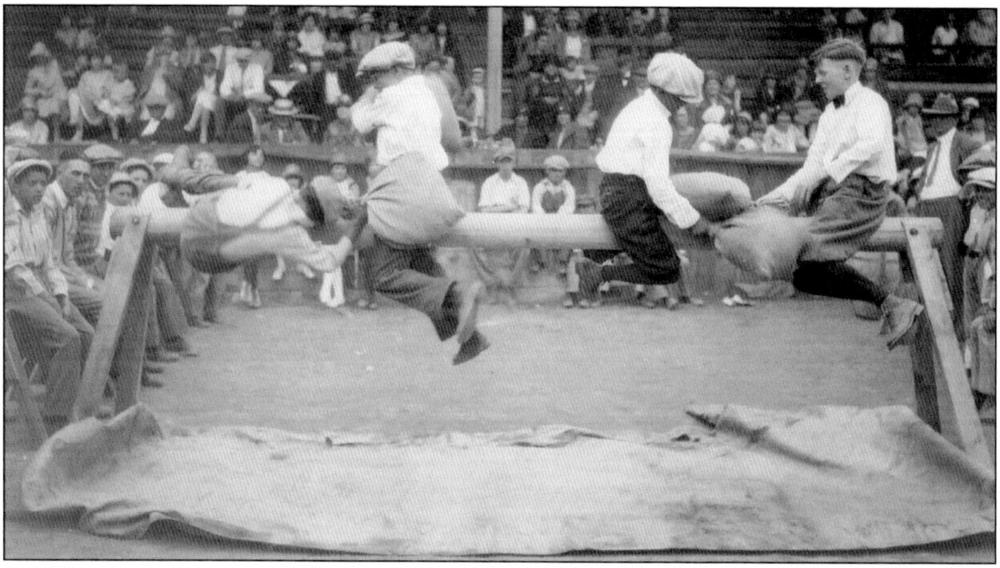

Field Day exercises were implemented under the Employee Representation Plan beginning in 1915. During Field Day, all work ceased for one day at the Minnequa Steelworks and in the mining communities, and workers and their families enjoyed a variety of games, contests, food, socialization, and relaxation. Shown here, a contest in 1920 involves knocking one's opponent off the pole with a pillow, and women race to see who can drive a nail into a board first. Contests varied through the years, but some of the more popular included "most children," in which the winner would get a pair of shoes for each of his/her children; the "saltine cracker and whistle" contest; and "climb a greasy pole." Prizes ranged from handkerchiefs to candy and, in later years, washing machines.

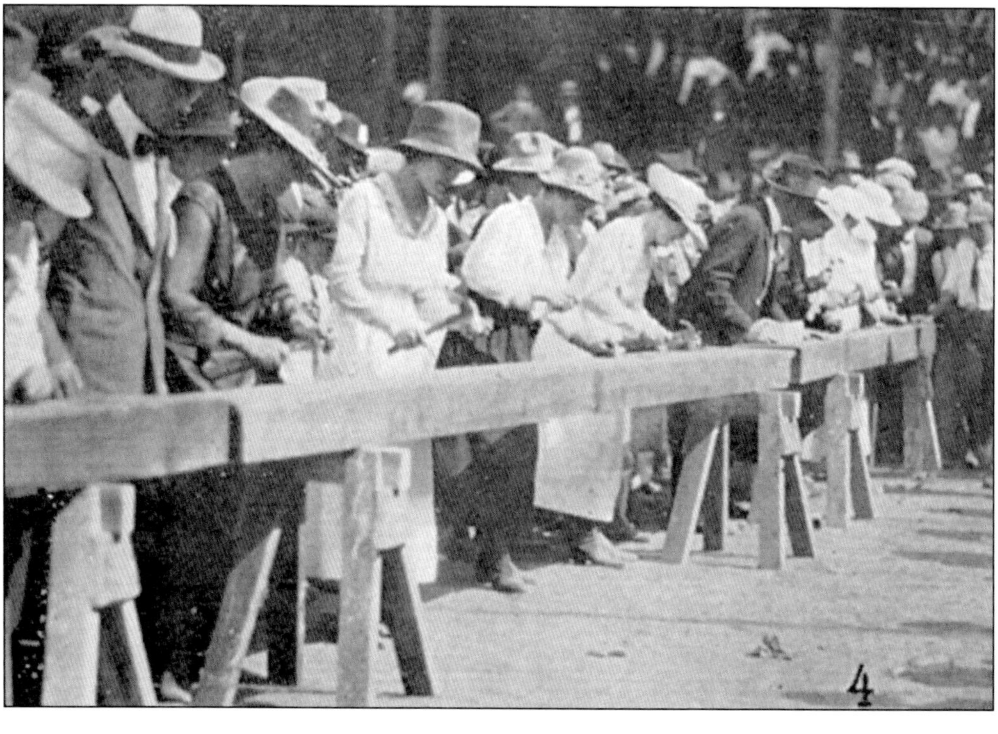

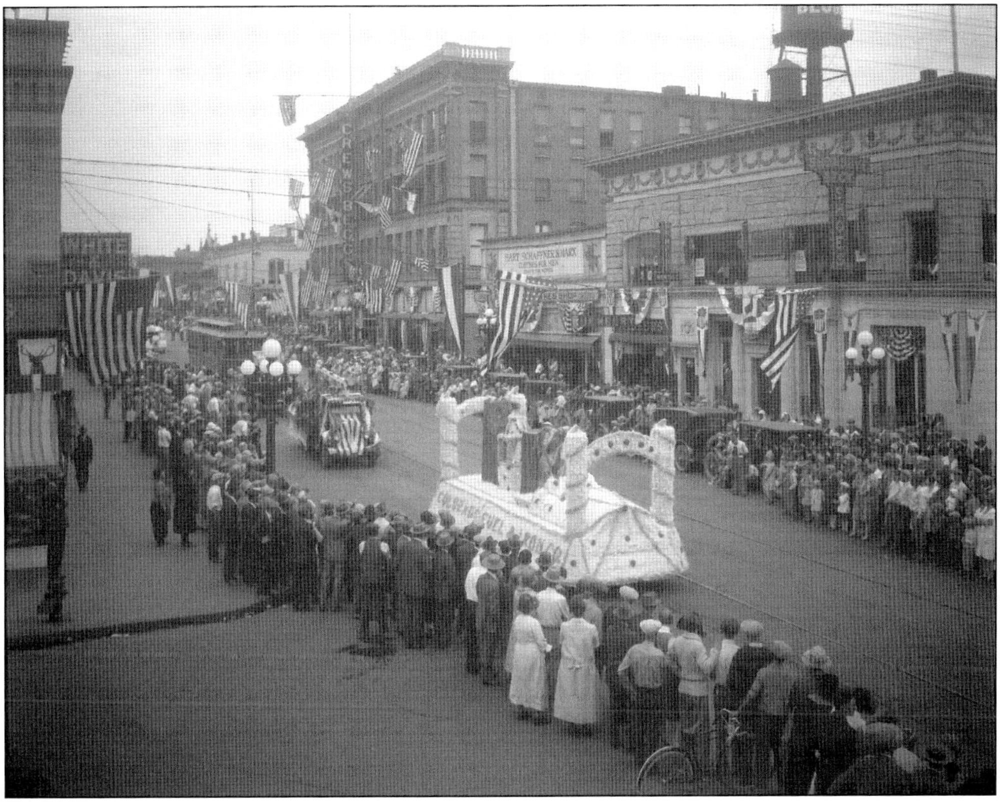

For those on the payroll, CF&I was more than just a place to work. The company served as the lifeblood of their communities. In their eyes, the company unified neighborhoods and ethnic groups and provided health care, shopping, education, entertainment, and other opportunities unimaginable just a few generations earlier. During the early 20th century, the company served as the common bond between members of a diverse community. Shown here are a parade float in downtown Pueblo in 1926 and the 1923 graduating class from Berwind High School, located in a company mining town in Las Animas County.

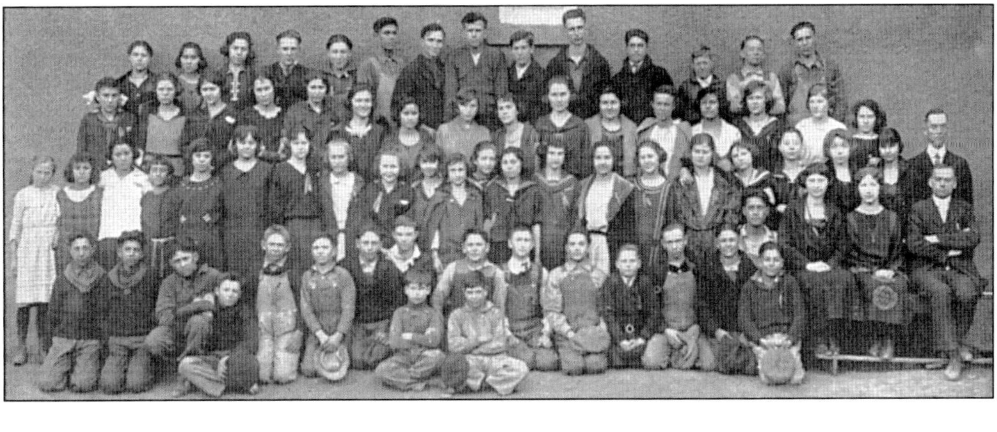

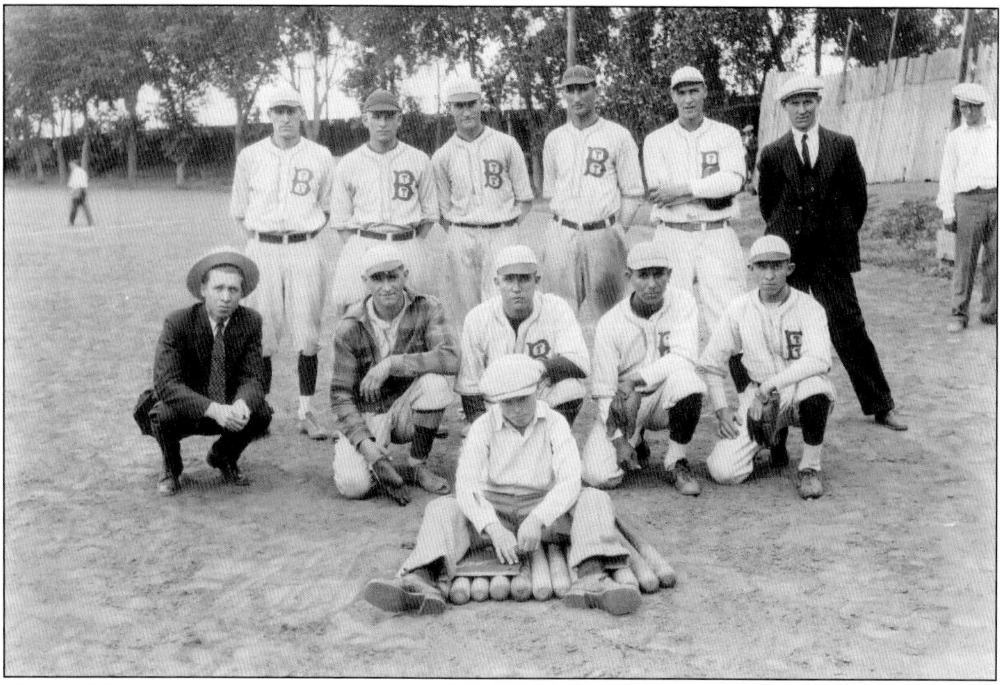

The CF&I community atmosphere extended beyond the walls of the Pueblo mill into the company mining districts. Company YMCAs and sports teams allowed workers to temporarily escape the perils they faced on a day-to-day basis and created a community environment for the workers. Shown here are the YMCA building at the company iron ore mine at Sunrise, Wyoming, and the Rouse coal mine baseball team in Huerfano County, Colorado. Activities at company YMCAs included billiards and swimming, and in some cases, the YMCAs possessed soda fountains. The YMCAs also served as community gathering places for dances and parties.

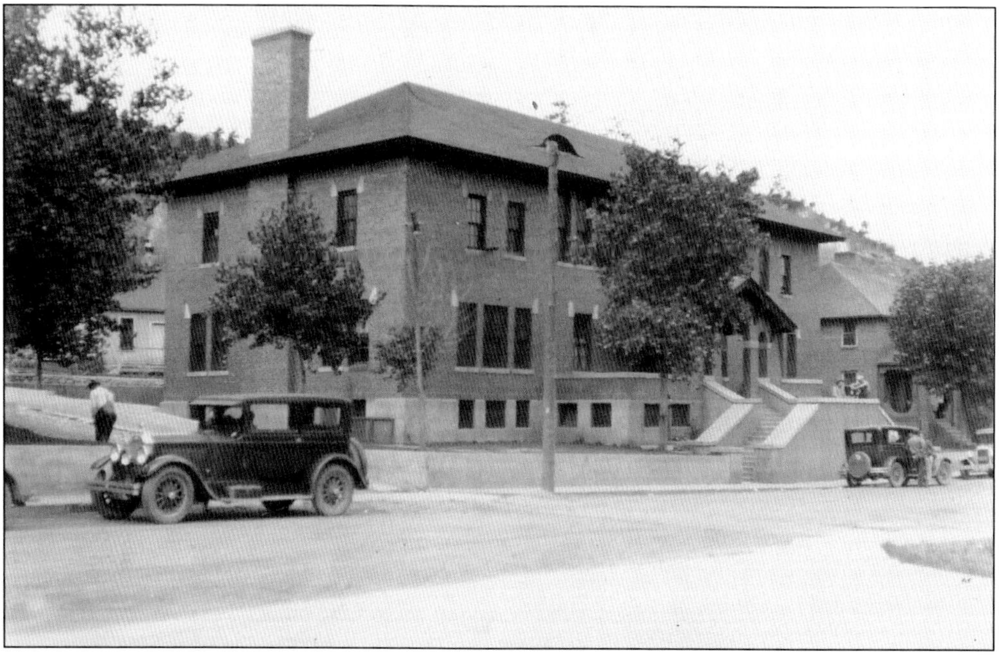

Three

The Late Rockefeller Years

After years of prosperity, the demand for steel products, especially rails, dropped sharply in the wake of the Great Depression. Rail output peaked at 600,000 tons in 1929, dropped to 351,078 tons in 1931, and then dropped again to 191,147 tons in 1932.

At the same time, natural gas was becoming more popular both with domestic users and in heavy industry, which led to a significant drop in coal sales, a vital income stream for CF&I. Many of the planned upgrades that were set to take place at the Pueblo mill, such as the construction of a larger blast furnace and improvements to the rolling mills, were abandoned.

By the mid-1930s, John D. Rockefeller Jr. had distanced himself from Colorado Fuel and Iron. His Employee Representation Plan was abandoned in the mining camps in favor of unionization in 1933, the same year that the company was forced into bankruptcy and reorganization. The company reemerged three years later with a new name, the Colorado Fuel and Iron Corporation, and a brighter outlook on the future.

With the economy beginning to recover from almost a decade of economic turmoil and a second world war on the horizon, the output of steel products once again reached levels not seen since the 1920s. Another round of unprecedented growth occurred over the next several years, with net profits reaching from $1.4 million to well over $2 million per year between 1941 and 1944. These profits led to a new round of plant modernization, increasing the overall value of the company. In December 1944, Charles Allen Jr. agreed to purchase the company from John Rockefeller Jr., ushering in a new era in CF&I history.

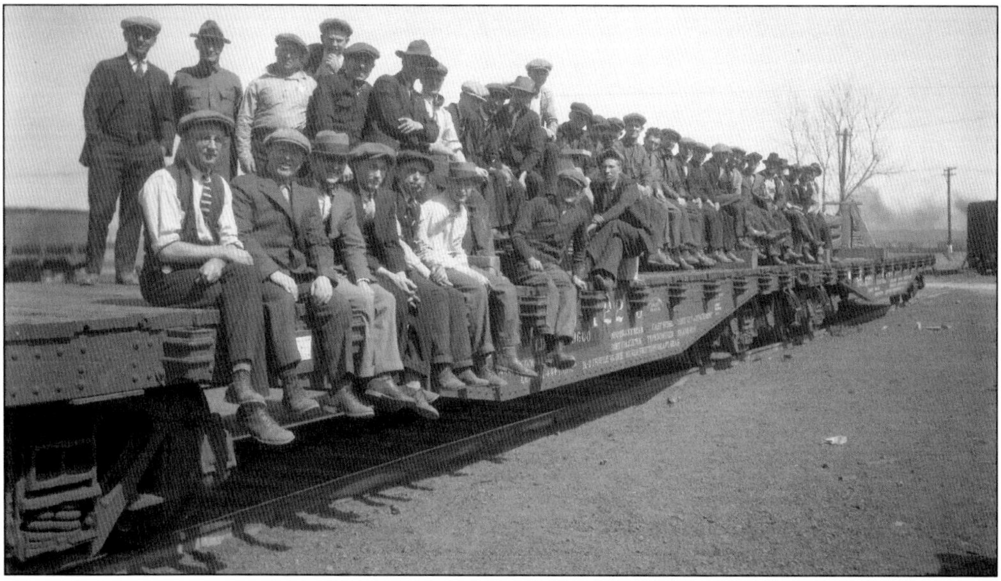

The 1920s was a period of economic gains and losses for the company. At the beginning of the decade, a general business slump marked the start of the metallurgical department operating at less than two-thirds capacity, with production dedicated largely to rails and rail accessories. By the 1930s, demand for rail products declined significantly. Shipping department employees pose on a rail transport car in 1926, when times were better.

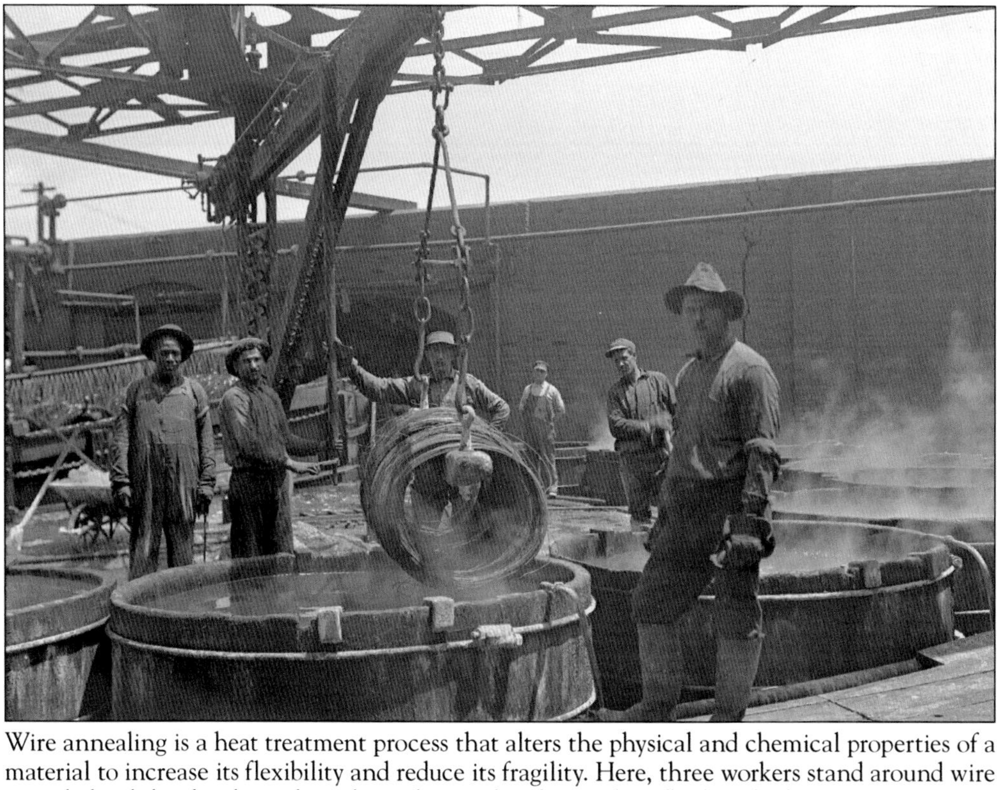

Wire annealing is a heat treatment process that alters the physical and chemical properties of a material to increase its flexibility and reduce its fragility. Here, three workers stand around wire or coiled rod that has been dipped into large tubs of annealing fluid in the late 1920s.

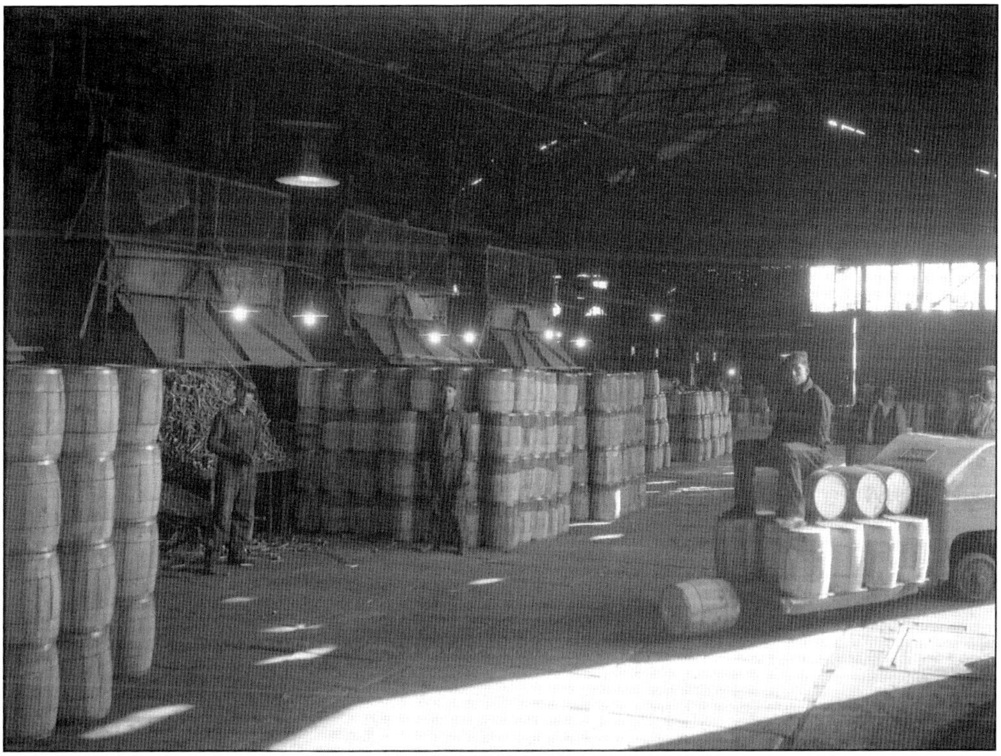

Spikes used to secure railroad plates to railroad ties were a profitable product earlier in the Rockefeller era. By the end of the 1930s, customer buying habits shifted away from rail transportation, and sales dramatically dropped. Here, some workers take a break from loading railroad spikes into barrels for shipping.

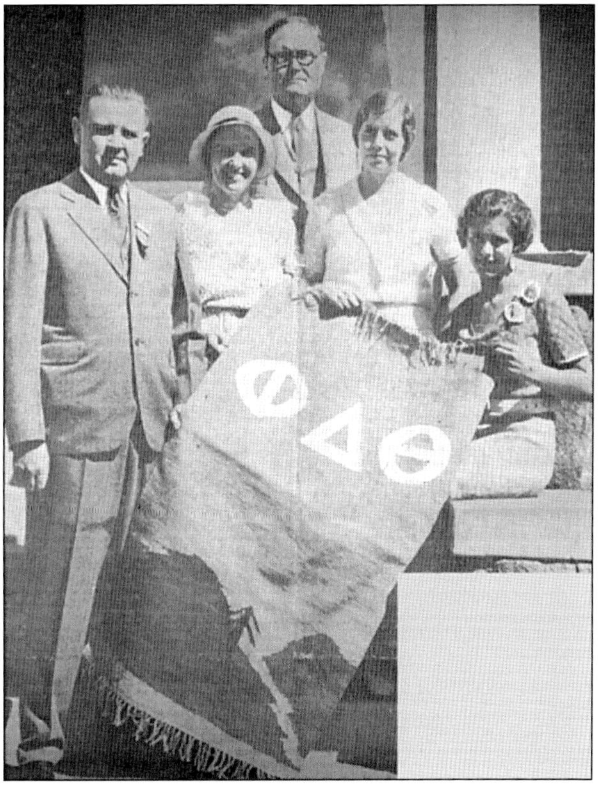

With the collapse of the steel industry and cutbacks on company mining activities, CF&I provided relief services to the thousands of dependents who found themselves unemployed. Gardening, cooking, basket and rug weaving classes, and other welfare activities were offered to those affected in hopes that workers would lead a more self-sustainable lifestyle. From left to right, George Banta, Mrs. Banta, D.A. Millet, Mrs. J. Hershel, and Ruth Millet show a rug created for a Phi Delta Theta convention in 1932.

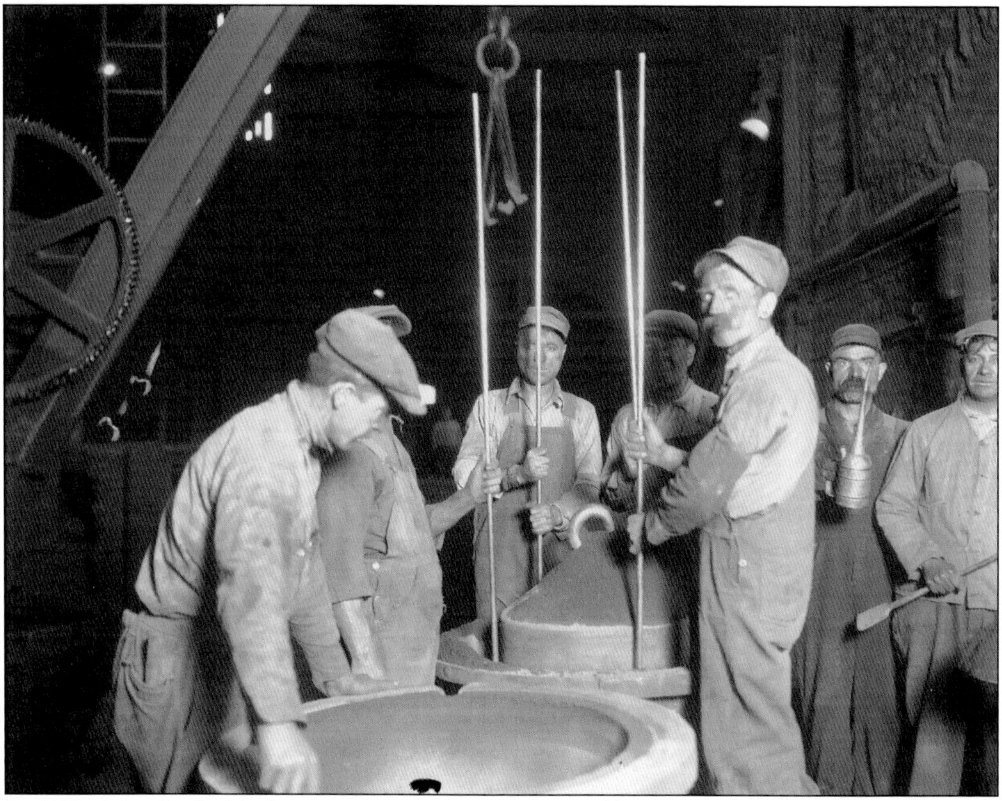

In 1933, federal relief and recovery programs encouraged businesses to reopen idle plants and expand operations. To assist with this development, the National Recovery Administration adopted industry-wide codes for fair competition, which in turn encouraged competitiveness and higher employment. The result of these programs called 3,000 people back to work at the steelworks and several hundred back to work in the company's coal- and iron-mining operations.

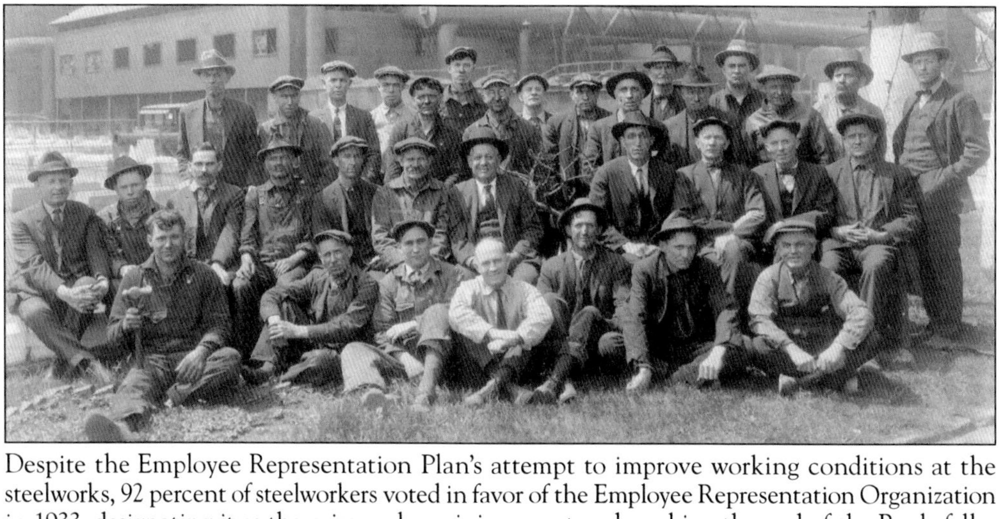

Despite the Employee Representation Plan's attempt to improve working conditions at the steelworks, 92 percent of steelworkers voted in favor of the Employee Representation Organization in 1933, designating it as the primary bargaining agent and marking the end of the Rockefeller plan. By 1942, the Pueblo mill formally unionized under guidance from the United Steelworkers of America.

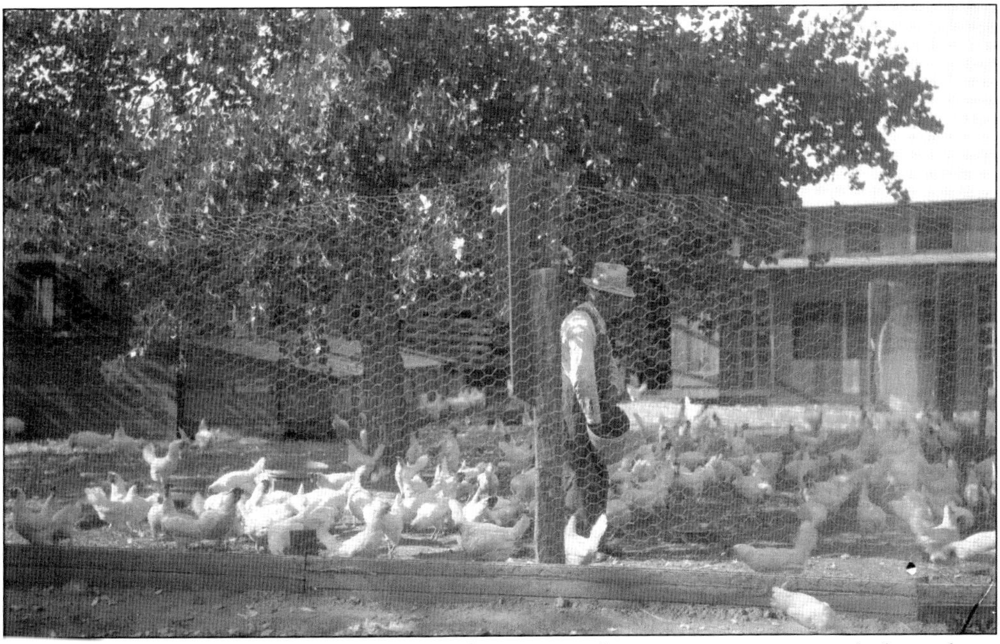

In an effort to recoup some financial losses, the company began to experiment with diversifying its product line to reduce its dependence on rail and accessories. In this effort, the company began producing ornamental fencing, farm wire, and highway guard fencing in 1929 and expanded to road grader blades in 1931.

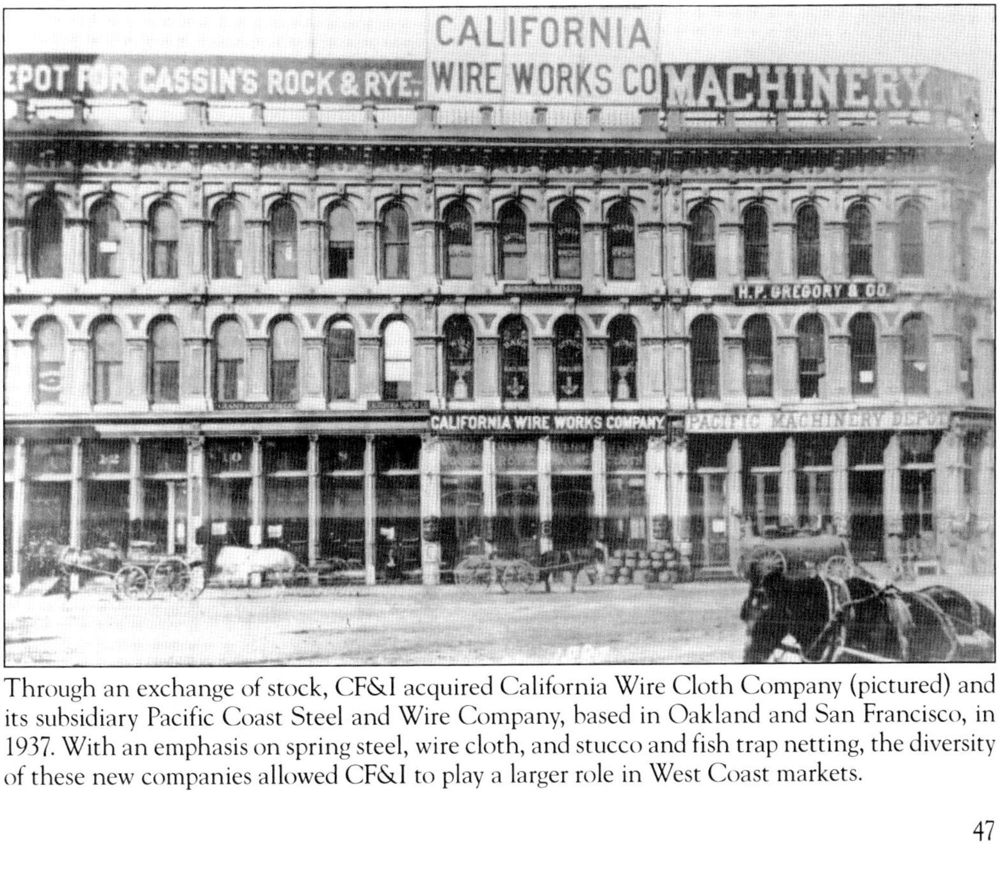

Through an exchange of stock, CF&I acquired California Wire Cloth Company (pictured) and its subsidiary Pacific Coast Steel and Wire Company, based in Oakland and San Francisco, in 1937. With an emphasis on spring steel, wire cloth, and stucco and fish trap netting, the diversity of these new companies allowed CF&I to play a larger role in West Coast markets.

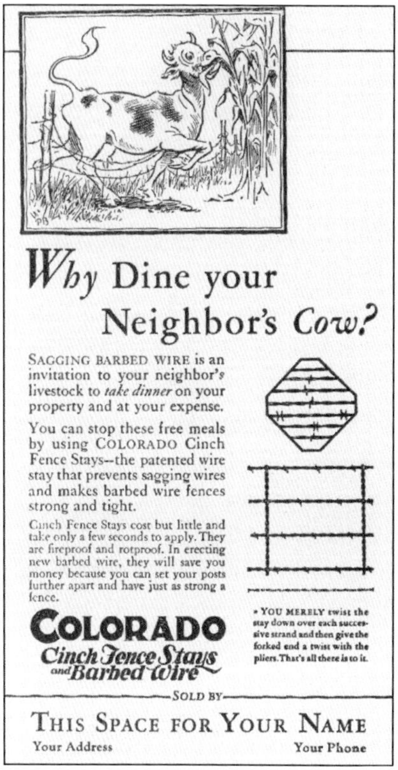

Turnover, a company sales magazine, was published bimonthly between 1929 and 1931 for retail merchants selling CF&I steel and coal products. Its articles included tips to increase profits, how to set up storefront displays, and hints to become a better merchandiser. This advertisement appears in a 1930 issue marketing CF&I's Colorado brand of cinch fence stays in barbed wire fencing products.

With an increase in staffing, annex extensions were built onto the main office building in Pueblo and the medical dispensary building in the late 1920s. Architect William J. Stickney was commissioned to continue the architectural style set by his predecessor, Frederick Sterner.

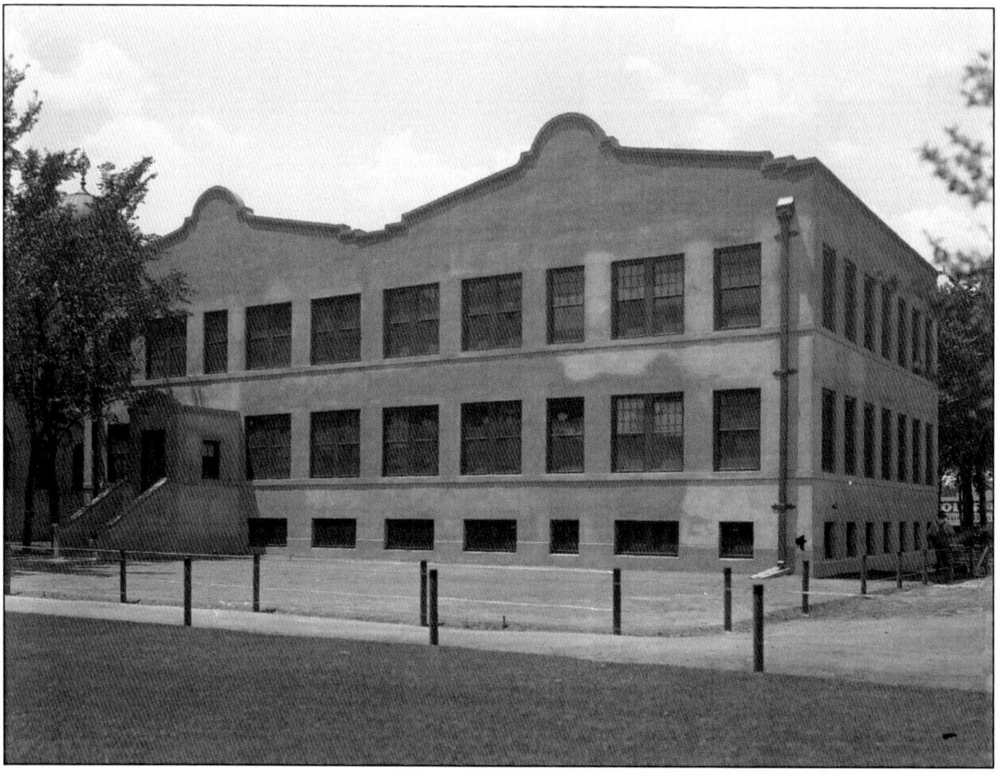

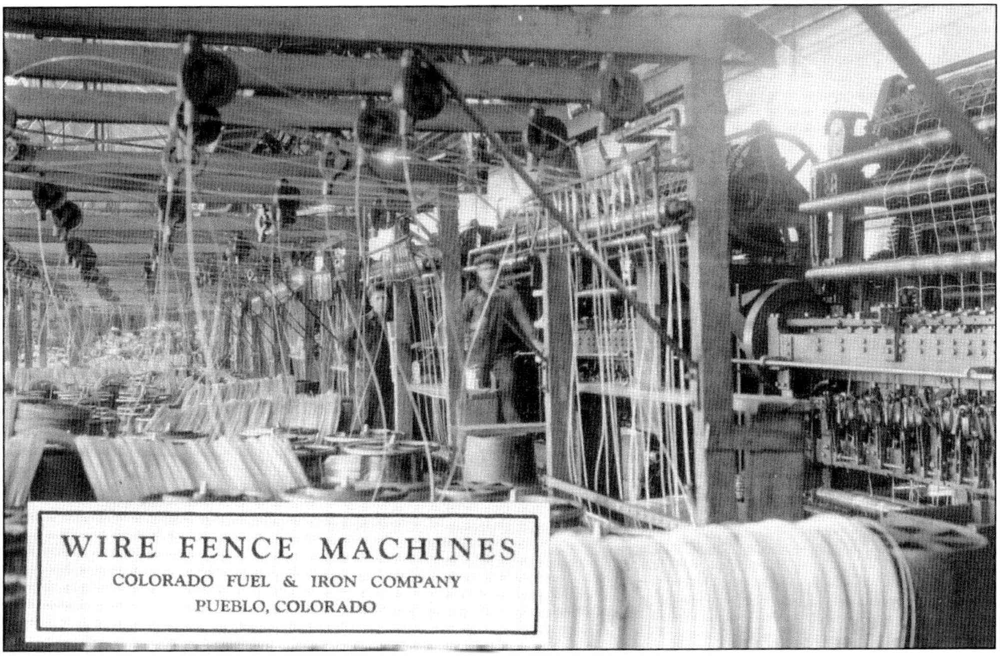

In 1928, improvements were made to the wire mill, including new machines to make ornamental fence. Fencing alterations to the V-mesh machines and newer and faster motor-driven nail machines were also installed, replacing the long shaft that previously ran the full length of the wire drawing room and allowed multiple machines to operate off one central engine.

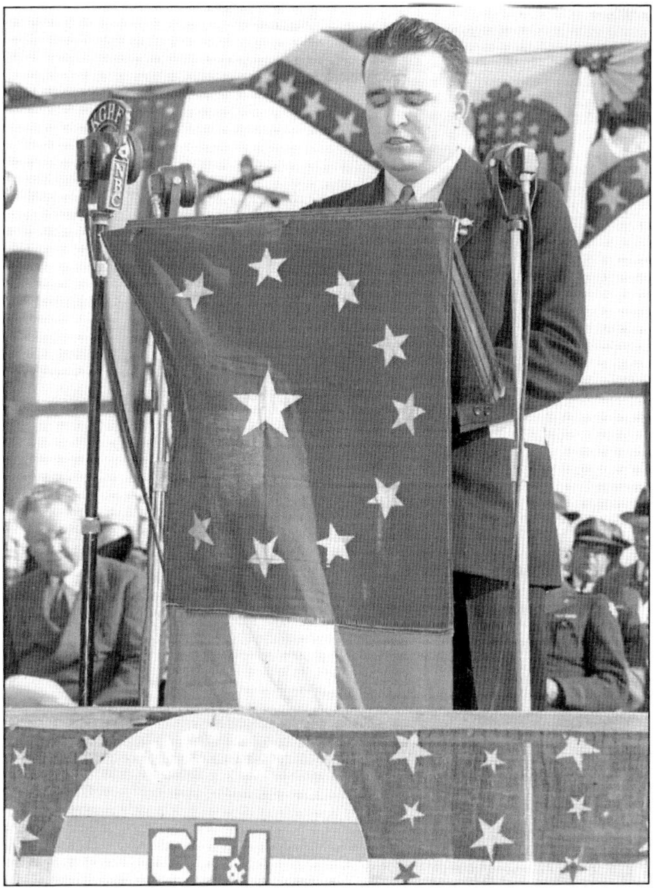

An active local member on the National Labor Relations Board, Alexander Bonata, was elected as the first president of the local branch of the United Steelworkers of America in 1942. Giving a speech at the dedication ceremony that spring, Bonata reiterated the common value of the steelworkers union that "united we stand, divided we fall," to uproarious applause. Bonata worked at CF&I's rod mill for 40 years, retiring in 1975.

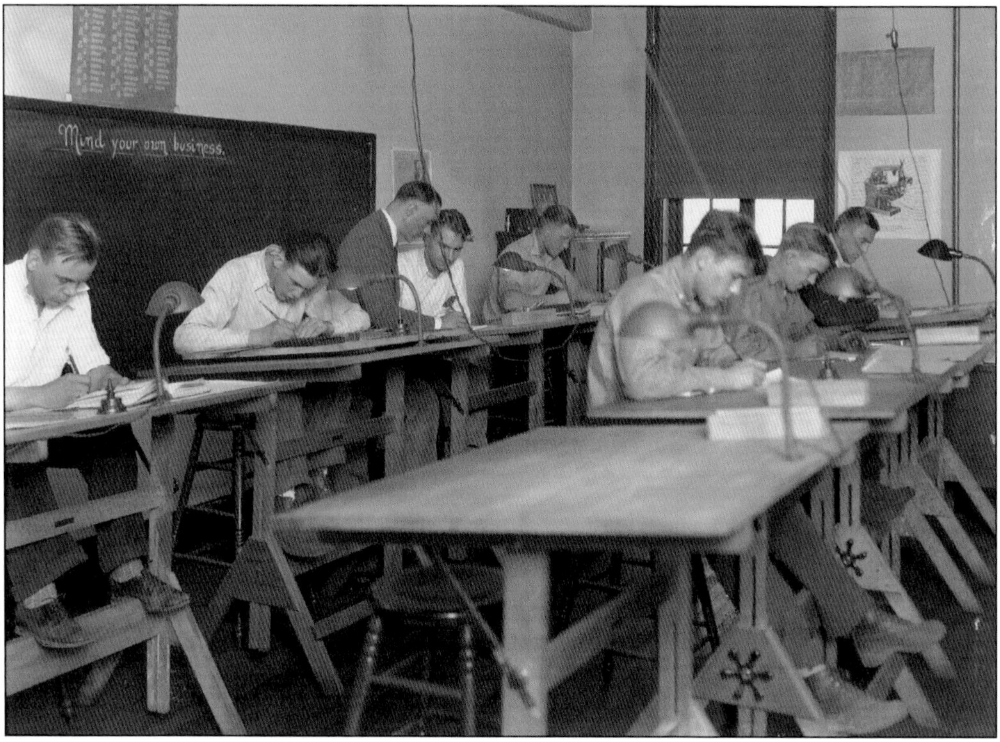

In 1925, the company's YMCA offered technical educational classes. Examples of courses included blueprint reading, typing, mechanical drawing, salesmanship, and advertising. Tuition for each class was $1 paid by the employee and $1.50 paid by the company. On-the-job training was also available. Through the program, apprentices earned 25¢ per hour with a 5¢ increase each year. Once trained, apprentices committed to working for the company for four years, at which time they earned a $100 bonus. The apprentice program at CF&I trained thousands of workers over the next five decades.

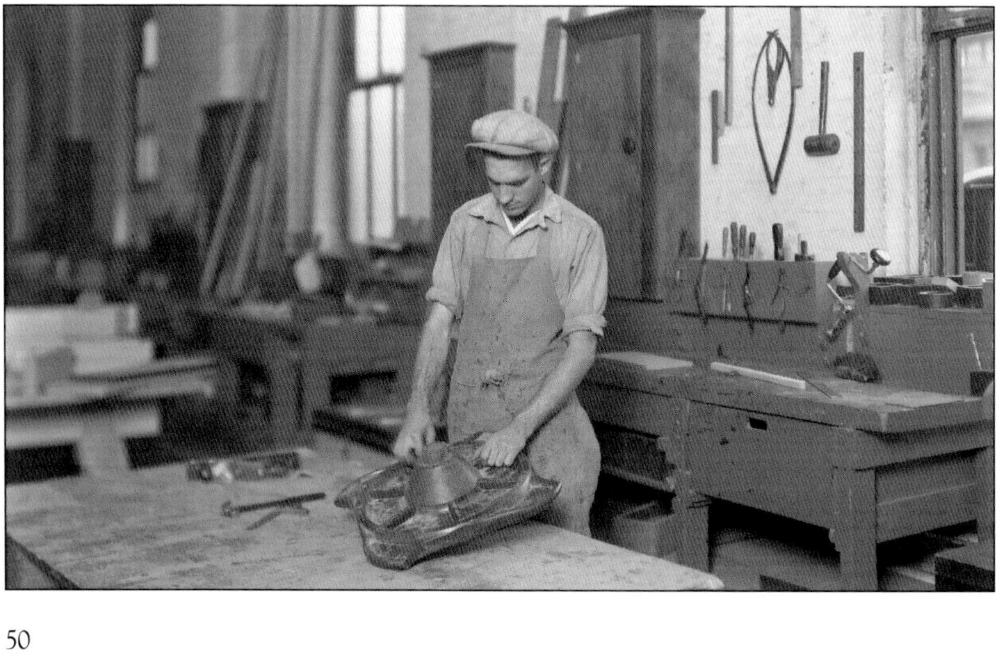

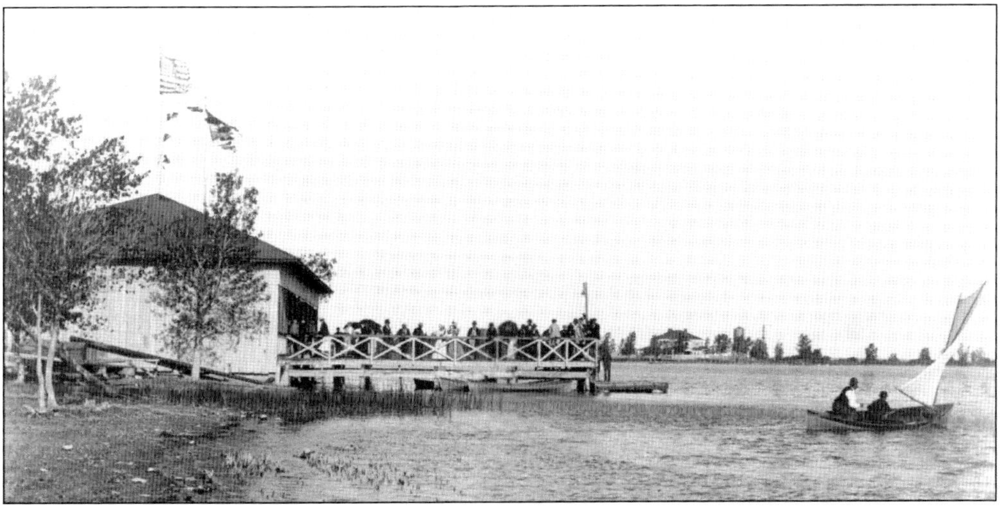

The artificial reservoir known as Lake Minnequa was quite the gathering place in the spring and summer months. By the beginning of the 20th century, trees and flowerbeds were set around the reservoir and a boathouse and dock were built for those enjoying boating, fishing, and swimming. An amusement setting within the larger park opened in 1902 and included a carousel, roller-skating rink, and dance pavilion. Celebrities entertaining inside the 1,200-seat theater included politician Eugene Debs and actors Sarah Bernhardt and Lon Chaney. For a fare of just a few pennies, families could ride a streetcar from the downtown areas to the park. With competition from other amusements and a lack of funding, the park closed in the late 1930s. The 30-acre site was razed in 1940, subdivided, and sold for residence properties.

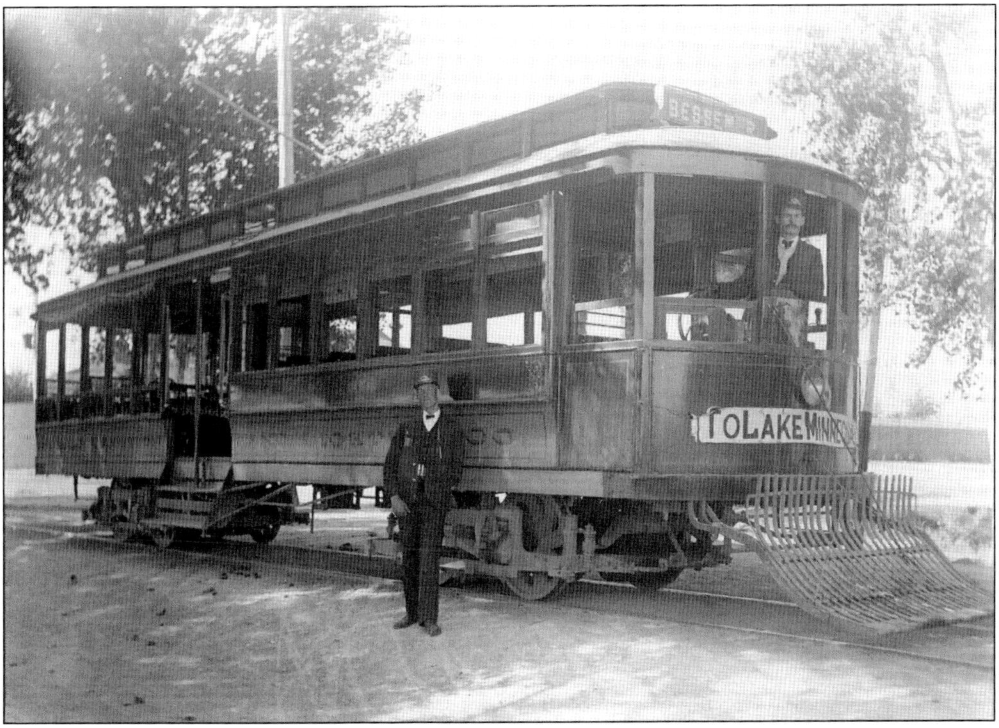

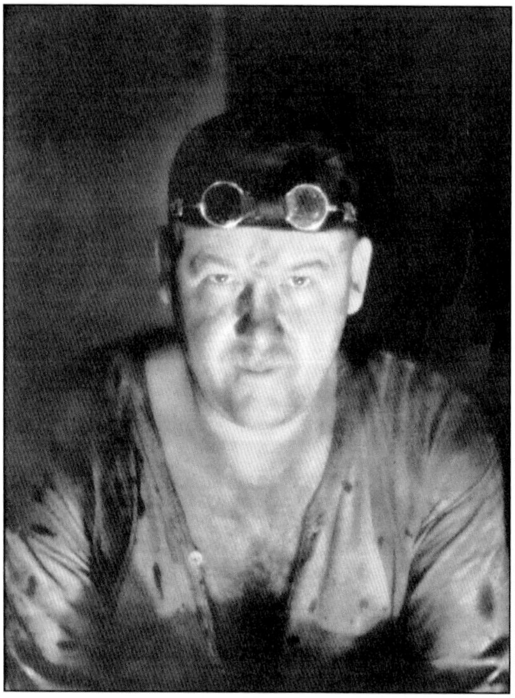

American photographer Eugene Hutchison, whose work in the 1930s focused on industrial subjects, found inspiration among CF&I employees. The subject in this photograph, titled *Gaze of Steel*, is James Comiskey, an open hearth worker. Hutchison described the composition of the photograph: "Years of looking into the seething mass of boiling metal has given the eyes of this open-hearth worker something of the hardness, the keenness and the power that is the soul of steel."

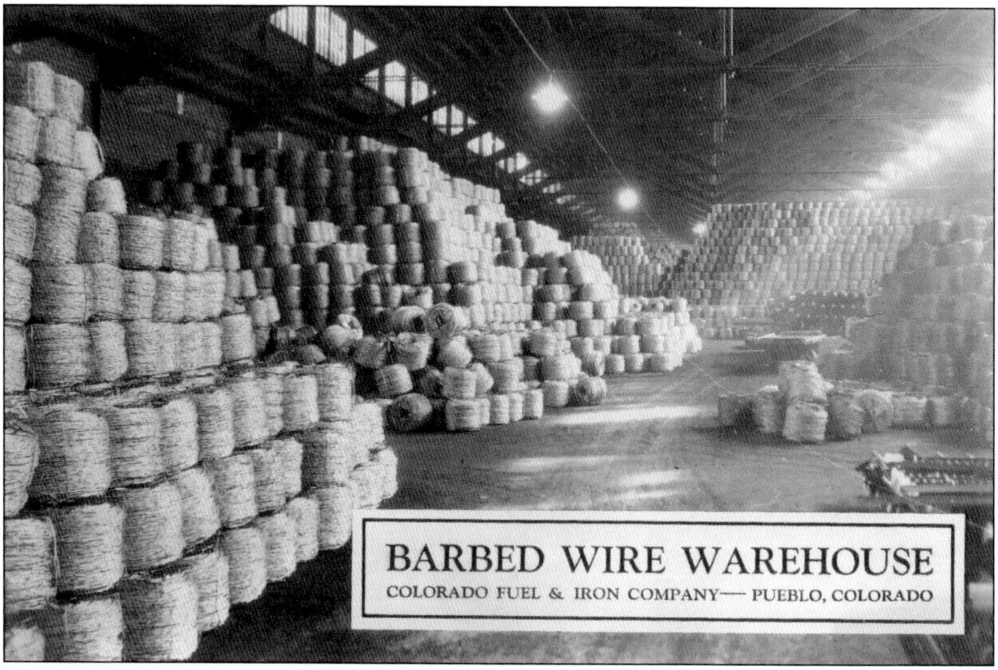

With marketing strategies aimed at farmers and ranchers of the West, barbed wire became one of CF&I's more profitable products in the 1930s. The wire, originally invented by Michael Kelly in 1864 and improved upon by Joseph Glidden in the 1870s, locked a simple barb onto a double wire and attached to a fence post. Thousands of farmers and ranchers purchased the special wire to keep their cattle and other livestock on their property. Shown here, the barbed wire warehouse stored the product until it was purchased by the customer.

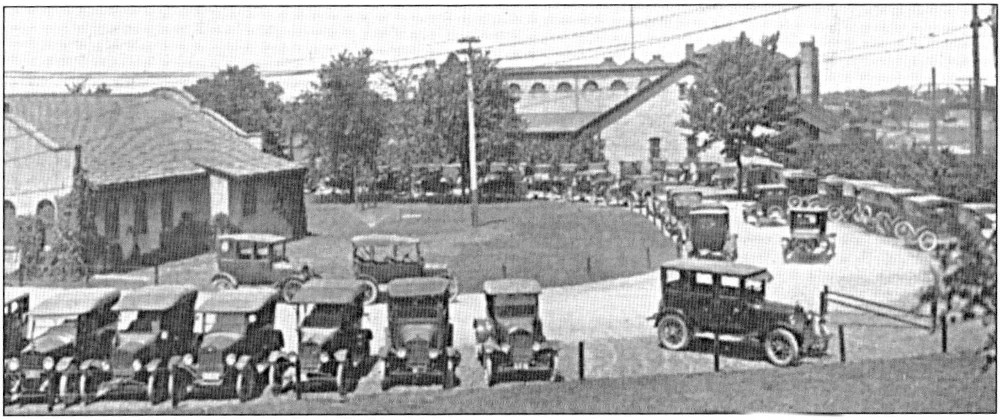

The popularity of automobile ownership in the 1920s and 1930s led to a new management challenge: how to encourage workers' good driving habits as well as good work habits. In 1931, the problems of speeding, parking too close to intersections, and double parking near work buildings became so severe that classes were offered for repeated infractions on company property.

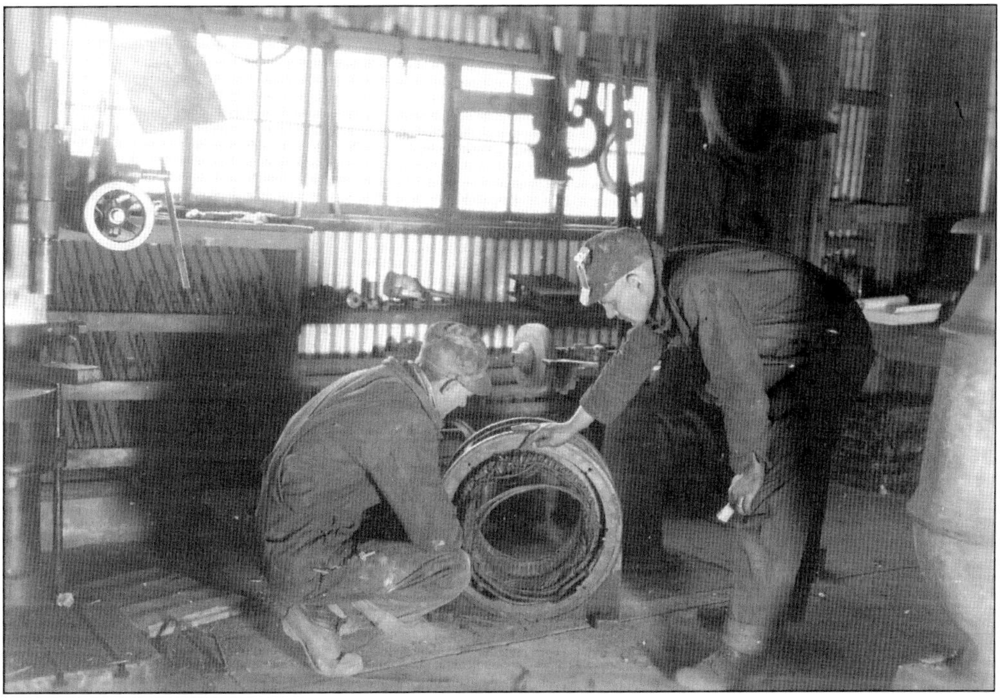

Those who worked in the shops department were responsible for repairing broken parts and maintaining equipment and spare parts to keep operations running smoothly. Shops included carpentry, rolling and smithing, machine, boiler, electrical, welding, pattern and pipe. Company mining operations also maintained their own shops to avoid bringing needed repairs to Pueblo. Two shopworkers at the Kebler Mine examine a piece of equipment in 1928.

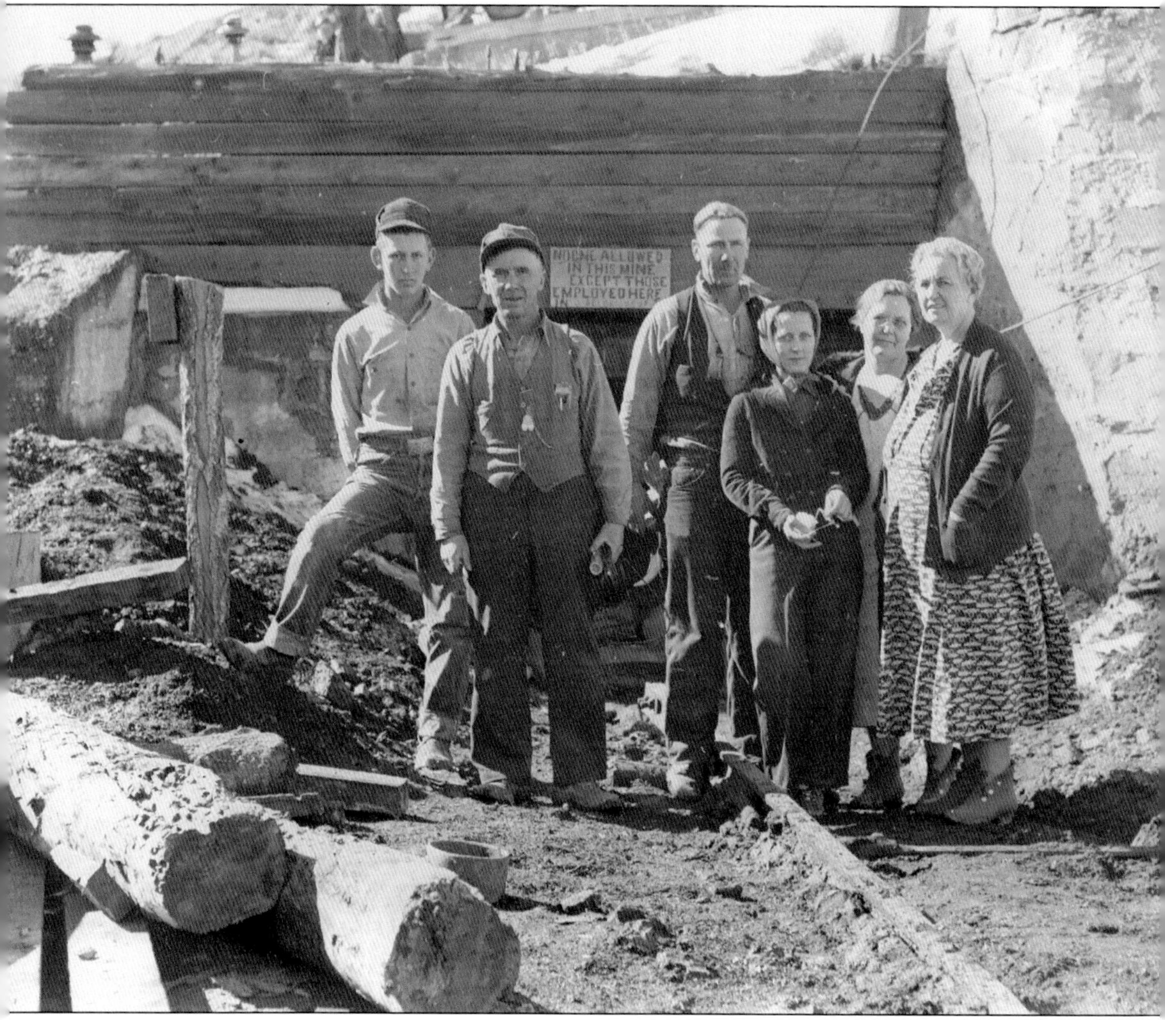

Throughout the late 19th and 20th centuries, CF&I depended heavily on coal extraction, not only for fuel in steelmaking but also for the income generated from customers for domestic heating. Between 1922 and 1930, competition from other, cleaner forms of domestic heating fuels, mainly propane and natural gas, dropped the demand for coal, forcing CF&I to close 21 of its mining properties. With the closing of the mines, many of the company's properties scattered throughout Colorado and New Mexico were shuttered, and buildings were moved to larger towns. The Deldosso family stands outside the Sopris Mine in Colorado's Las Animas County shortly before it was blasted shut. From left to right are Jack Deldosso Jr., Jack Deldosso Sr., Tom Deldosso, Dorothy Deldosso, Mrs. Tom Deldosso, and Mrs. Jack Deldosso.

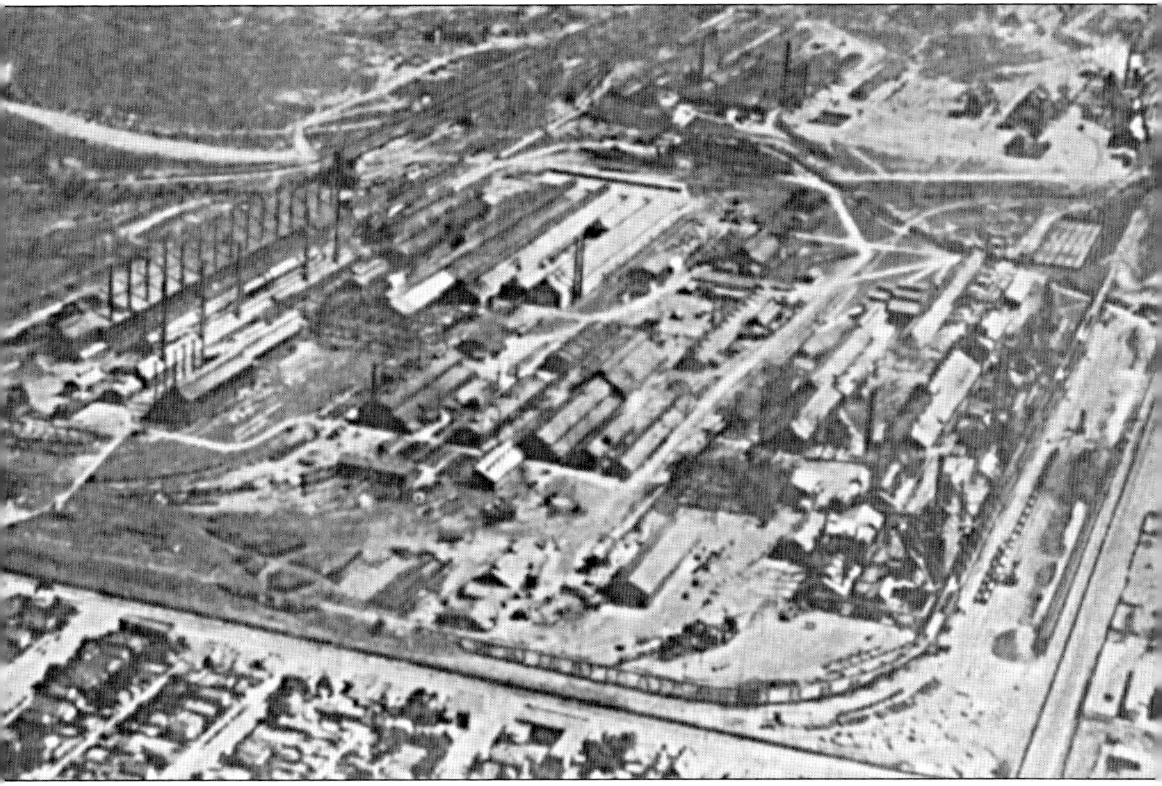

In 1872, when Palmer and his associates first planned to build an iron and steelworks at Pueblo, the investors purchased 71,000 acres of land in Pueblo County south of the Arkansas River on which they would build their empire. This aerial image, taken by the publicity department in 1932 for the company's 60th anniversary, shows about 6,000 acres used directly for mill operations. The mill property at the time included more than 50 buildings used in the preparation, production, and finishing processes of products; administrative functions; and the storage of materials and supplies. Today, Interstate 25 divides the property, with the east side of the interstate used for production purposes and the west side for administrative functions.

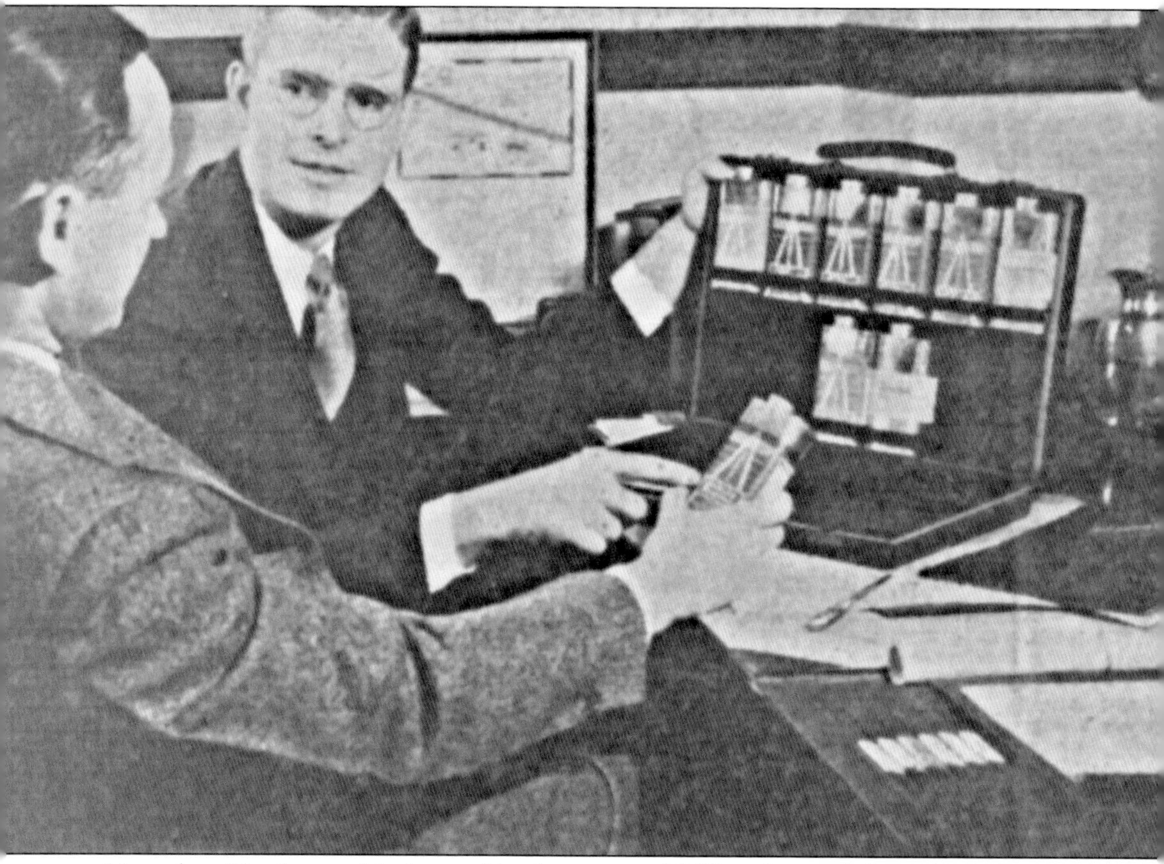

More than 50 salesmen hit the road in the winter of 1933 with sample kits of CF&I's newest product at the time, Silver Fly-Tip Spray, a by-product from the coke plant. Known for the previous 50 years as a company focusing on steel and mining of ores, CF&I expanded its product base to include insecticides beginning in 1932. Silver Fly-Tip sprays, ant control, chicken coop and rabbit hutch disinfectant, cattle spray, fly repellant, and similar products were available to customers in sales catalogs until the 1950s. Salesman M.J. Aurelius shows a potential customer the benefits of the fly spray.

Four

The War Years

Both world wars had a profound impact on company operations. During the Great War, more than 1,600 men left service with CF&I to fight in the trenches. The commercial sale of steel was suspended in 1918 to make room for government orders, and the company and employees purchased over $1 million in Liberty bonds.

World War II injected new prosperity in most of America's heavy industry enterprises, and company employees served a more active role in the United States' victory abroad and on the home front. During the nearly four years the United States was involved in the war, the company increased its production by more than 60 percent. Rail manufacturing played a major role in the war effort, with 22 percent of the nation's rails rolled at the Pueblo plant.

Between 1942 and 1945, CF&I produced nearly four million 155-millimeter and eight-inch shells, metal coils, and springs in addition to its regular catalog of products. In 1944 alone, 917,948 tons of finished steel products were rolled at the Minnequa Works in Pueblo. Besides supplying the needs of domestic customers, CF&I rails were purchased by railroads in North Africa, used in the Normandy invasion, laid on the Trans-Iranian Railway, and were a vital link for shipping Lend-Lease supplies to Russia during the early part of the war. In addition to their regular workload, CF&I employees and their families found time to engage in other activities to aid in the war effort on the home front.

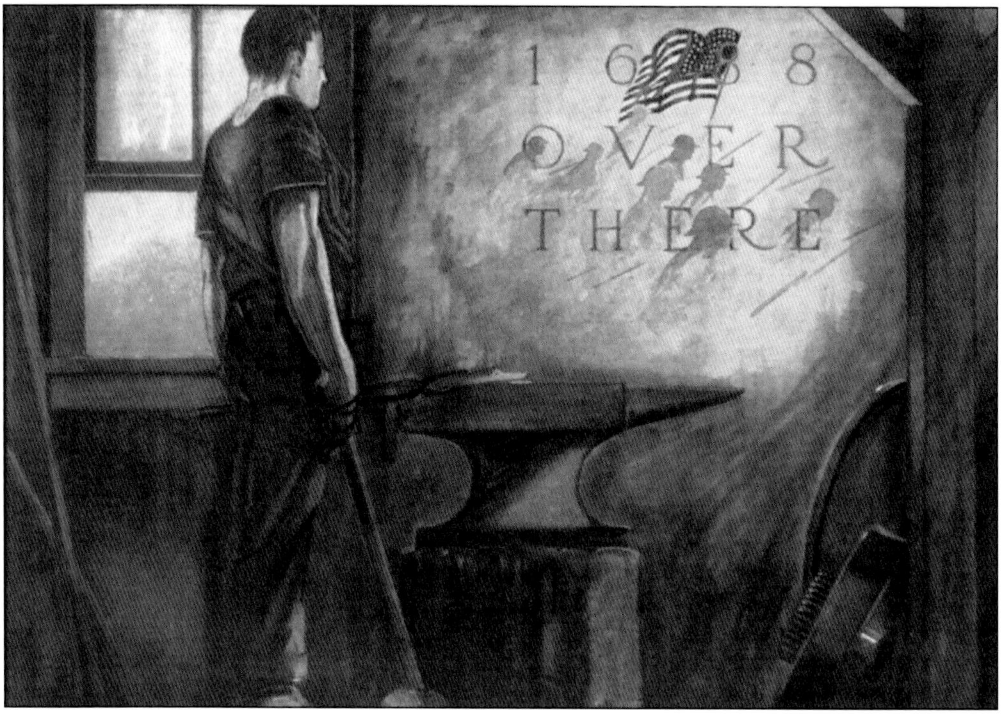

The *Industrial Bulletin*, a monthly CF&I newsmagazine between 1915 and 1928, printed a sketch of a steelworker thinking of his 1,688 fellow coworkers who left the company to serve in the war in the autumn of 1918. Many of these soldiers returned from Europe and resumed their work as miners, steelworkers, and office personnel.

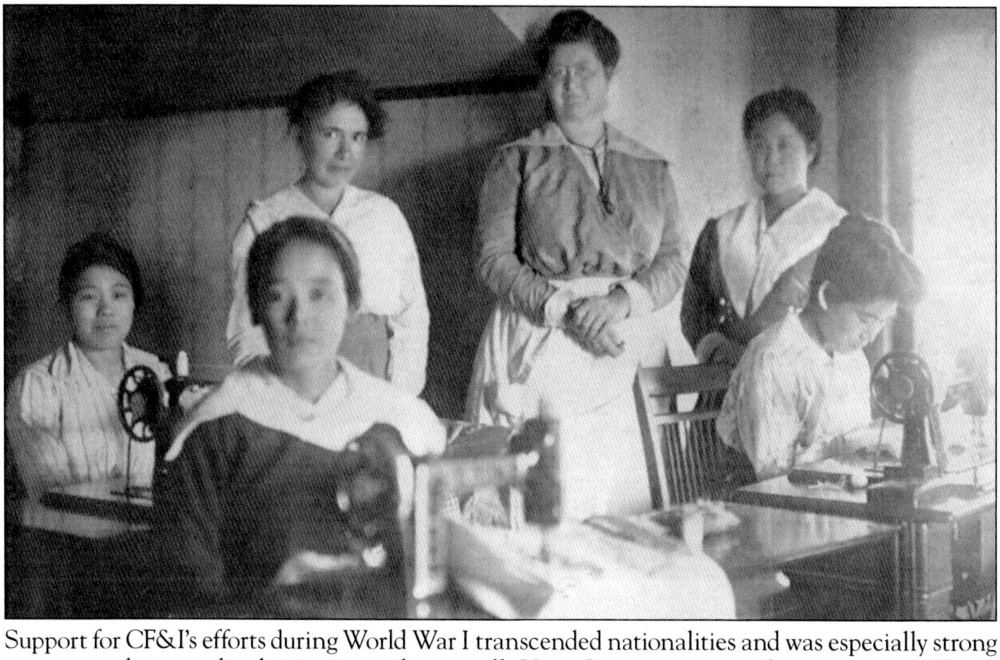

Support for CF&I's efforts during World War I transcended nationalities and was especially strong among newly naturalized citizens on the payroll. Here, Japanese women learn to sew uniforms for the Red Cross at the Steelworks YMCA in 1918.

The *Industrial Bulletin* stated that "the most patriotic duty for a young woman was to learn the proper methods of caring for the sick and safeguarding the health of the community." From left to right, Bertha Perry, Merwyn Darby, Bertha Solberg, Vivian Flager, Stella Ackelbein, and Lela Henery comprise the company's Minnequa School of Nursing class of 1917.

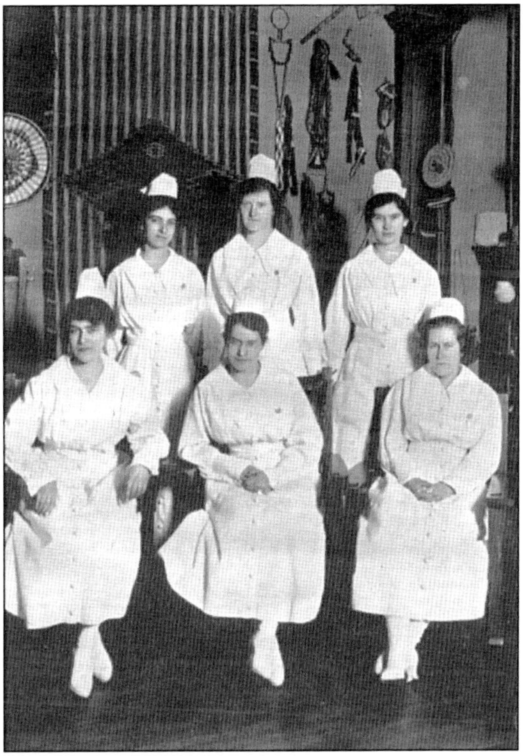

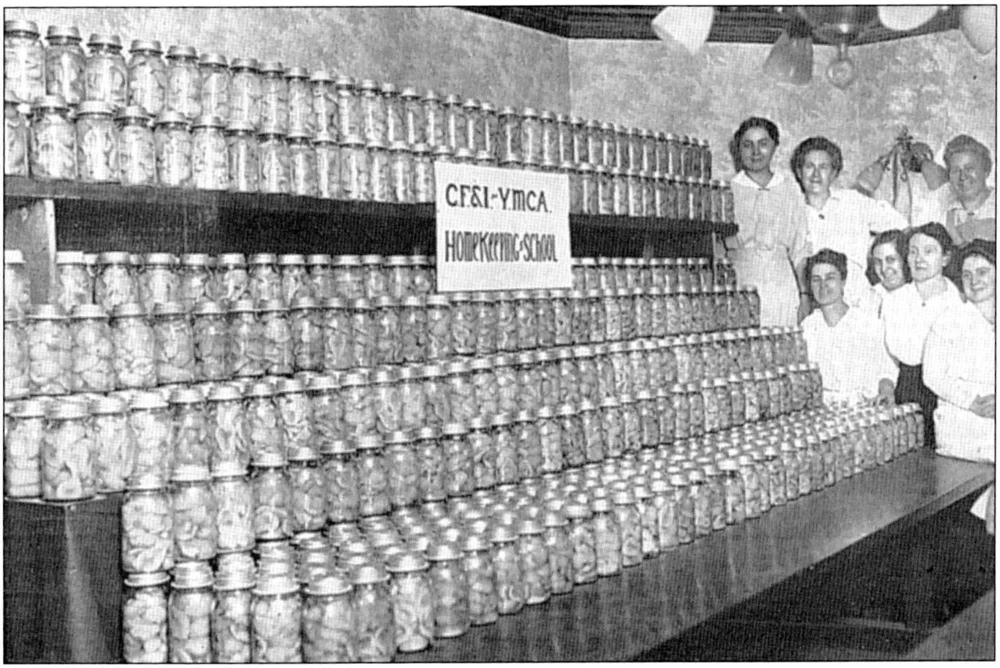

Wives and daughters of CF&I employees were encouraged to grow Victory gardens at home, preserve their produce, and send any extra food overseas to servicemen. In 1918, YMCA employees taught classes relating to food preservation. Their efforts canned 697 quarts of Bartlett pears to send to American army bases in Europe.

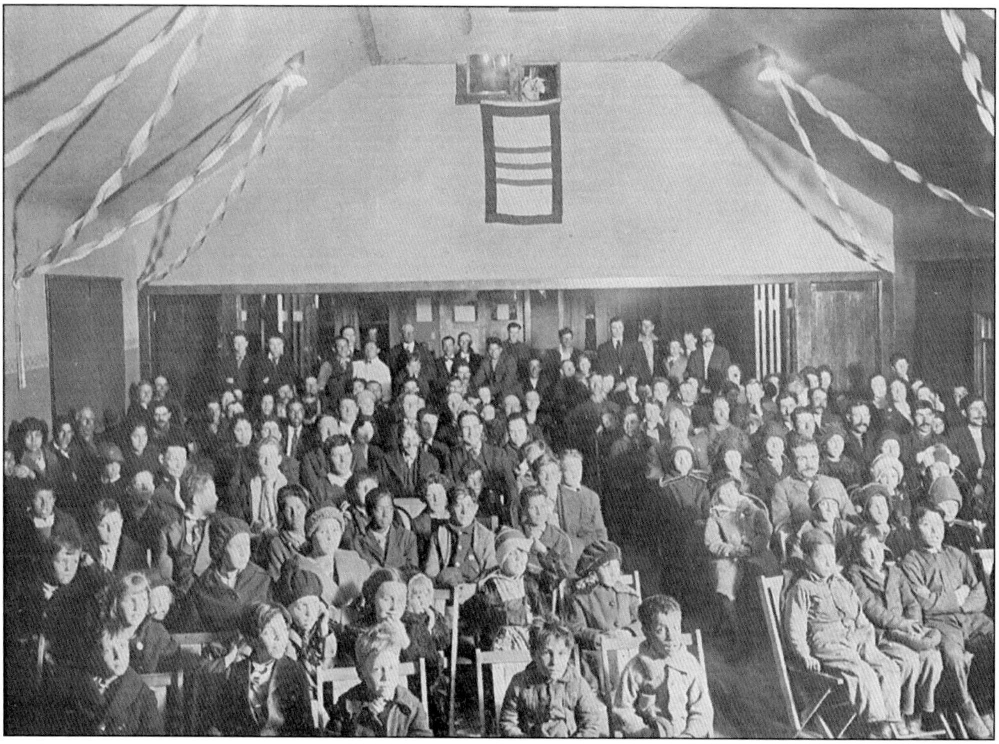

During the final days of World War I and the months that followed, the America's First Club organized in the Steelworks YMCA and in the company mining camps, stimulating patriotism and good citizenship. Patriotism rallies, flag raisings, and America-themed parties were common.

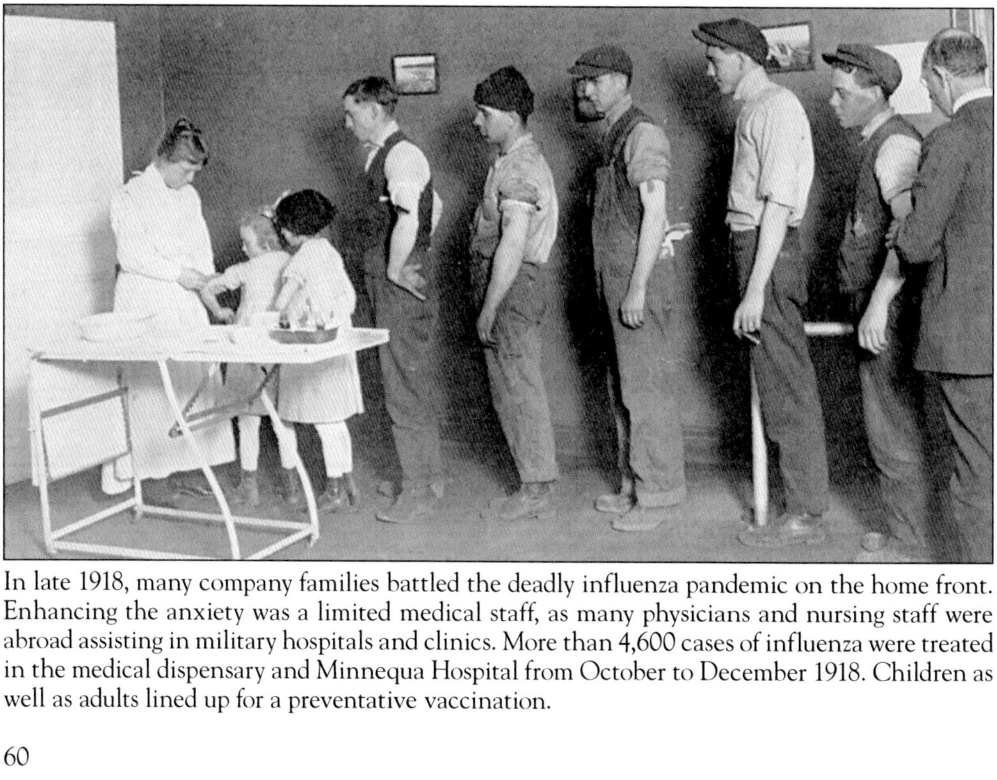

In late 1918, many company families battled the deadly influenza pandemic on the home front. Enhancing the anxiety was a limited medical staff, as many physicians and nursing staff were abroad assisting in military hospitals and clinics. More than 4,600 cases of influenza were treated in the medical dispensary and Minnequa Hospital from October to December 1918. Children as well as adults lined up for a preventative vaccination.

CF&I publications regularly reported on the activities of former employees or the children of employees as they conducted their military service. Arthur Murray, a former crane operator in the open hearth furnace, gave his life in service of his country while assigned to the shipping docks in Bordeaux, France, where military supplies were unloaded. His father, John H. Murray, was also employed at the Minnequa Steelworks in the brass foundry.

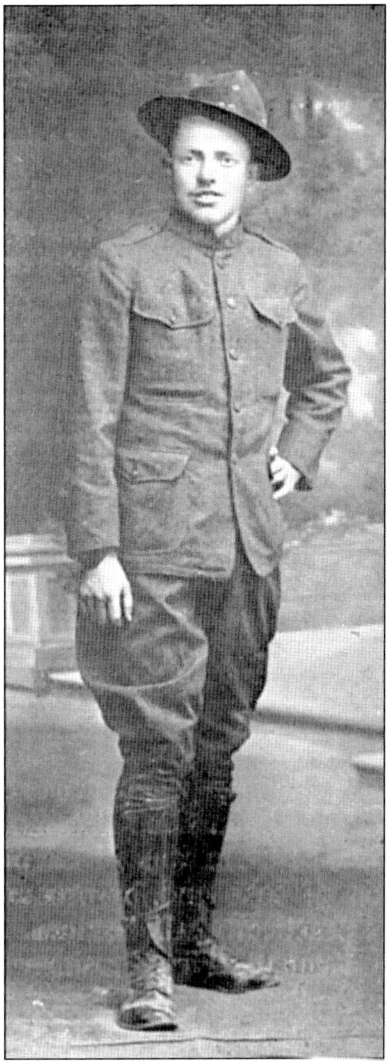

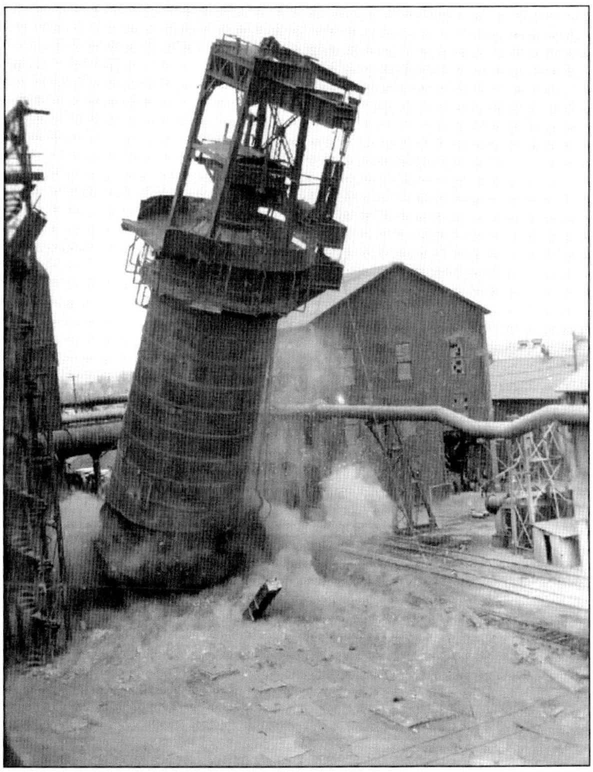

Governmental war contracts signed in 1941 provided funding to build a new blast furnace, new water and ore preparation facilities, a battery of coke ovens, and a steam-powered electric plant. The steel coming from this blast furnace, originally built in the 1890s as part of a modernization campaign, was re-melted in the open hearth furnace to create new steel.

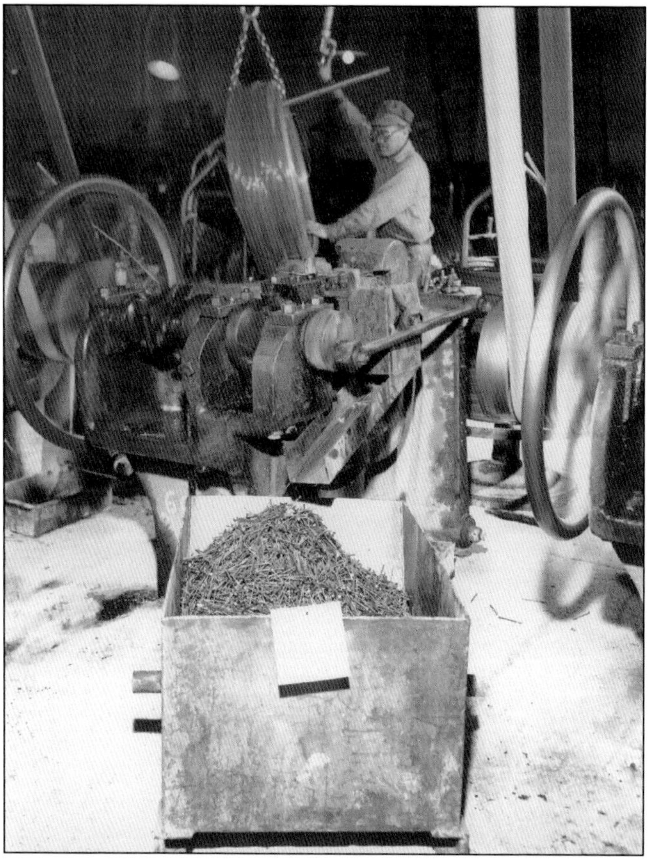

Opening in 1903, the wire mill serviced CF&I until the 1990s, when it was purchased by Davis Wire of Irvine, California. In this mill, dozens of different grades of wire were created for use in making metal springs and coils, barbed wire, field fence, and much more during World War II. A worker is assisted in lifting a 750-pound bundle of wire with the aid of a crane around 1945.

In 1940, CF&I signed an agreement with the US Army Ordnance Department to produce forgings for 155-millimeter shells. By the end of the war, CF&I had produced 3.5 million projectiles. Larger, previously used artillery rounds were used as scrap metal and melted in the open hearth furnace. The new steel created in the process was then used for the shell forgings.

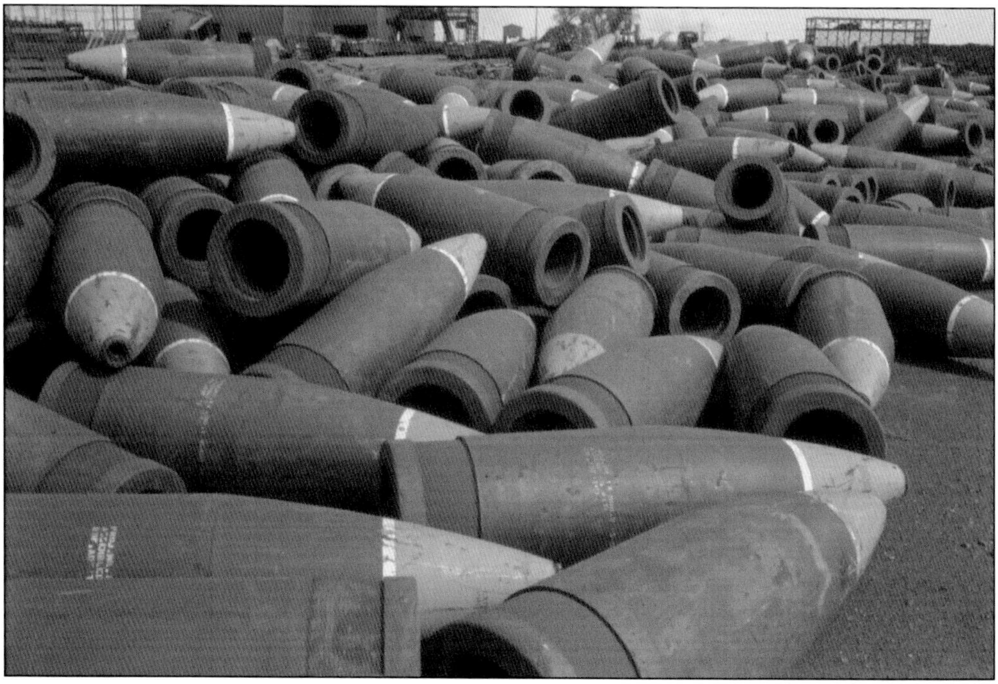

Open hearth furnaces produced heat around 3,000 degrees Fahrenheit, which further purified the pig iron created in the blast furnace. Fires blazed at both sides of the hearth, passing heated currents of air and gas alternately from each fire over the molten iron. The extreme heat eventually burned any impurities in the iron, resulting in pure steel.

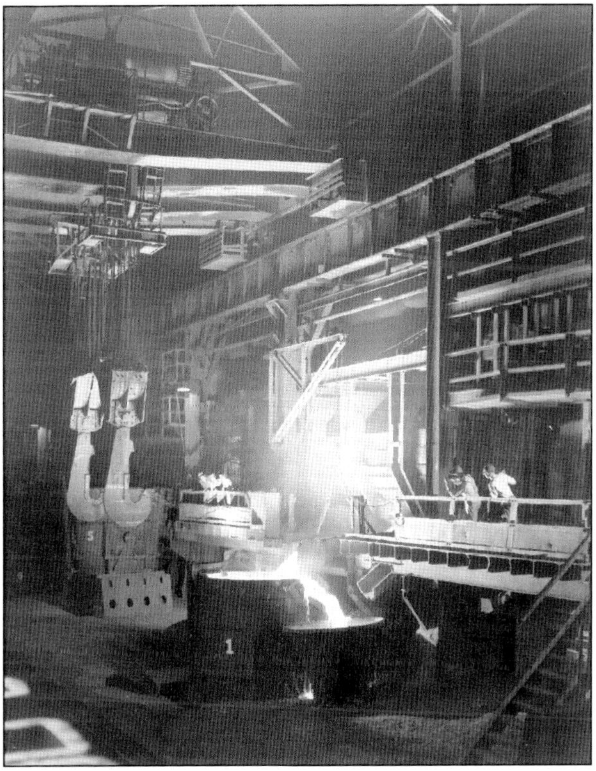

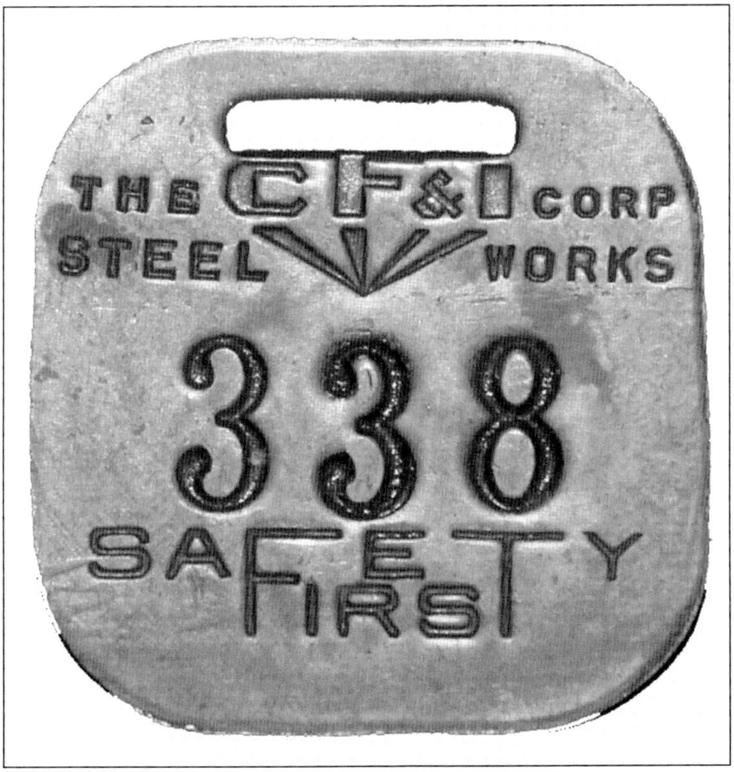

Beginning in the early part of the 20th century, each CF&I employee was assigned a number for payroll purposes and employee identification. These numbers were stamped on brass checks, small squares of brass the employees carried on a belt loop or key fob. In the 1940s, security tightened at the Minnequa Steelworks, and rules were enforced that employees must have identification with them at all times.

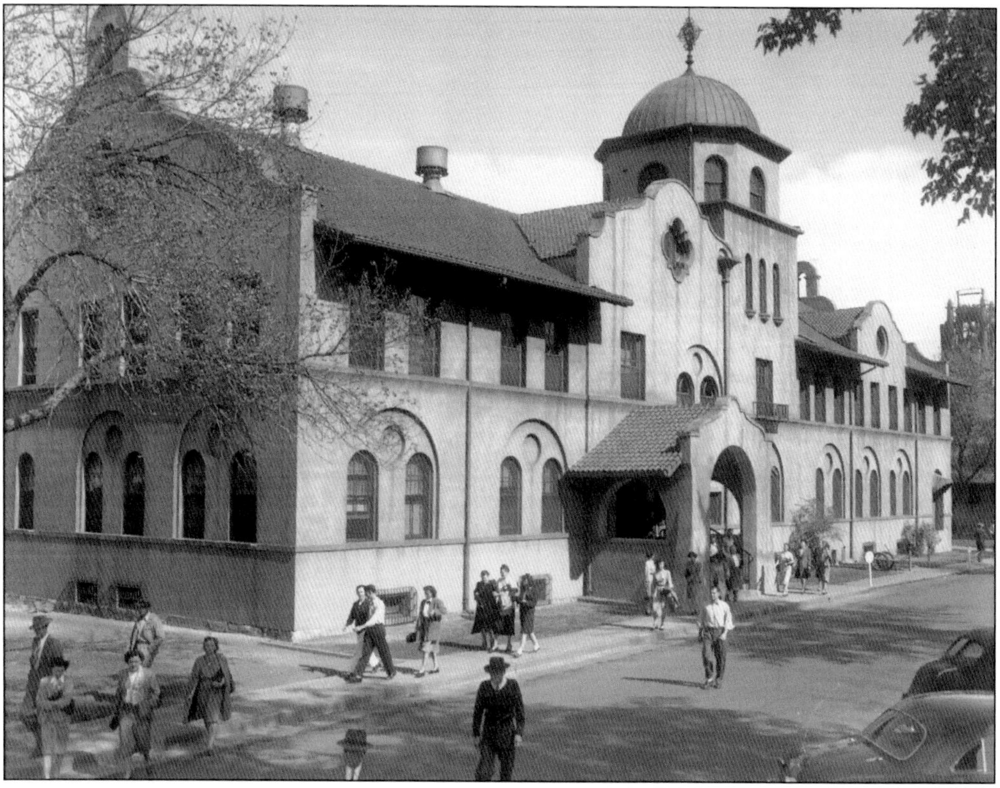

Built in 1901 by Frederick J. Sterner, the main office building to the west of the Minnequa Steelworks served local administration functions including payroll, finance, and engineering until the early 1990s, when the company entered into a bankruptcy. In the 1940s, the company also maintained administrative offices in Denver and, by the end of the decade, in New York City.

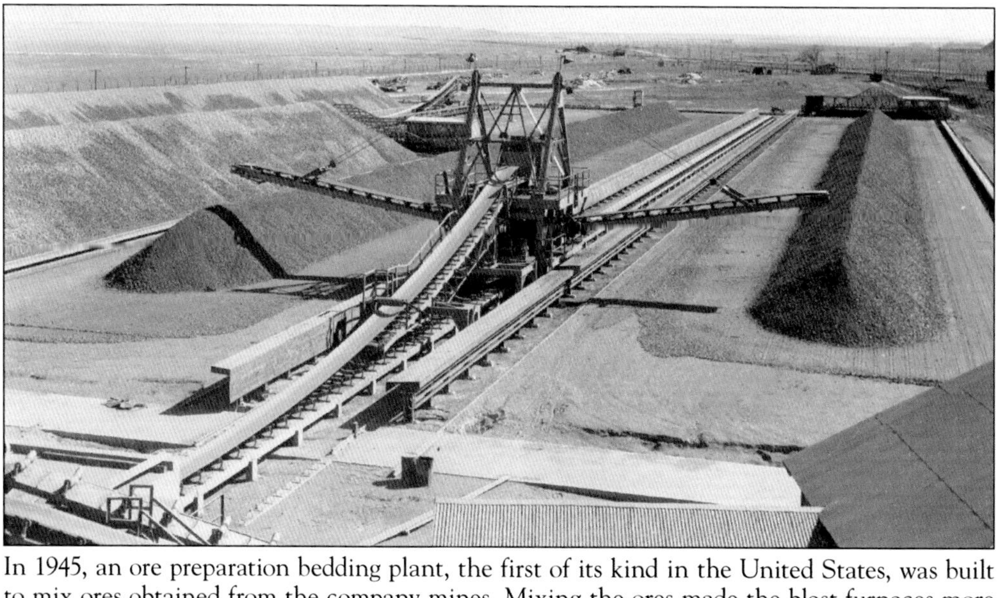

In 1945, an ore preparation bedding plant, the first of its kind in the United States, was built to mix ores obtained from the company mines. Mixing the ores made the blast furnaces more efficient by reducing the volume of coke consumed in the production of pig iron.

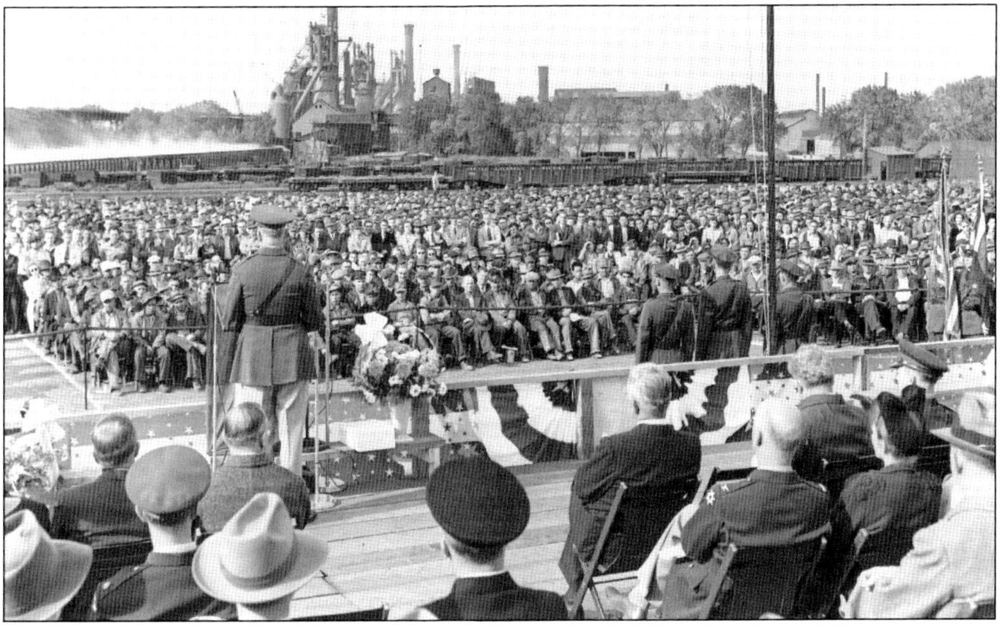

Employee dedication to success during a time of national crisis earned CF&I four prestigious Army-Navy Efficiency Awards. These awards were given to only five percent of the country's production plants for quality and quantity of products, maintaining a low rate of absenteeism, plant protection, and keeping exemplary records regarding number of accidents, health, and sanitation. Here, employees accept the award in 1942 near the blast furnaces.

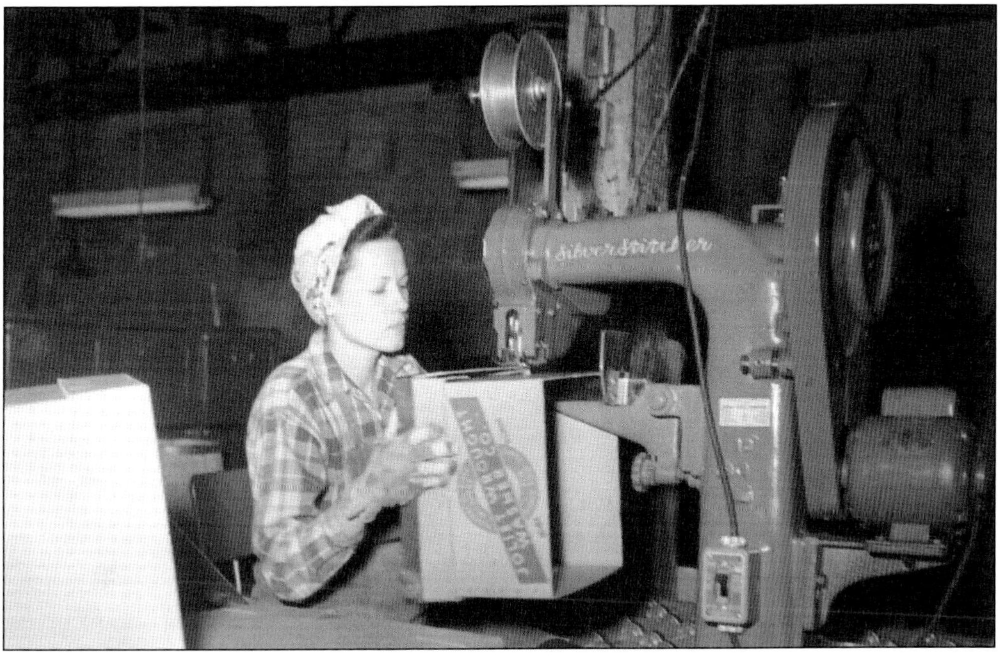

Keeping female workers' long hair out of machinery is a constant safety concern in industrial environments. A bandanna wrapped around the head solved the problem easily and inexpensively. Snoods, small bags attached to a band of cloth or hat and worn at the back of the head, turbans, and crocheted hairnets were also popular during the 1940s.

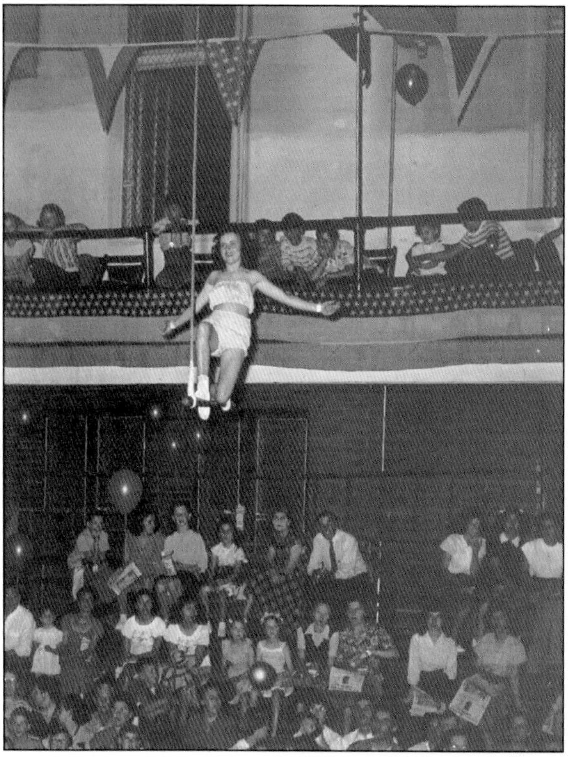

The Steelworks YMCA, built in 1920 to the west of the Pueblo mill, served as a gathering place for employees and their families to engage in recreational activities and forget about their troubles, even if for only an hour or two. Amateur acrobatics troupes the Kings and Queens of Balance and the Steel Y Flyers, consisting of employees and their families, entertained viewers in the 1940s with complicated balancing routines, flips and throws, and flying trapeze performances. Other employees supplemented the circus performances with clown routines and juggling demonstrations.

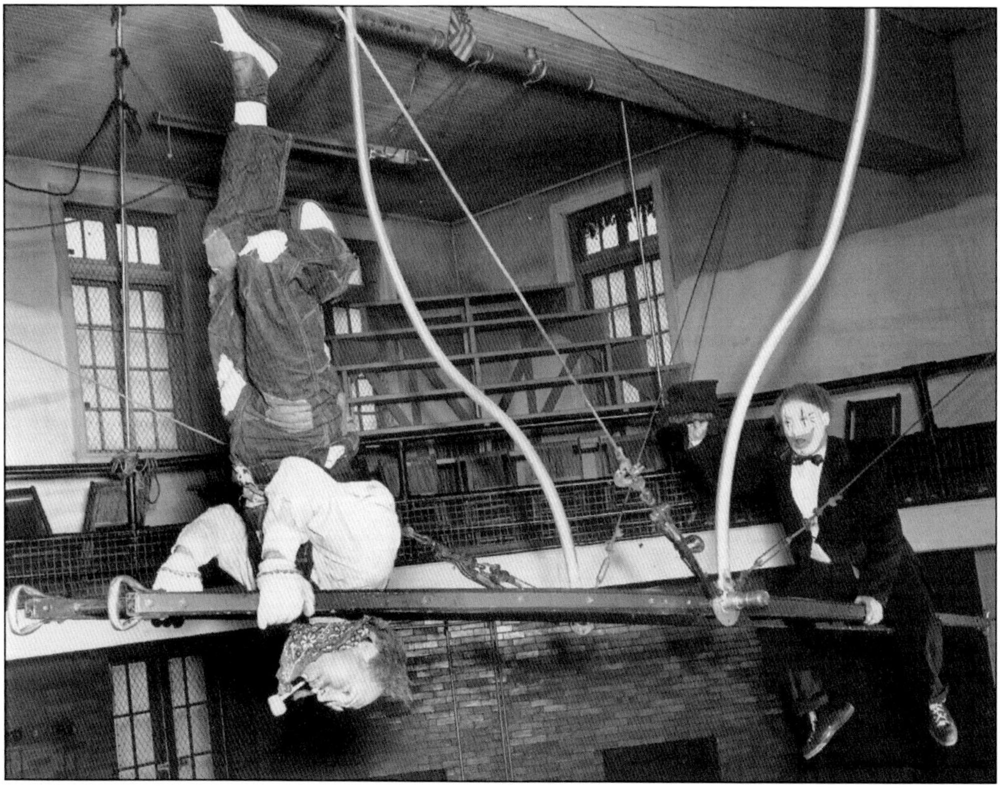

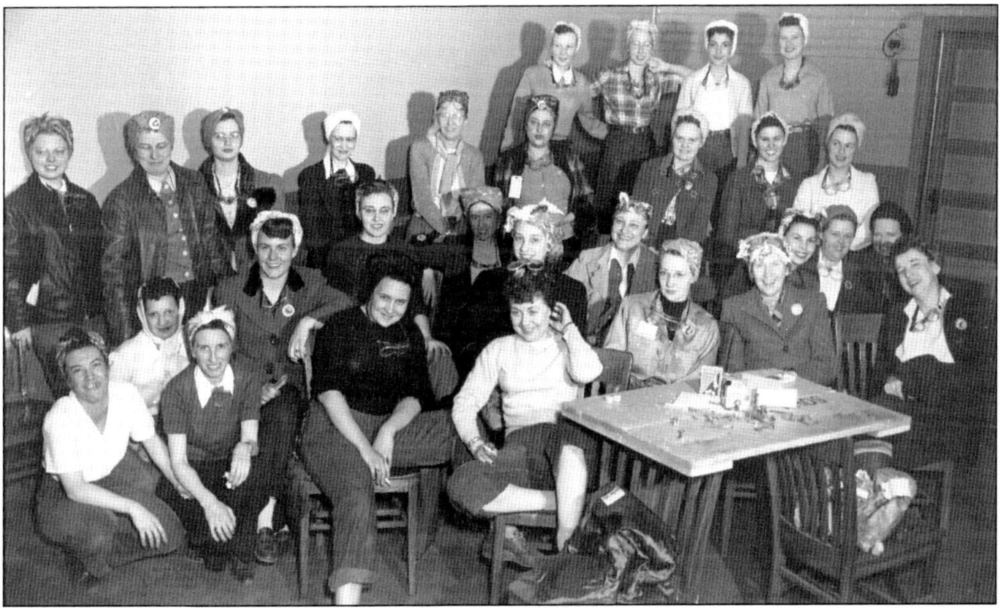

In the 1940s, dozens of women joined the Spark Plug Club, a social and philanthropic women's group sponsored by the company. Members maintained their normal work schedules and participated in club activities during their off hours. Charities the Spark Plug Club supported varied through the years but mainly focused on producing children's parties and activities at CF&I's YMCA and assisting needy local families with bedding, clothing, and food.

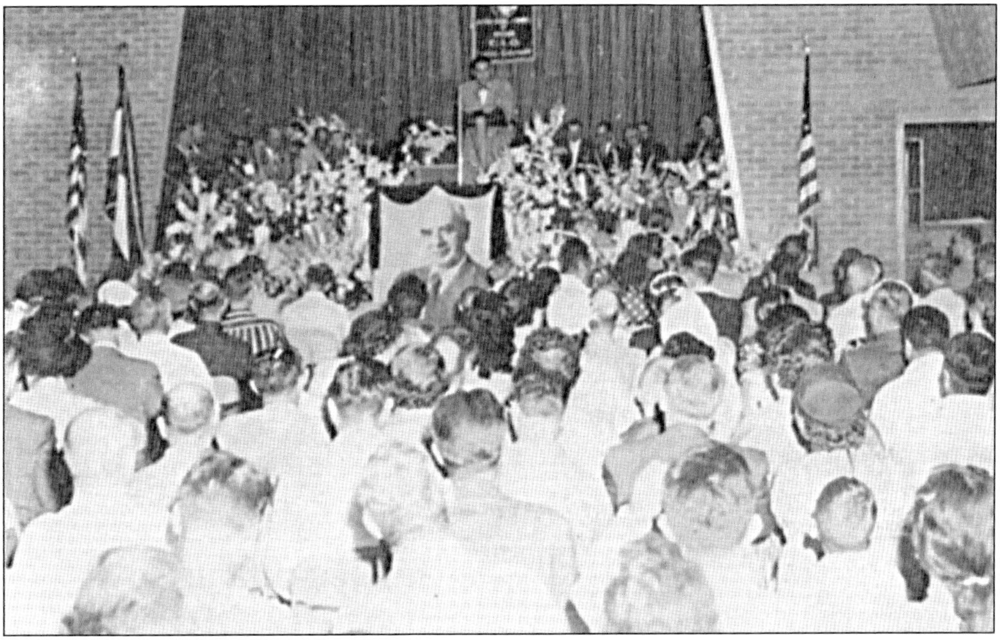

After decades of labor issues, American steelworkers, with the Amalgamated Association of Iron, Steel, and Tin Workers and the Aluminum Workers of America, organized into the United Steelworkers of America (USW). Steelworkers won in their first contract negotiations, which entitled veterans to full seniority rights upon completion of their military service. Built two blocks west of the plant's main gate, the USW Labor Union 2102 building was dedicated in May 1942.

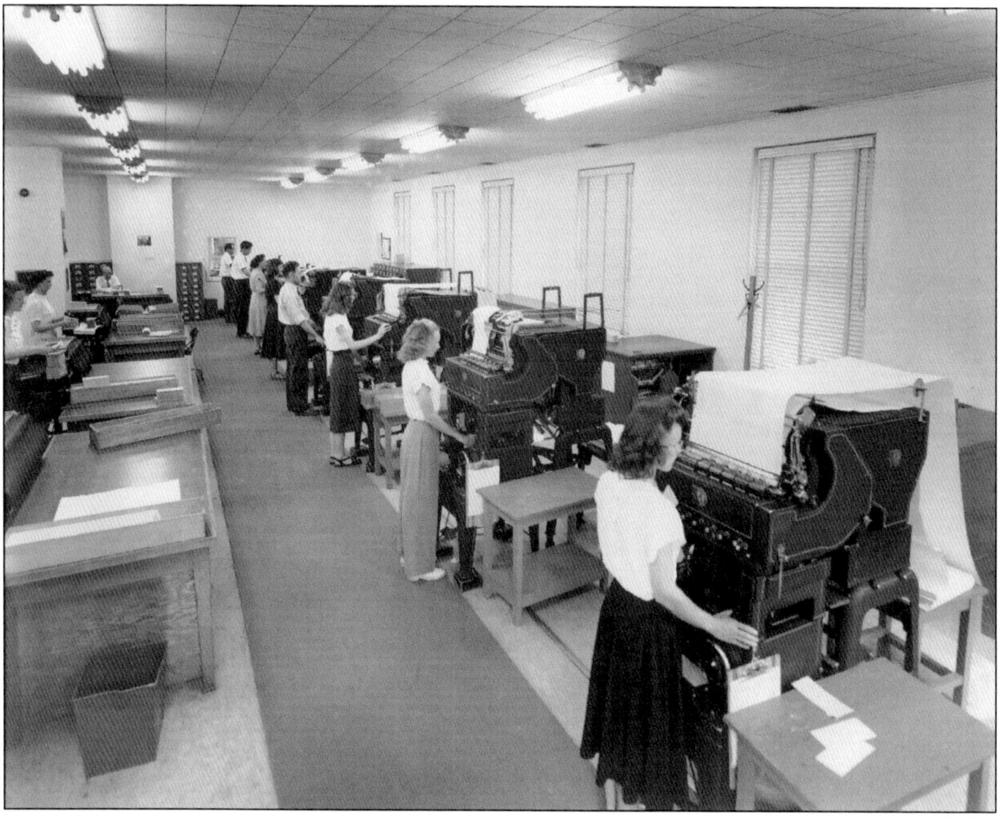

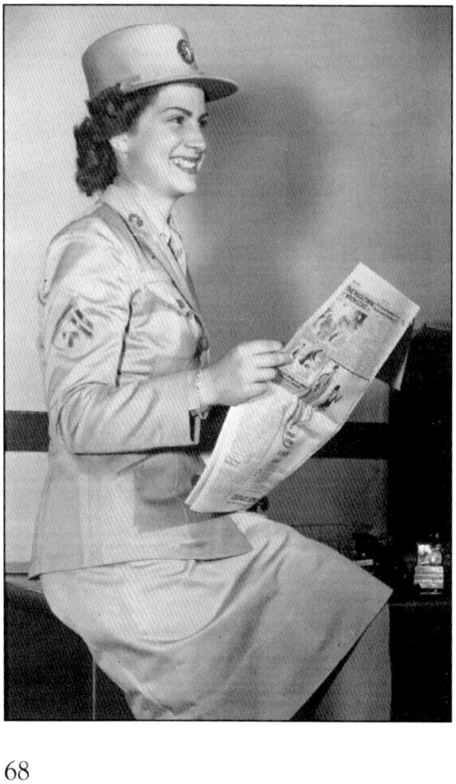

The 1940s saw several changes in office technology. Tabulating department employees, shown here working in the main office building, merely guided paperwork through new machines, Remington Rand Alphabetic Tabulators, which computed employees' net earnings and recorded all the deductions automatically on the stub of the check, a job once done by hand. Six thousand paychecks per hour could be turned out with this technology.

When World War II began, many young women, such as Helen "Sally" Thompson, were employed as clerks or office secretaries and joined one of the women's branches of the armed services. During the war, 18 women left service with the company to join the war effort. In contrast, 2,629 men left CF&I service for the war. Thompson joined the WAACs, the Women Army Auxiliary Corps.

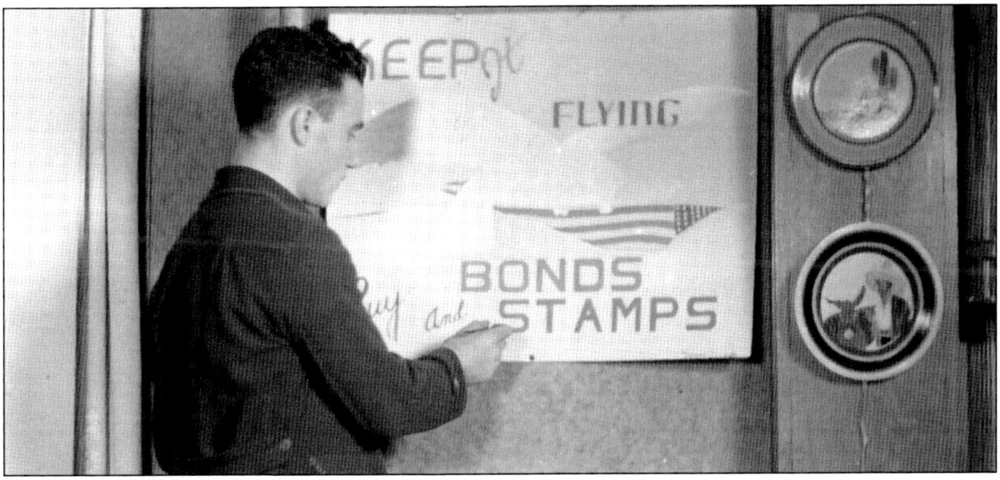

CF&I employees purchased bonds throughout the war to finance the effort. In February 1942, CF&I noted 9,859 people buying bonds. Banners hung in lunchrooms, offices, and work areas reminding workers to financially support the war effort. That year, the average price of a bond purchased was $9.42 per worker, quite a sum considering CF&I laborers earned an average of $1.47 per hour.

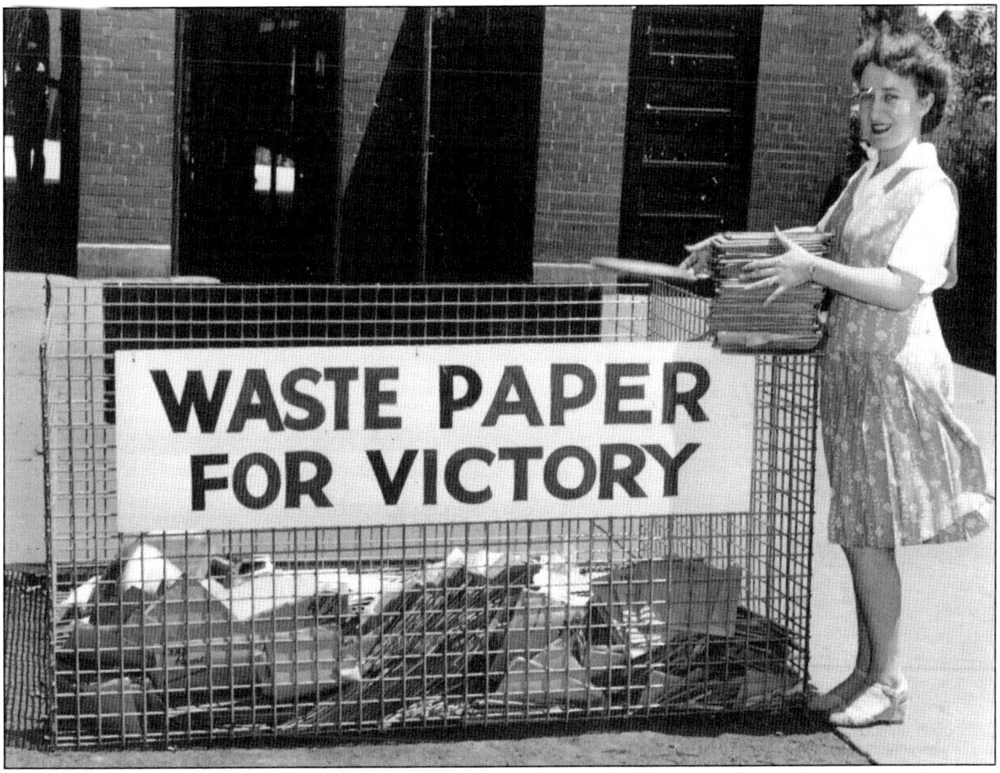

"Wanted for Victory" was a common slogan for community collection efforts throughout the war. Rubber, aluminum, rags, paper, and small metal objects were collected at various stations around Pueblo. After collection, items were cleaned, repaired, or melted if needed and repurposed for various military efforts. Salvaging was one way women on the home front could contribute to the war effort in concert with other wartime programs.

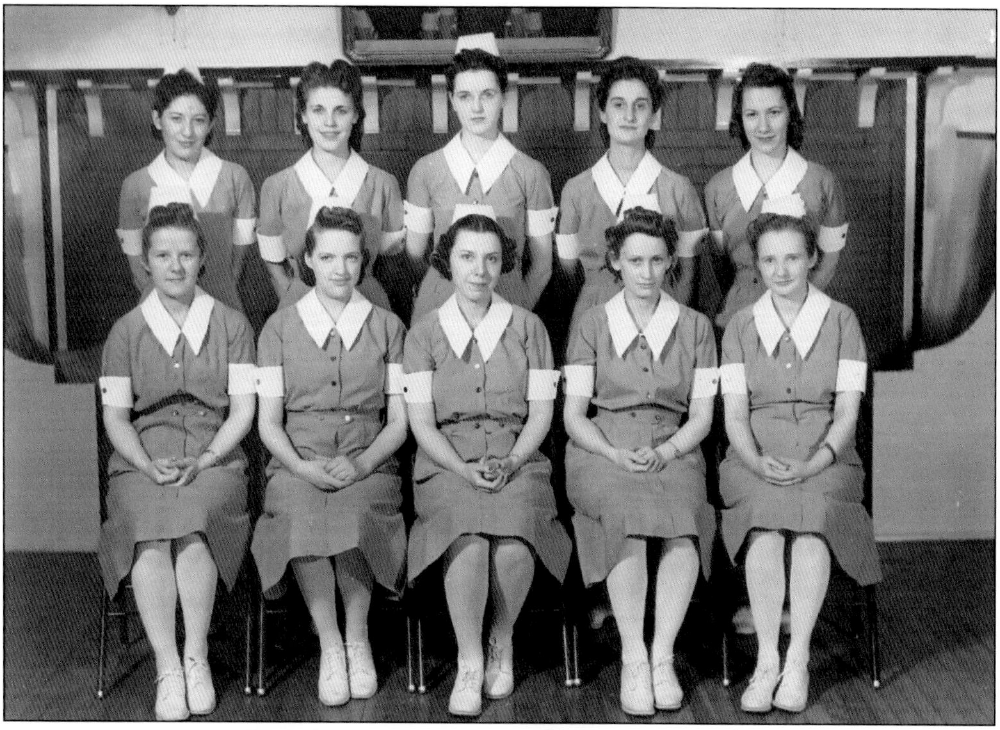

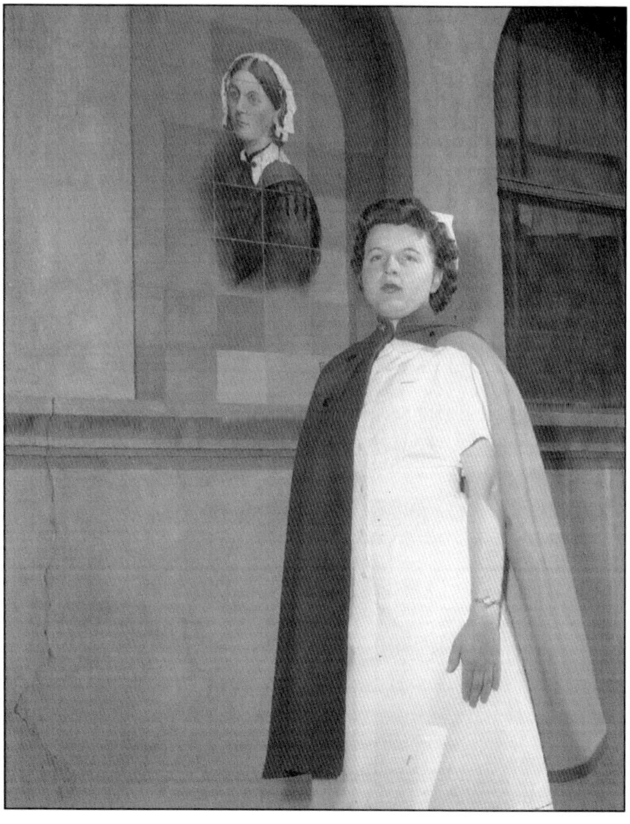

Particularly in 1943, CF&I publications emphasized the need for women to relieve the shortage of nurses nationwide. Throughout the war and a few years following, the Minnequa School of Nursing participated in the nationally sanctioned Cadet Nursing Program. Under this program, the US government paid the expenses of young women to train to become nurses in exchange for a commitment to work in a military hospital or remain in civilian nursing after graduation. In 1946, a partnership with the University of Colorado began, merging the school's curriculum with university standards. The Minnequa School of Nursing closed in 1949. Members of the class of 1942 are pictured in their student uniforms. Nora Lombardo is shown in her cadet nursing uniform shortly after graduation in 1948.

During World War II, women were hired as laborers, inspectors, and supervisors. The inspectors ensured quality products left their work space before moving on to other departments. From left to right, Ada Sullivan, Agnes Fitzpatrick, and Vivian Aileen Henley, the first three women inspectors hired by the company, stand with a newspaper reporter.

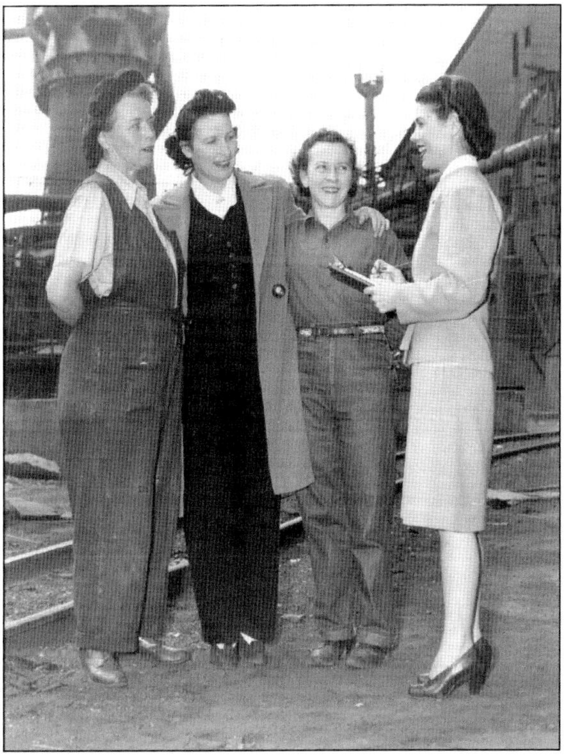

Many new construction projects ceased during the war but started again in 1946 with the construction of 12 new soaking pits, brick-lined ovens where ingots are kept for a certain length of time. Heated to 2,250 degrees Fahrenheit, the ingots were brought to a desirable temperature for rolling into the final product. Gas-fueled burners inside the pits assured uniform heating of the entire ingot.

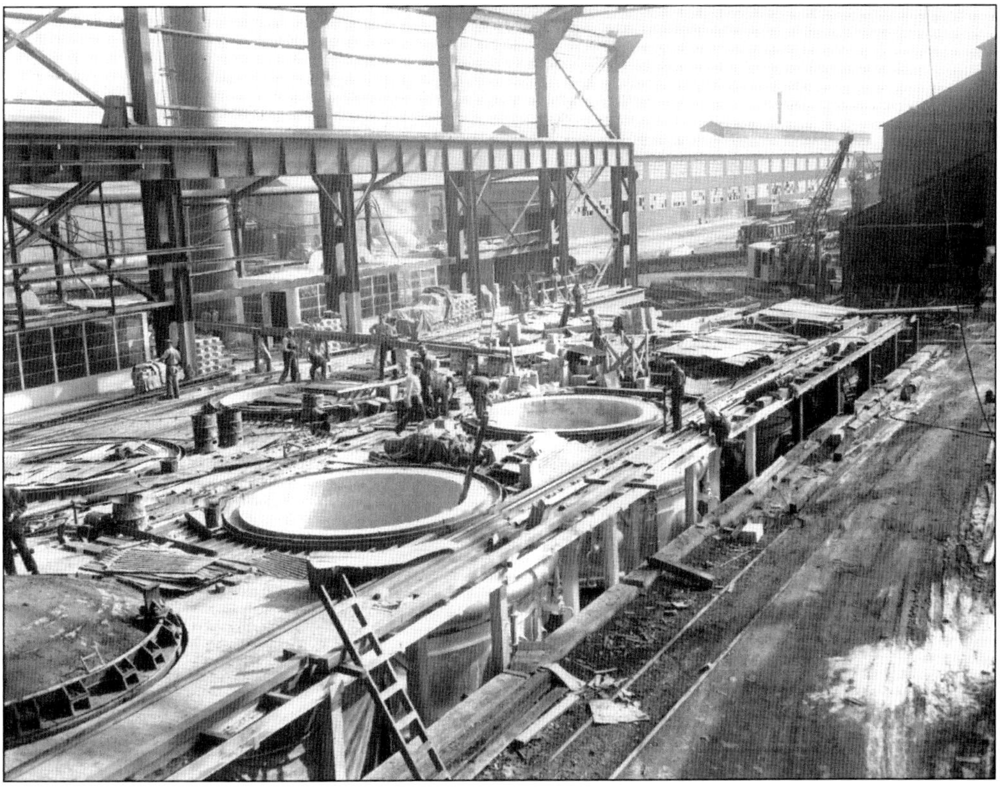

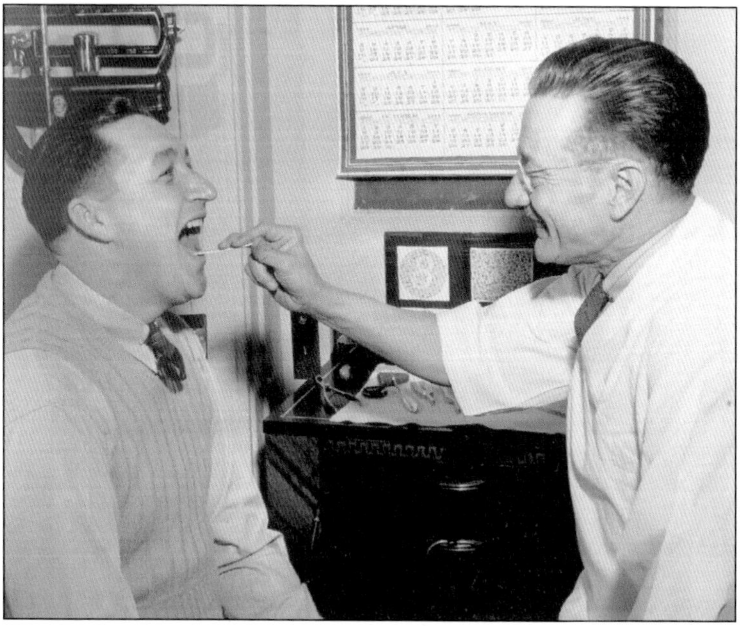

In the spring of 1943, a plan was introduced to provide free health exams in CF&I's medical dispensary by company medical staff. The clinic served a threefold purpose: to examine prospective employees and determine their fitness for work, discover any existing occupation-related diseases, and supervise industrial health control programs. Dr. Morris Clarke examines the throat of patient Otto S. Huber.

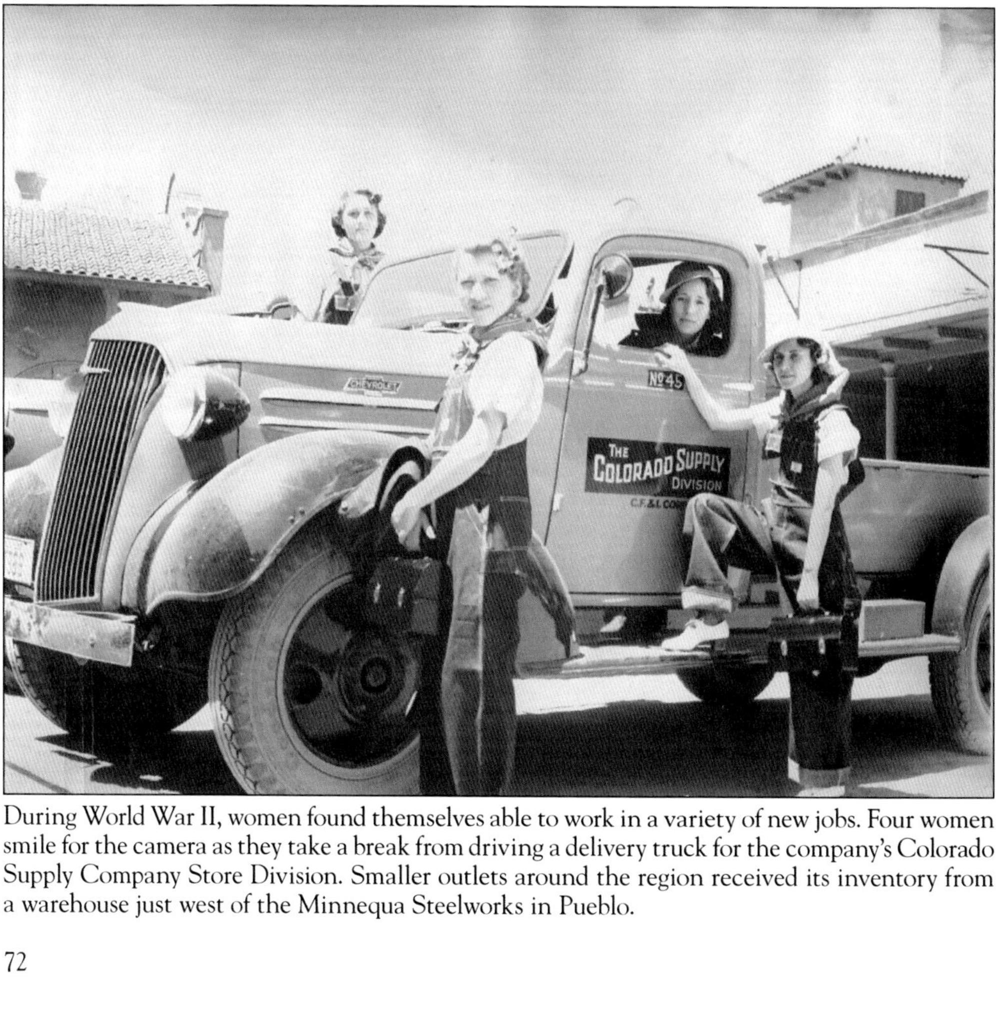

During World War II, women found themselves able to work in a variety of new jobs. Four women smile for the camera as they take a break from driving a delivery truck for the company's Colorado Supply Company Store Division. Smaller outlets around the region received its inventory from a warehouse just west of the Minnequa Steelworks in Pueblo.

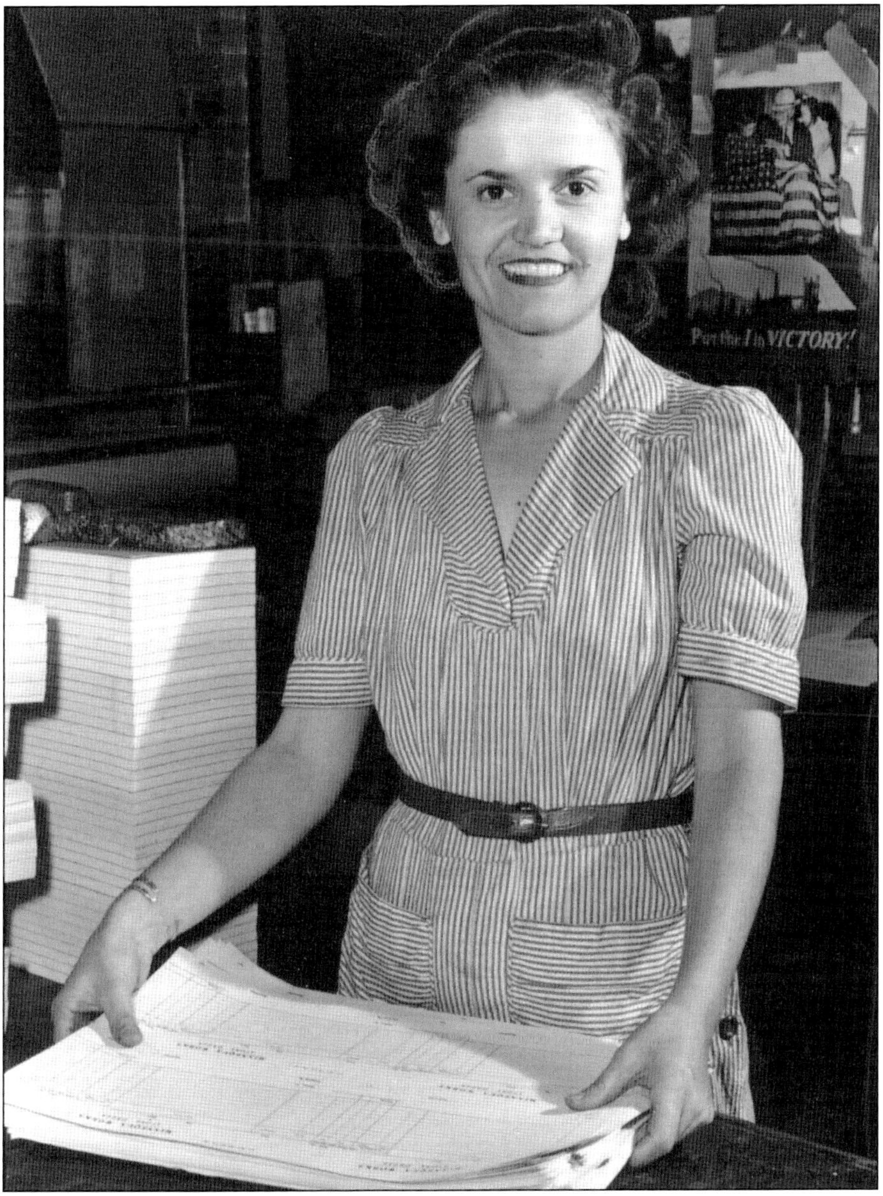

Dorothy Rodokovich holds a stack of papers while working in the print shop in 1944. CF&I maintained its own shop to print brochures, annual reports, and its newspaper. The first publication, *Camp and Plant*, was published under the direction of the sociological department. The weekly newsletter was printed until 1904, at which time it was cancelled to cut expenses. It featured news from the coal mines and the mill and included advertisements for the Colorado Supply Company Store. *Camp and Plant* was also published in multiple languages representing the workforce: German, Spanish, Slovenian, Italian, and English. With the development of the Employee Representation Plan, the *Industrial Bulletin* was published from 1915 to 1928 and reported not only news but also the minutes of the management and employee meetings. From 1928 to 1974, the *CF&I Blast* provided weekly updates to its readers relating to company, local, national, and international news. With a staff of reporters, photographers, salespeople, and delivery drivers, the *Blast* became an integral arm of the company.

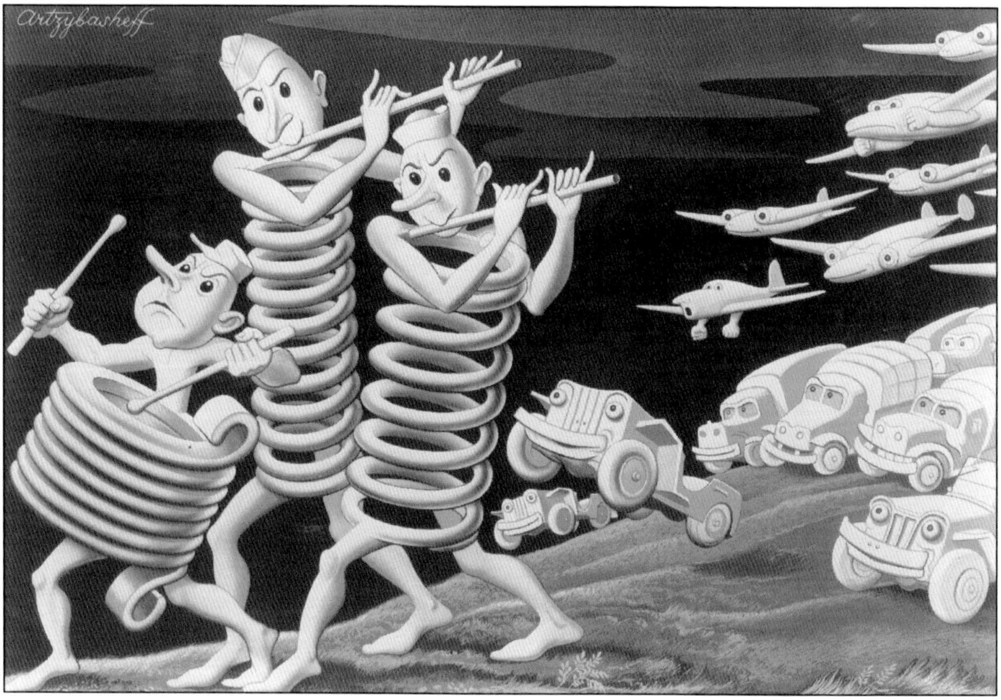

CF&I subsidiary Wickwire Spencer Steel Company wanted to demonstrate how the "hidden parts" produced at its factory were an essential component to the United States' victory during World War II. The company commissioned commercial artist Boris Artzybasheff to produce a series of 29 illustrations. Wickwire Spencer Steel provided more than 15,000 posters to assistance and salvage groups across the country.

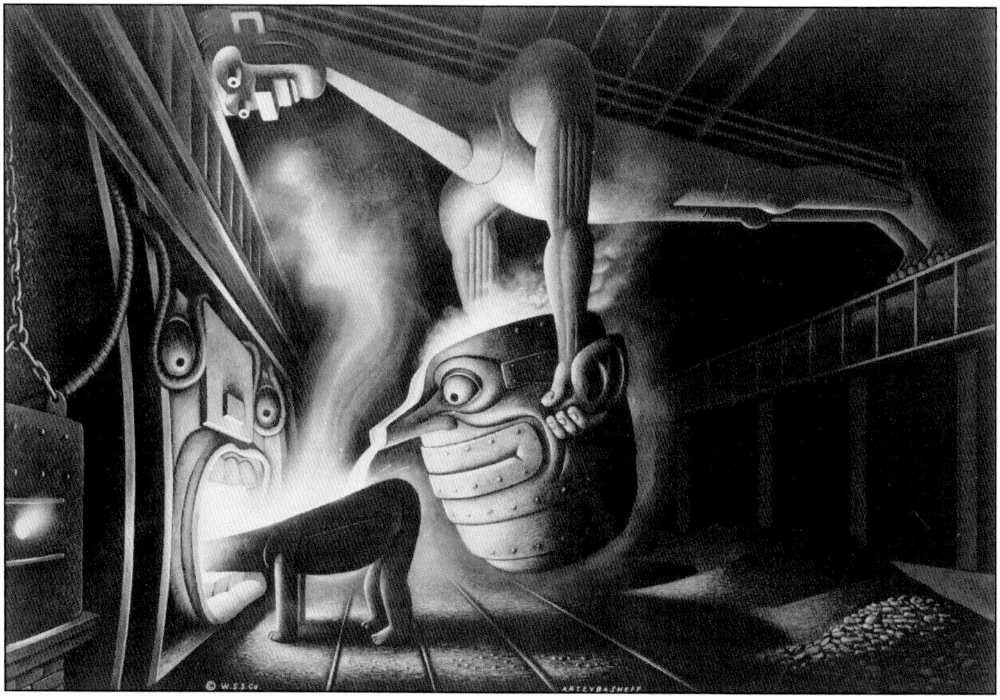

Five

The Allen Years

Three decades affected by instabilities in the economy, international stresses, and local labor challenges led John Rockefeller Jr. to remove himself from the company. Allen & Company, a commercial investment firm, purchased the majority of CF&I's common stock in late 1944. Under Charles Allen's leadership, the company grew to acquire five other subsidiary companies with plants and offices stretching CF&I's presence from New York to California. Locally, a new rod mill opened in 1949, and the seamless tube mill, the first of its kind in the United States, opened in 1953 to great celebration. The conversion from open hearth steelmaking to the first tap of the basic oxygen furnaces occurred in 1961. In 1957, the peak year of employment for the company, the payroll reached 22,715, including mining, steelmaking, office, and subsidiary operations. As a result of the expansion projects at the steel mill, a period of midcentury prosperity allowed for the building of multiple housing subdivisions and schools in Pueblo. Smaller independent businesses throughout the city sprang up in concert with postwar prosperity occurring across the United States.

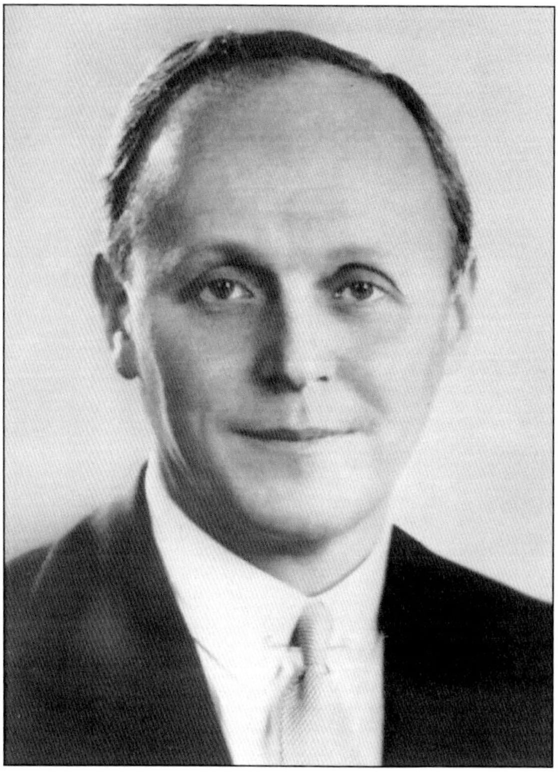

In December 1944, after several months of steady profits, wartime upgrades, and the completion of large-scale modernization projects in several buildings at the Pueblo mill, John Rockefeller Jr. agreed to sell a controlling interest in the company to Charles Allen of the Wall Street investment firm Allen & Company. The new owner sought to make CF&I a national manufacturer and distributor of a full line of steel products.

Built in Pueblo between 1951 and 1957, Interstate 25 bisects the mill property, with production buildings on the east side of the highway and the administration complex to the west. The Colorado Department of Transportation, along with CF&I engineers, designed a tunnel underneath the highway, allowing workers to safely walk from the parking lot on the west side to their work stations on the east.

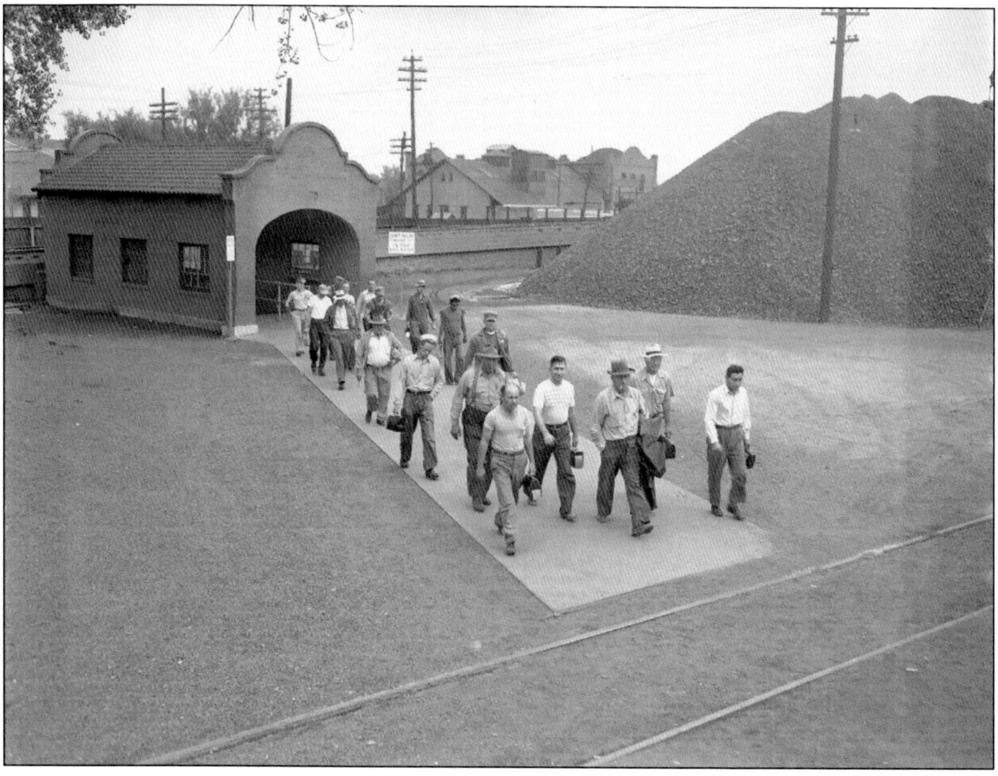

Suggested as far back as 1856 by British scientist Sir Henry Bessemer, the basic oxygen process involved blowing high-purity oxygen onto the surface of a mixture of scrap metal and molten pig iron. The resulting violent reaction and intense heat accelerates the refining of the newly created steel. Shown here is the first tap of the basic oxygen furnace on July 11, 1961. Samples of steel were taken throughout the process, as seen here. The samples were sent to a laboratory to ensure the steel's quality and, if needed, any adjustment to its composition was conducted at this stage. The basic oxygen furnace was the primary method utilized at the Minnequa Steelworks until the early 1970s, when the company converted to more efficient electric arc furnaces.

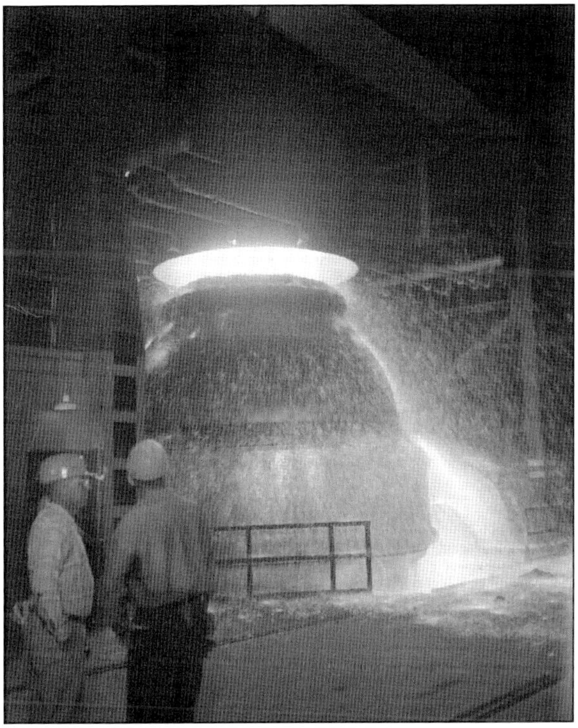

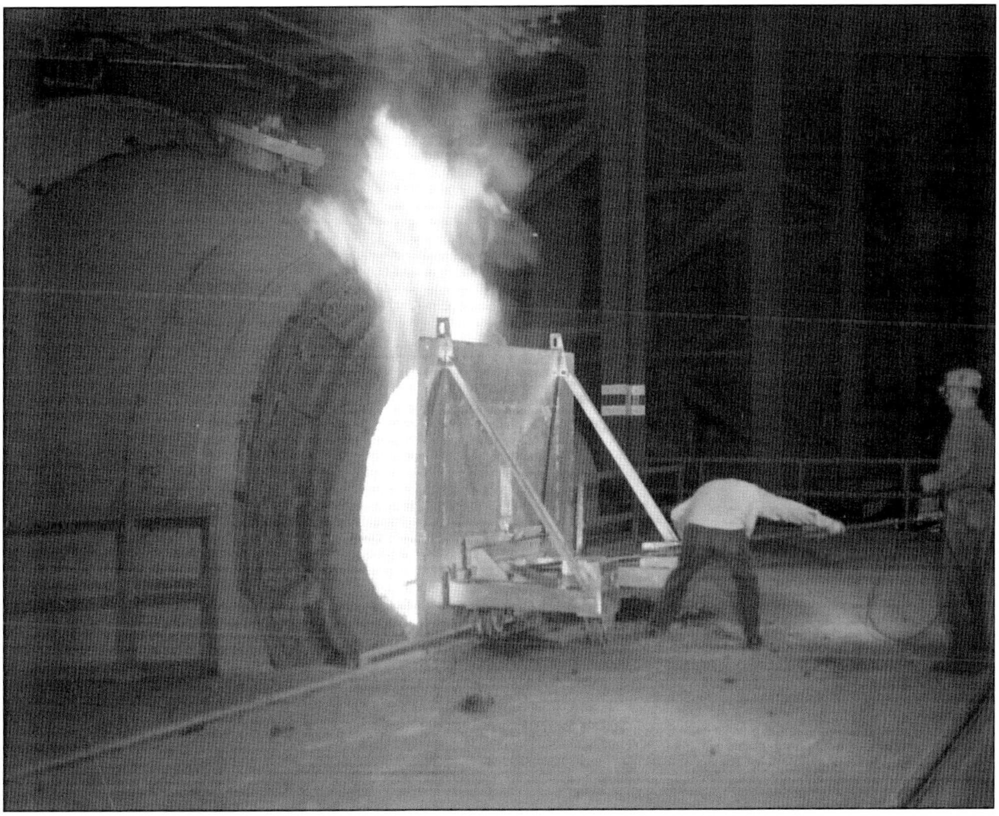

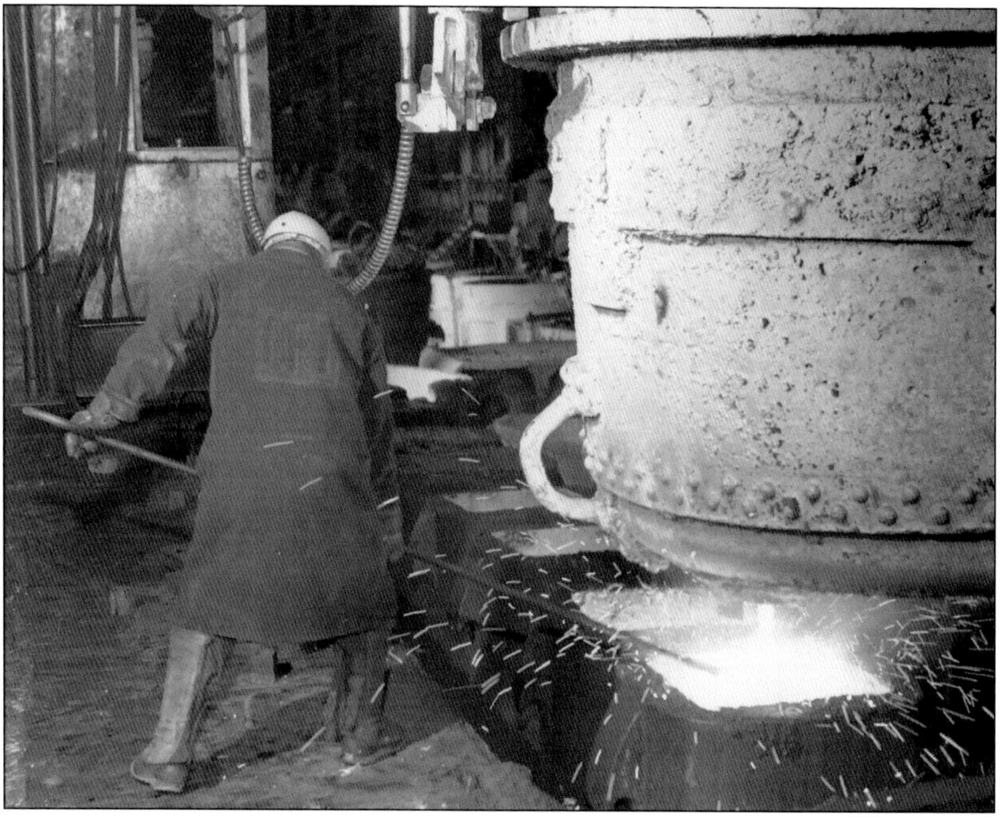

Controlled analyses were numerous throughout the steelmaking process to ensure adequate quality of the final products. Second helper Charles D. Espinoza takes a sample from an ingot mold in 1966. The sample was then shipped to an on-site laboratory, where it was analyzed for imperfections or potential defects in the iron.

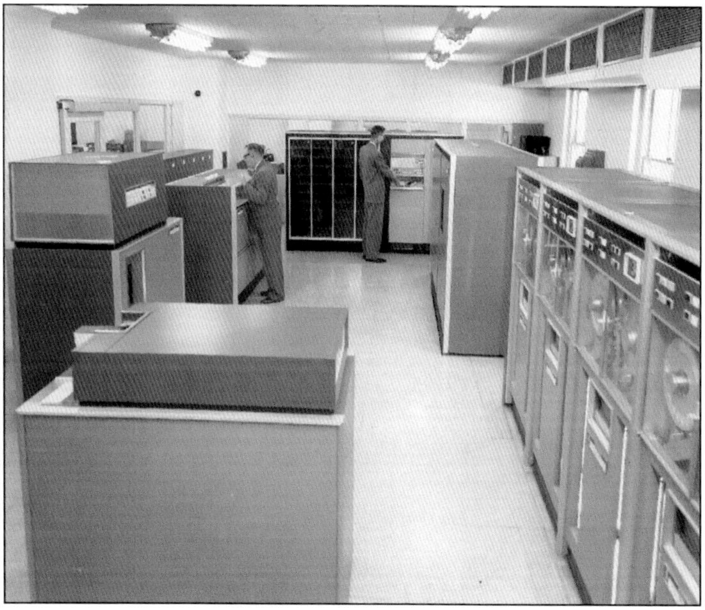

In 1962, William Campbell (left) and Jim Peterson work with CF&I's newest computer at the time, the Solid State 90. This computer, described in the *CF&I Blast*, could "do it all," assisting many departments, including iron ore prospecting and sales analysis. It generated payroll with speed and accuracy, kept track of property records, and recorded mill production figures and dispatches of the trucking and shipping departments.

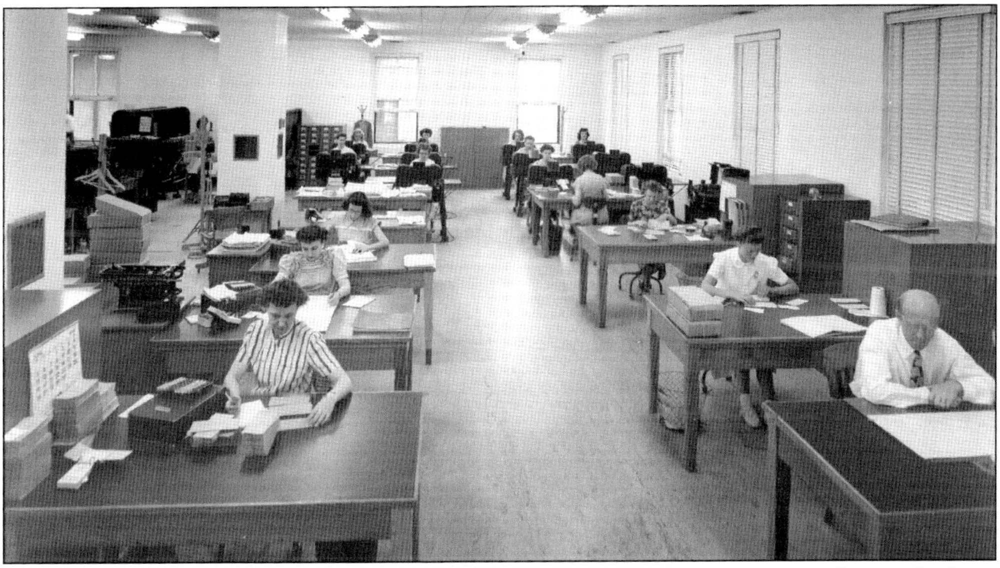

Product sales continued to climb during the Allen years due to the integration of new subsidiary companies, general postwar prosperity, and an overall stable economy. In 1949, CF&I operated at 98 percent capacity. Total sales of products exceeded $138,344,000, an increase of 16 percent from the year before. Tabulating workers kept busy tallying income and expenses on comptometers and adding machines in the sales department.

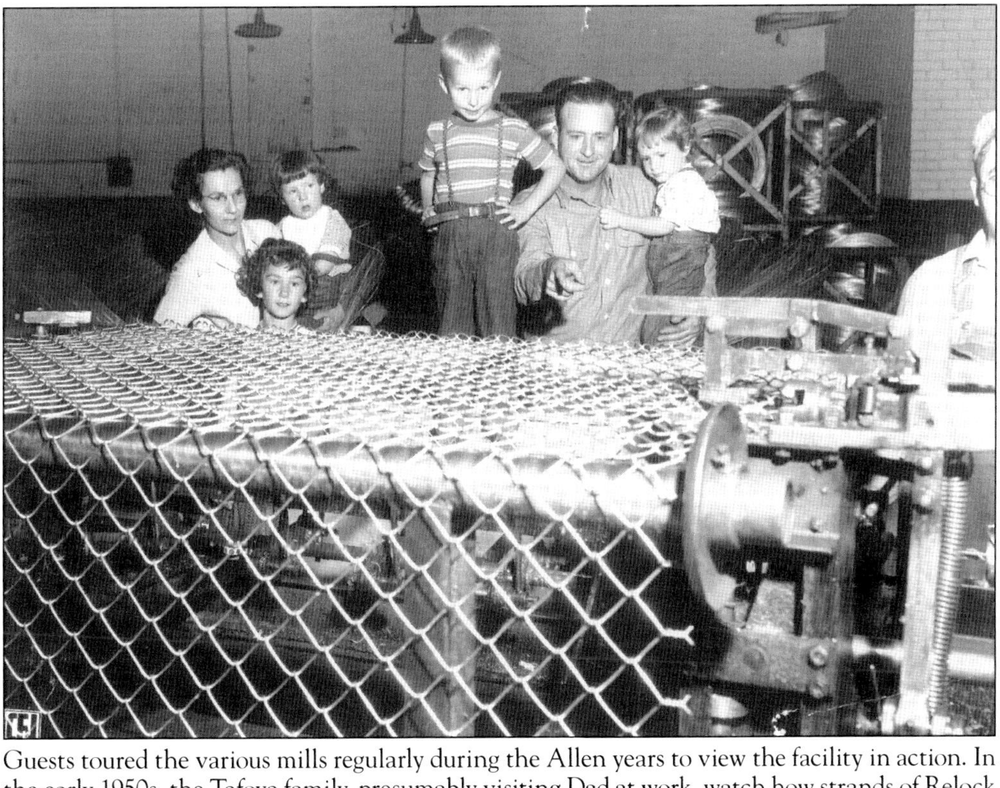

Guests toured the various mills regularly during the Allen years to view the facility in action. In the early 1950s, the Tafoya family, presumably visiting Dad at work, watch how strands of Relock Fence, CF&I's brand of chain-link fence, are twisted together.

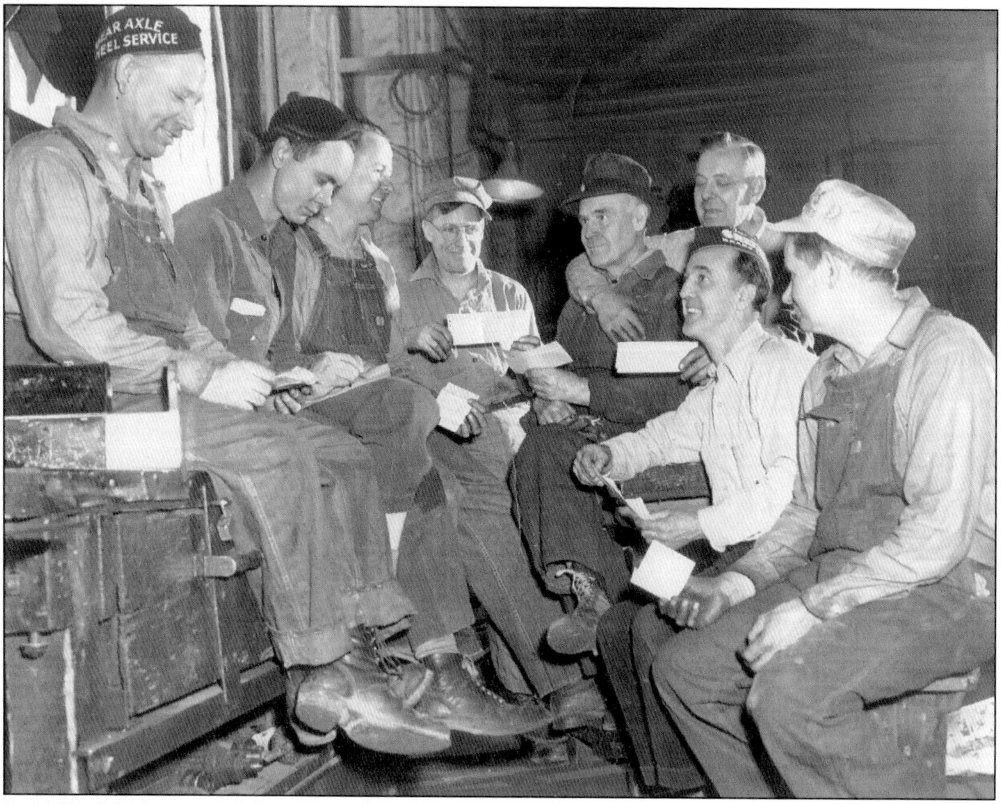

In 1953, CF&I reported that its employees in Pueblo and at its 38 plants and subsidiary companies were eligible for a raise of 8¢ per hour and the company would provide 100 percent funding for the pension plan and social insurance program. With cash in their pockets and a retirement program in place, workers celebrated payday as a joyous time.

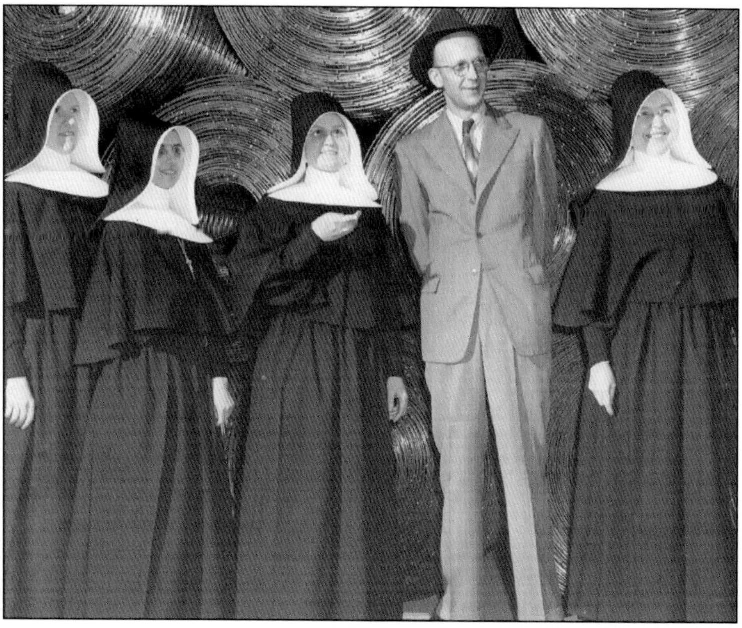

Ready to distance itself from its hospital operations and convinced of the good work of the local order of the Cincinnati, Ohio–based Sisters of Charity, CF&I's board of directors voted to transfer ownership of its Corwin Hospital to the order for $1 in 1948. Here, sisters tour the wire mill with foreman Ford Frederick. Today, the hospital operates as St. Mary–Corwin Medical Center.

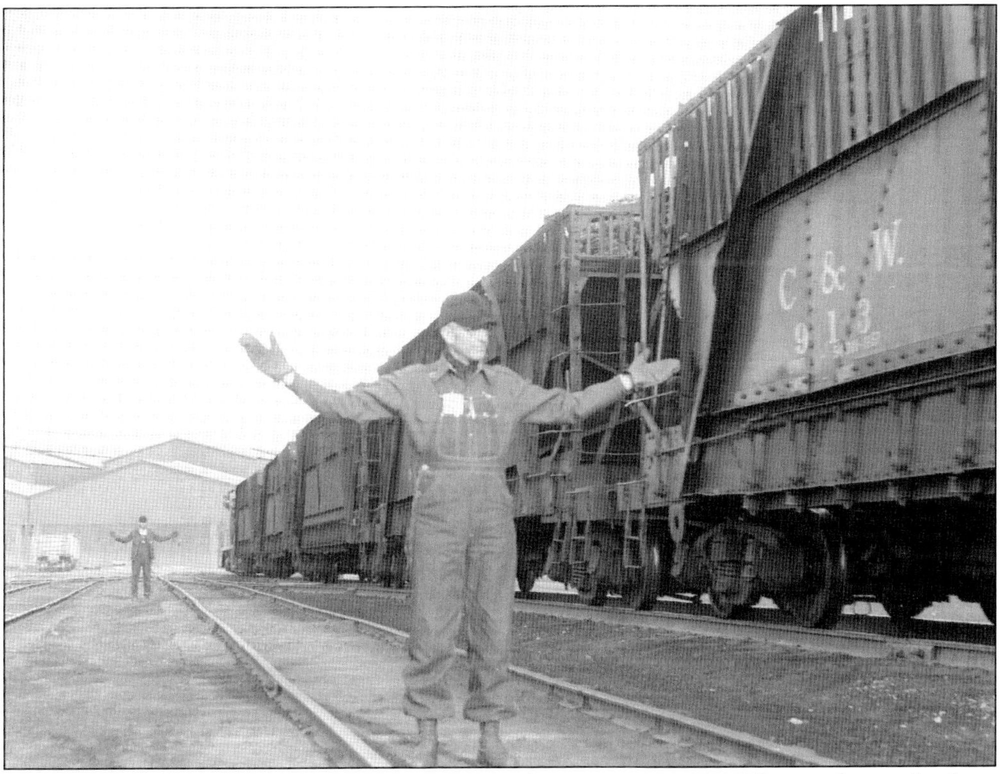

Organized in 1899, the Colorado & Wyoming Railway Company (C&W) served as a subsidiary company of the Colorado Fuel and Iron Company. Its main function was to haul heavy loads of mineral wealth from the mining districts to the Pueblo mill (though for a short time it was also a passenger line). It also serviced the mill yard by moving heavy loads of steel products from one area to another. With the advent of diesel power, the C&W, like many other carriers, converted from steam to diesel locomotives, completing the transition in April 1952. The C&W continues to service the mill today, running throughout the mill property hauling and delivering heavy loads.

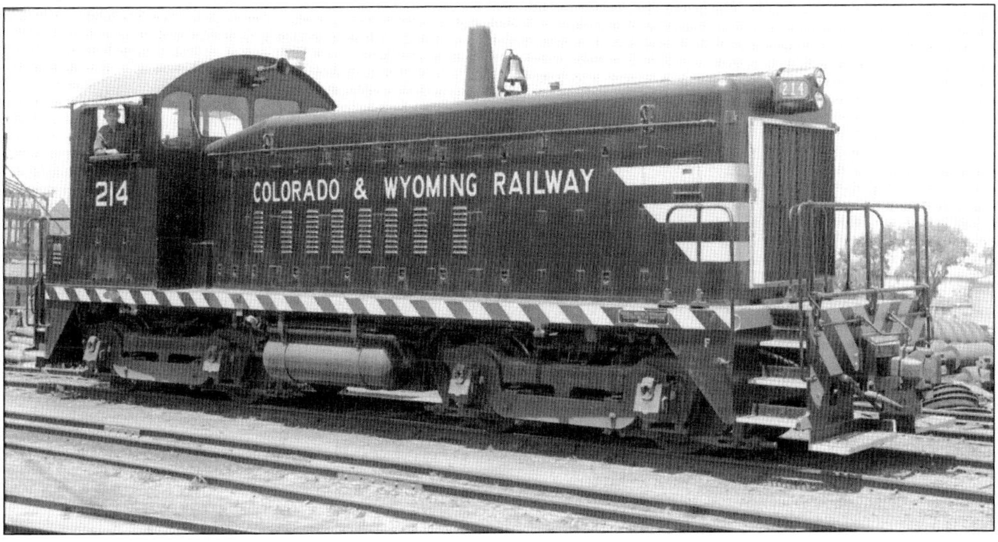

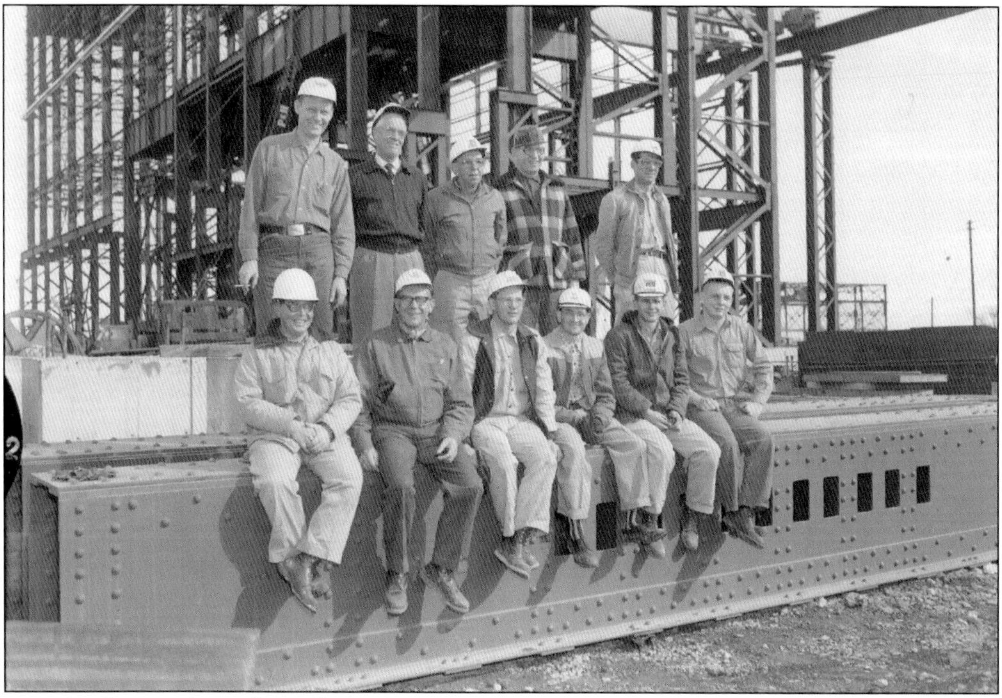

In 1953, the seamless tube mill, the first of its kind west of the Mississippi River, opened at the Minnequa Steelworks at Pueblo. This new facility created seamless steel pipes, mainly to supply customers in the oil and gas industries. The new mill, built on 10 acres, was constructed using 37,000 cubic yards of concrete, 240 miles of electrical wire, and 6,000 tons of steel.

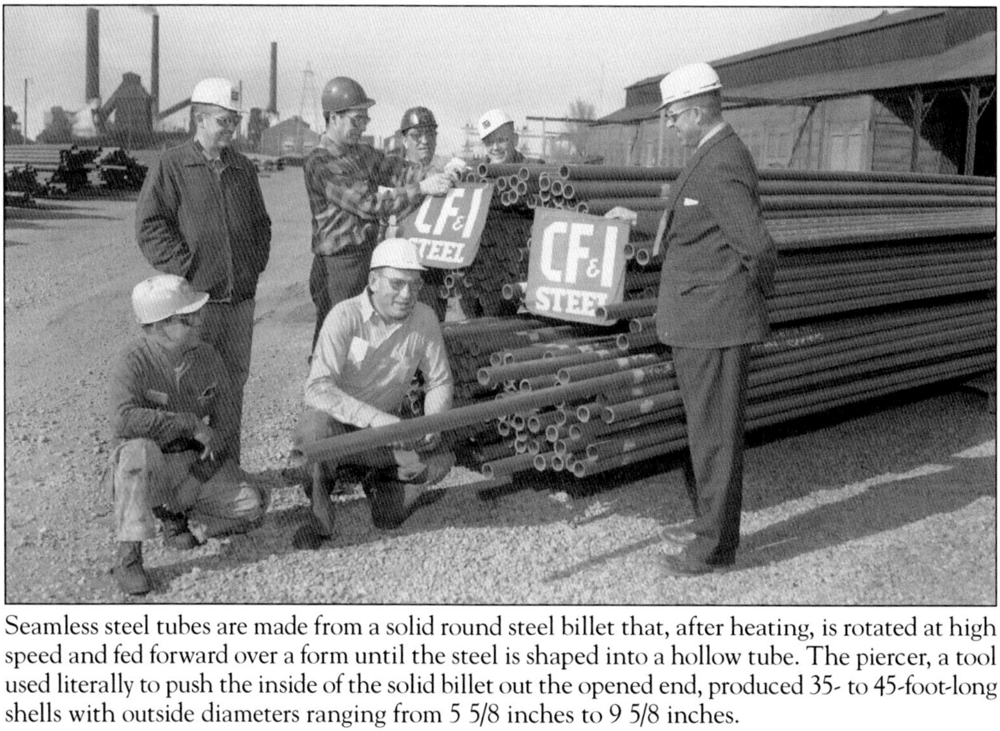

Seamless steel tubes are made from a solid round steel billet that, after heating, is rotated at high speed and fed forward over a form until the steel is shaped into a hollow tube. The piercer, a tool used literally to push the inside of the solid billet out the opened end, produced 35- to 45-foot-long shells with outside diameters ranging from 5 5/8 inches to 9 5/8 inches.

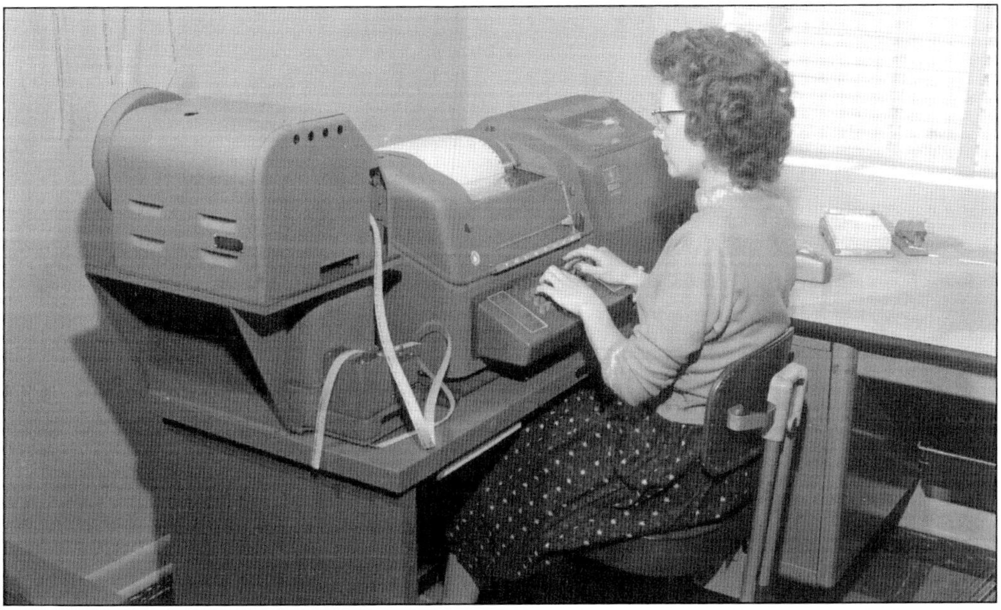

Teletypewriters allowed for greater communication to the company's 38 plants and offices. The machines provided service through circuits that allowed one machine to instantly reproduce a typed message on any teletypewriter to which it was connected. The roll of fed paper would be used for recording keystrokes. The teletypewriter was made obsolete by the fax in the 1980s. Willa Dee Van Zandt worked as a teletypewriter transcriptionist in 1959.

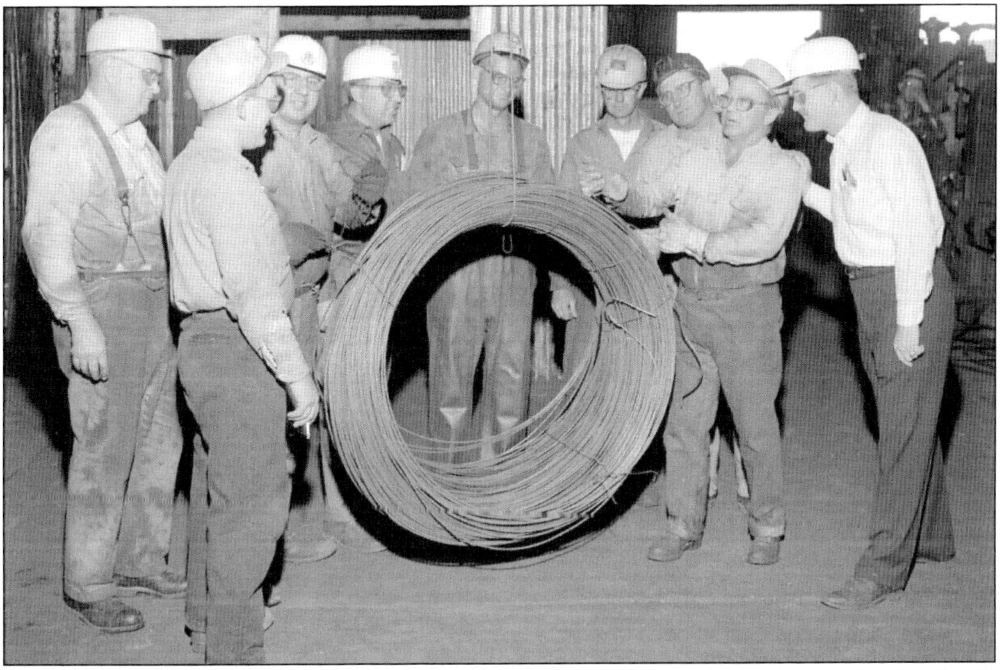

CF&I's Pueblo plant opened its new Morgan rod mill in 1949, replacing the outdated rod mill built in 1903. This new mill produced steel rods, which could be drawn into final products of heavy welded fabric, stucco netting, or poultry netting, in addition to rebar products. Workers examine the four-millionth ton of coiled rod in 1966.

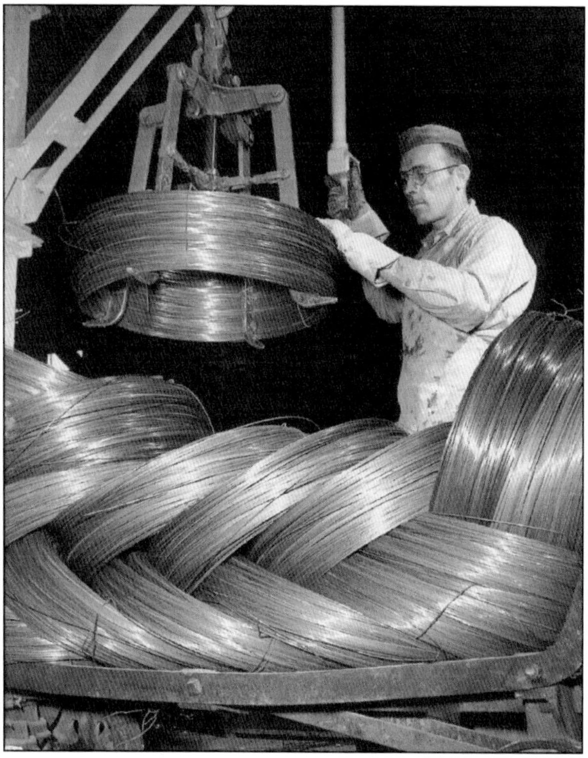

The 1945 acquisition of the Wickwire Spencer Steel Company, based in Buffalo, New York, and California Wire Cloth Company, based in San Francisco, allowed CF&I to offer more than 100 types of wire products, including dozens of sizes of nails, fencing, netting, welded fabric, and wire, reducing CF&I's longtime dependence on sale of rails and rail accessories.

Crucial to its operations, CF&I employed hundreds of engineers and draftsmen through the decades. Shown here in 1950, engineers worked on developing new ideas for machinery within buildings as well as new exterior structures. These draftsmen might be designing parts of the seamless tube mill, which opened three years after this photograph was taken.

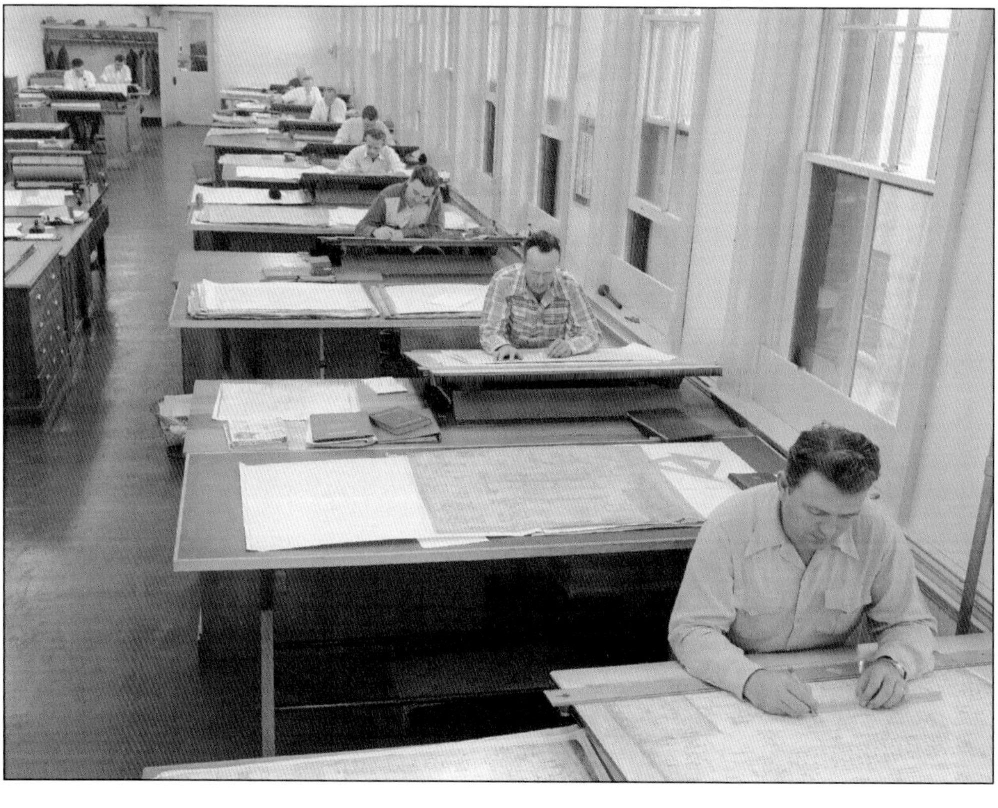

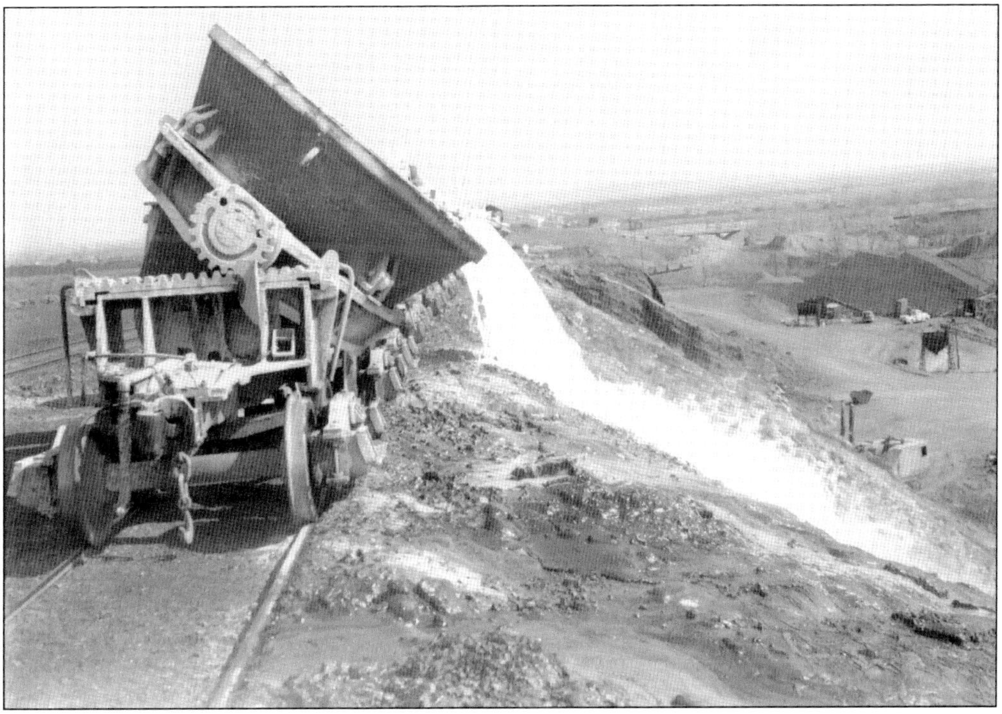

Slag, a by-product of the smelting and refining process, was poured into containers known as slag pots. The pots were then tipped on their sides, releasing a glowing hot liquid. As it was released, the slag lit up the nighttime sky. Once cooled, it was crunched into smaller pieces and resold as railroad ballast, roadbed material, and driveway aggregate.

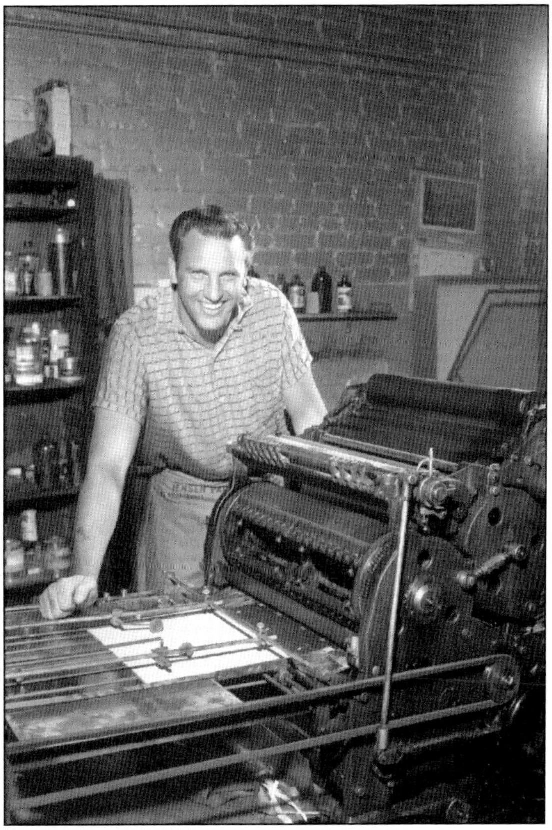

Opened in the 1920s, the print shop produced the company newsletter and safety reminder posters. The department soon grew to produce all printed materials required by the company, including sales brochures and annual reports, stationery and envelopes, writing tablets, forms, and booklets. In addition to printing, the department also was involved in binding, stapling, collating, and punching materials as necessary. Here, Bob Lawson oversees a run of brochures in 1961.

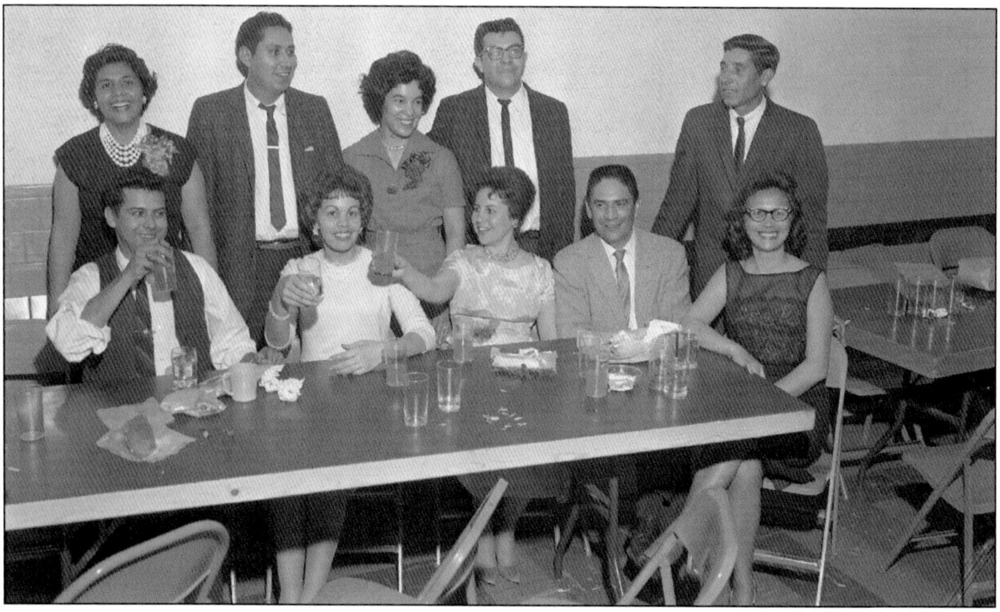

Opened in 1942, the local union hall of the United Steelworkers of America, Labor Union 2102, serves as a gathering place for Pueblo steelworkers to relax after work or on the weekends. Inside the hall are a kitchen and dining room, office space, auditorium, and meeting rooms. A group of steelworkers and the men's wives celebrate in the dining hall in 1963 following the company's annual apprenticeship graduation ceremony.

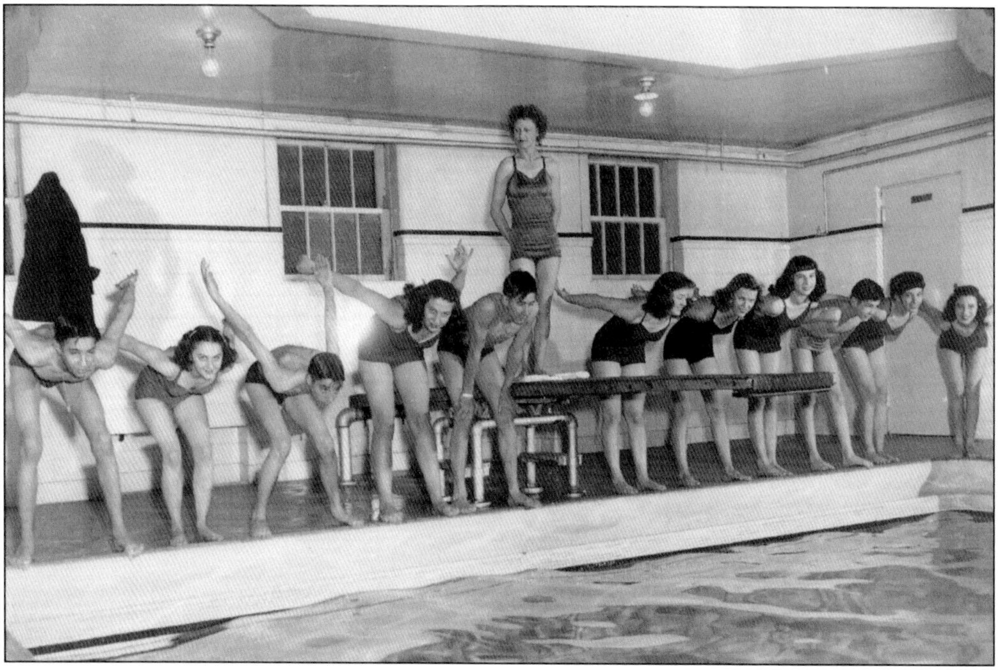

One of the highlights within the Steelworks YMCA was the 60,000-gallon, 21-by-60-foot swimming pool. Open from 9:00 a.m. to 10:00 p.m. daily and 1:00 to 4:00 on Sundays, it offered beginning, intermediate, and advanced swim lessons. Competitive diving teams were popular in 1948 after the installation of a diving platform.

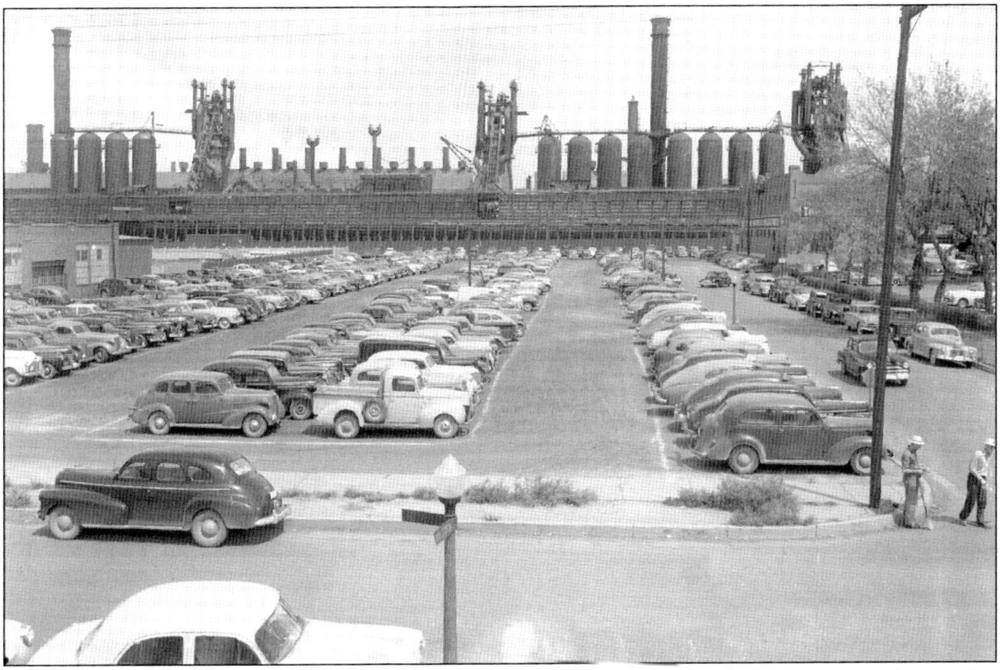

As car ownership became more popular and affordable, parking lots became crowded near the entrance to the mill. To avoid traffic jams and difficulties finding a parking stall, many families resorted to dropping steelworkers off at the company's main gate and then picking them up at the end of the shift. Many current Pueblo residents still reminiscence about this daily routine.

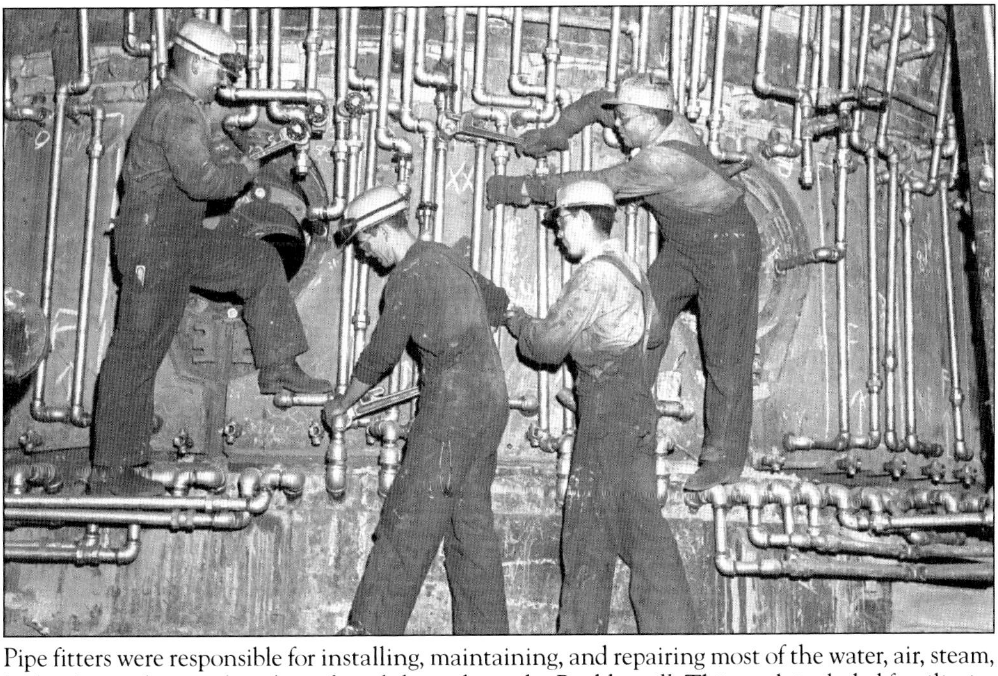

Pipe fitters were responsible for installing, maintaining, and repairing most of the water, air, steam, hydraulic, and natural gas lines found throughout the Pueblo mill. This work included familiarity with component parts of automatic control equipment, valves, furnace burners, traps, siphons, and filters. In 1964, these pipe fitters rebuilt plumbing lines in a blast furnace.

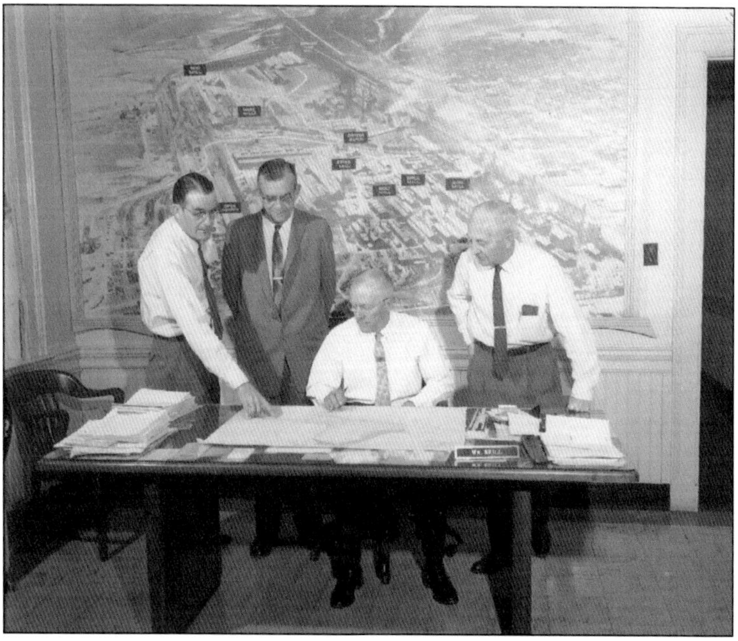

Land acquisition and development in the mid-20th century included only one mine, the Allen Mine, located in Colorado's Las Animas County. William Brill (center, seated) and other engineers survey company maps in the Pueblo office in 1961. In the 1970s, CF&I felt the financial pinch of the industry and sold much of the western land rights it had acquired over the previous century.

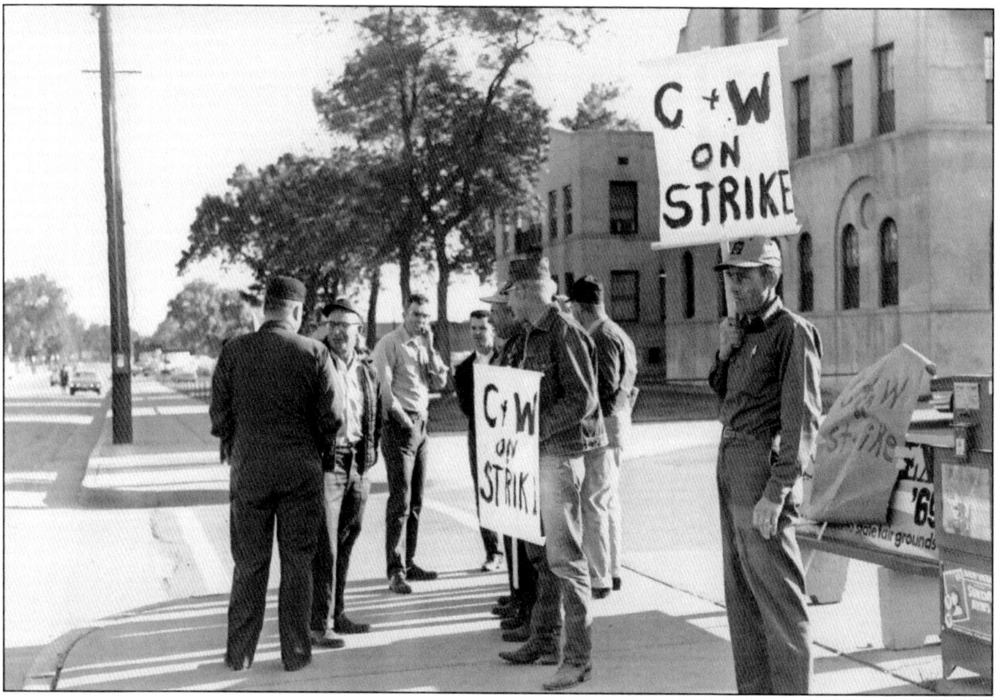

CF&I experienced many cases of labor upset and resolution throughout its history. In July 1959, the United Steelworkers of America called for a strike affecting 500,000 steelworkers, including those employed at the company. Steelmakers demanded higher salaries and changes to the language in their contract, which allowed certain machines in the workplace, resulting in reduced hours and numbers of employees. The strike lasted 116 days, the longest US steel strike until that point. Employees of the CF&I subsidiary Colorado & Wyoming Railroad protested for higher pay for skilled workers and improvements to their working conditions just 10 years later.

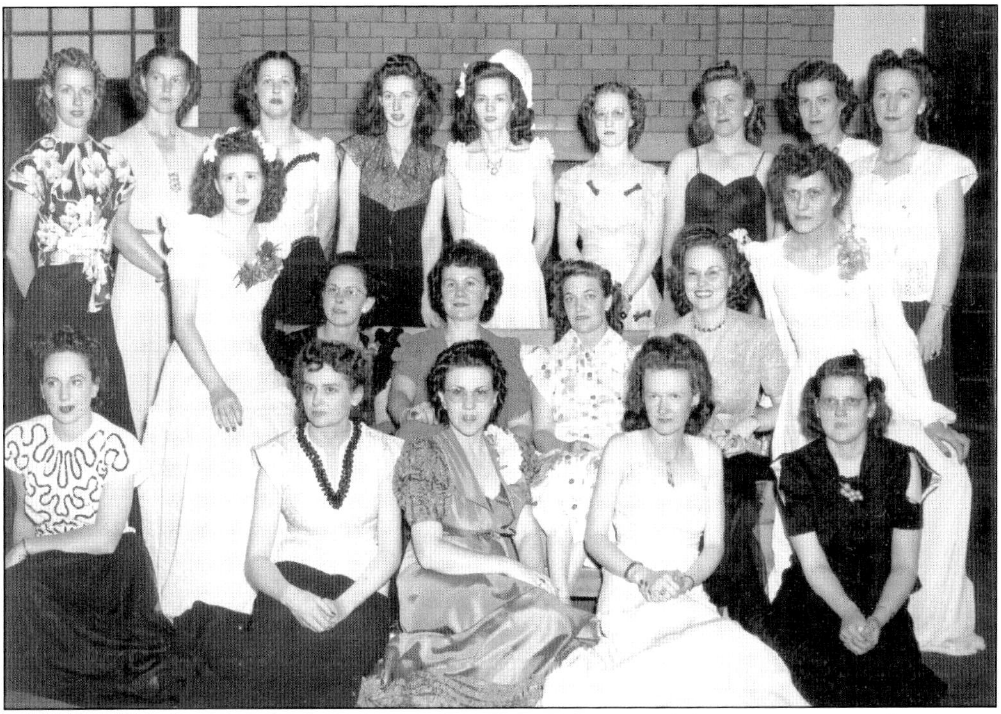

The Spark Plug Club celebrated its 25th anniversary in 1948, and the group continued to donate and support needy families and youth around Pueblo through its Community Chest Fund. One way in which the "Sparkies" raised funds for their charitable acts was through hosting and charging admission to dances, tea parties, and musical performances at the Steelworks YMCA and the Minnequa Club, CF&I's management social club.

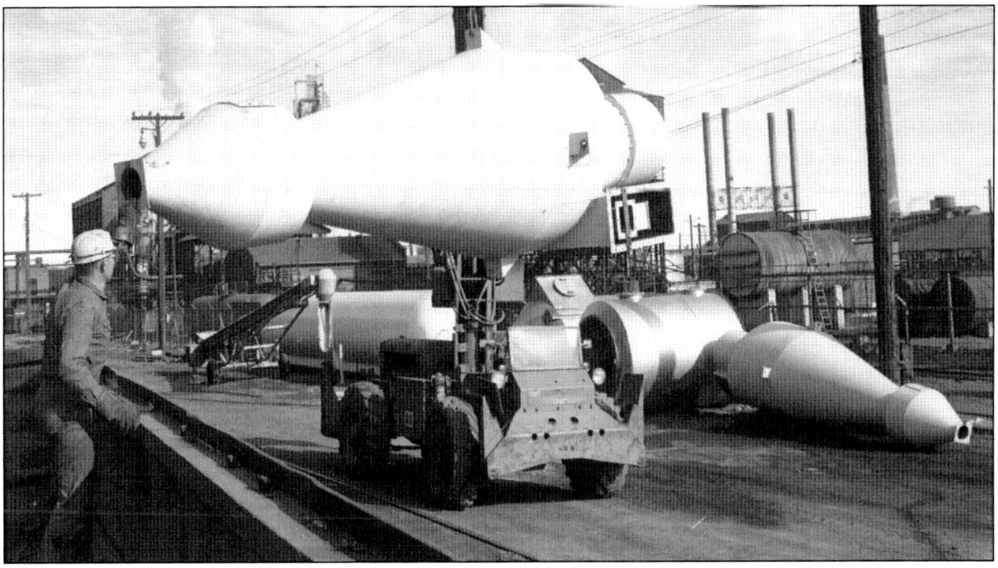

Pesticides were not the only products sold by CF&I that were derived from by-products of the steelmaking process. In 1968, CF&I constructed a new fertilizer plant that utilized by-products of the coke plant. In this photograph, workers are installing air cleaners for the plant. The new fertilizer was sold under the brand name Envy, with the slogan "Your lawn will turn green with Envy."

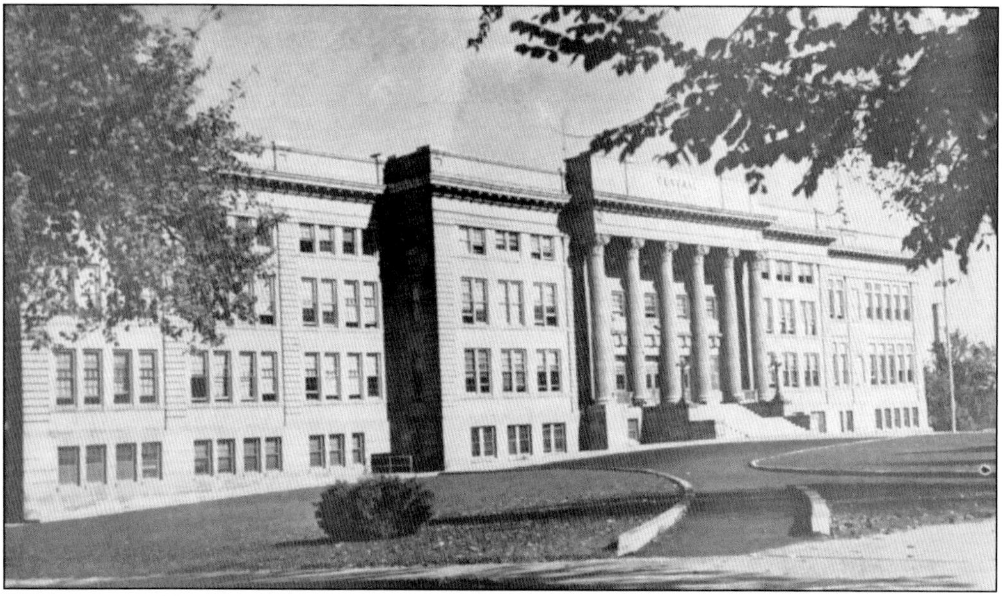

Since 1880, Pueblo's Central High School has provided public education to students in the Bessemer neighborhood. The home of the Wildcats continues to provide traditional, vocational, and advanced college prep courses, and extracurricular activities, and, with Pueblo's Centennial High School, it serves as one half of Colorado's oldest and arguably most intense high school rivalries.

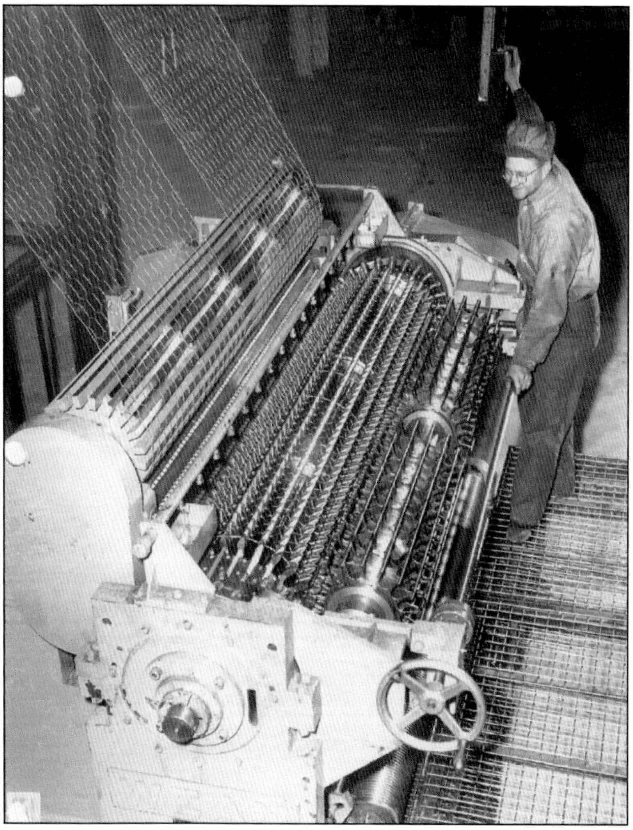

Joe Anzick, operator of the lock-twist poultry netting machine at the wire mill's fence department, supervises his machine. The new machine incorporated a completely new product for western farmers by twisting together two-inch meshes on the fencing. At the time of installation in 1948, it was the only machine of its kind in the world.

Six

The End of an Era

With heavy competition from foreign imports in the 1970s, CF&I managers saw a declining demand for American-made steel products looming in the distance. Additionally, increased pressure to meet clean air and water legislation forced steel companies throughout the United States to update their operations. In many companies, including CF&I, blast furnaces were shut down, product mills sat idle or ran on reduced schedules, and mining operations ceased. About 4,000 employees at the Pueblo mill were released from duty in a four-year period from 1981 to 1985. Unemployment in Pueblo reached an all-time high of 20 percent in 1982.

Unable to meet the demands of its creditors, CF&I reorganized and filed for Chapter 11 bankruptcy protection in 1990. Oregon Steel Mills, based in Portland, purchased CF&I's assets in 1993. During this transitional time, work never completely stopped. With the heavy impact of the steel recession and significant reduction of the company's operations, Pueblo community leaders created a civic organization, Pueblo Economic Development Corporation (PEDCO) in 1982 to attract new enterprises to the city and provide employment opportunities. In its first year of operation, 14 different companies relocated, providing jobs and a new permanent base of economic stability in Pueblo. PEDCO continues today to attract new businesses to the city.

The official name of the company changed from the Colorado Fuel and Iron Corporation to CF&I Steel Corporation on August 1, 1966. The company stated that this reflected the change in its operations; it was no longer producing coal and coke for the fuel trade and declared it was committed to new product lines and company acquisitions including metal scrapyards, asphalt paving, and a sand, gravel, and metalwork company.

The modernization of the rail mill was the largest single capital improvement program carried out at the Pueblo mill. Completely financed from within with no governmental assistance, the new and improved plant could turn out 82-foot-long rails of high-performance alloy steel in addition to traditional 39-foot-long rail sections. Workers watch a glowing hot 39-foot-long rail section on the rollers in 1979.

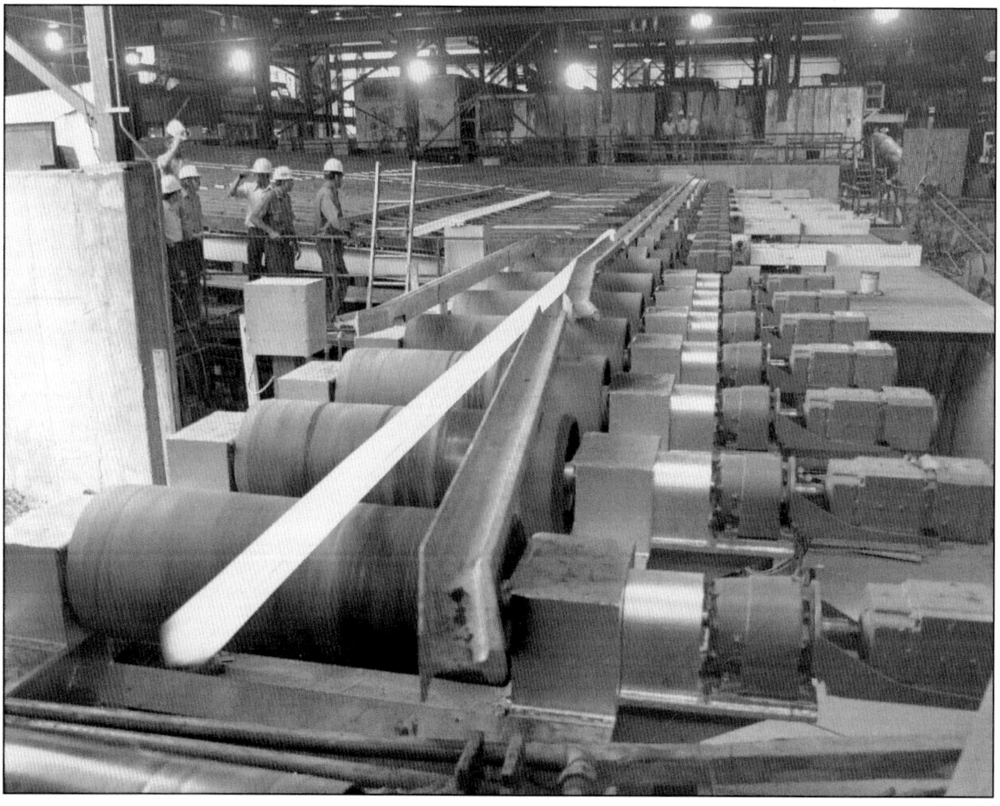

To remain compliant with clean air legislation, the electric arc furnace facility was completed in 1973. Designed to complement steel produced in the basic oxygen furnace, this new furnace transformed 135 tons of scrap metal into steel in just a few hours using electrodes as the primary energy source.

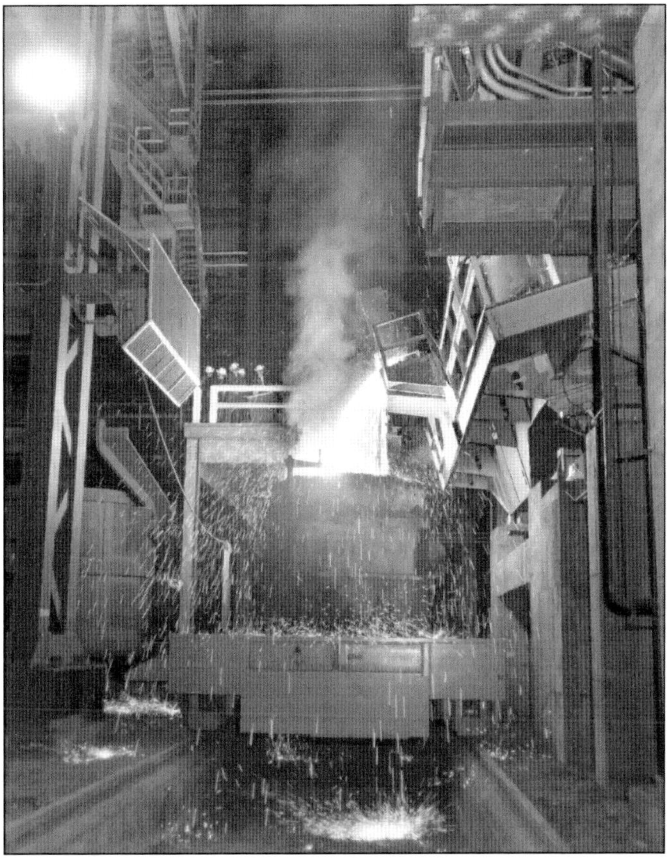

One of the metallurgical properties of steel is that it can be recycled continually with no lessening of performance when remade into another product. Examples of scrap metal used include old cars, air conditioner units, and railroad tracks. Due to its intense weight, workers move crushed scrap metal with the aid of a crane. The crushed metal is melted in a furnace for reuse.

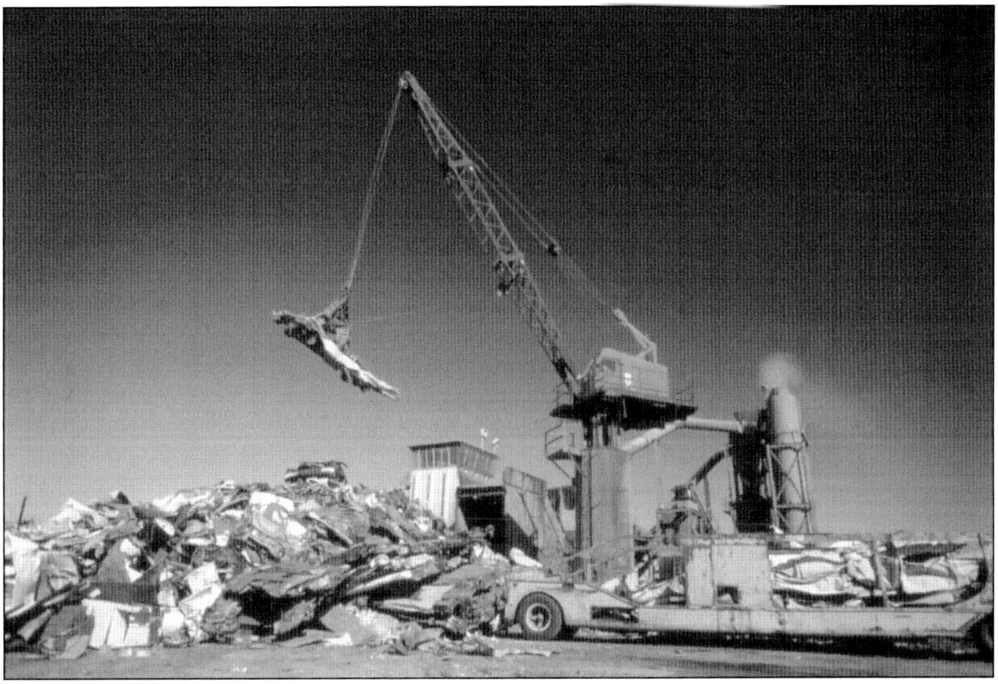

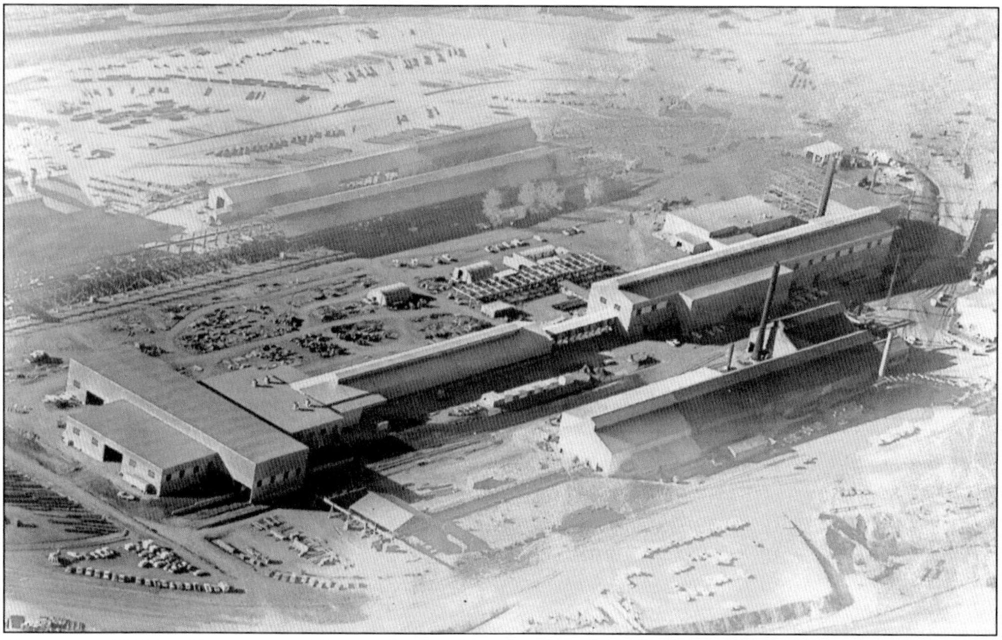

At a cost of $41 million, a new 11-inch bar mill opened in October 1970. This new mill treated steel in 11-inch widths in a continuous process, creating a variety of end shapes including hexagons, squares, rods, and angles.

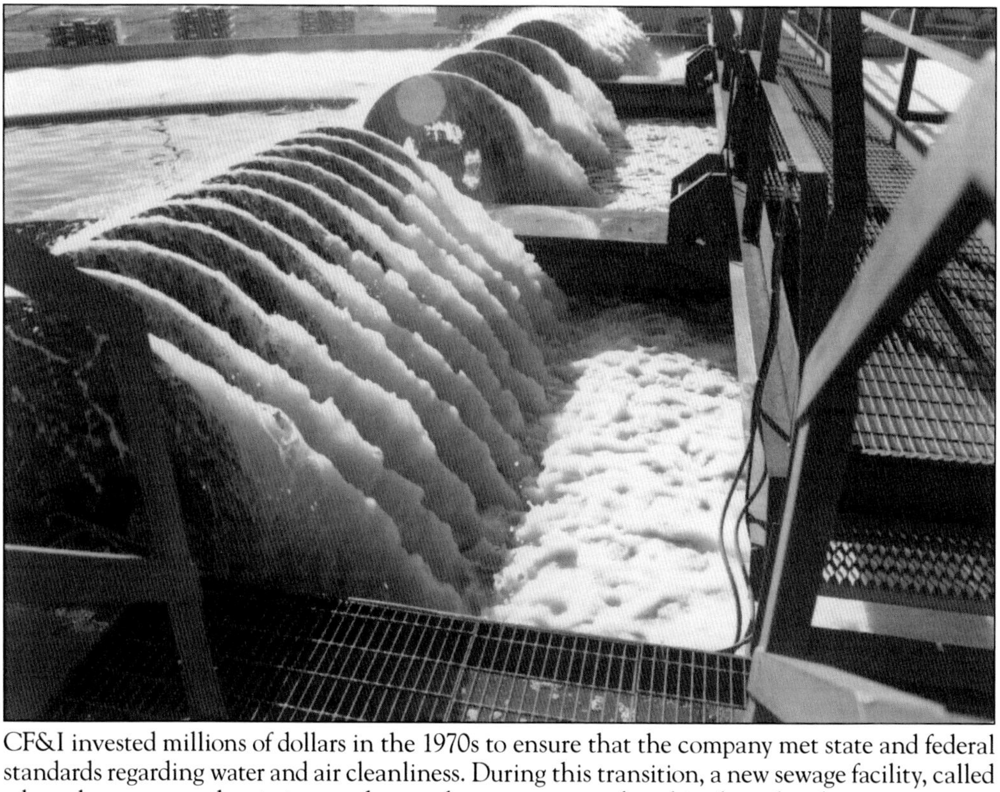

CF&I invested millions of dollars in the 1970s to ensure that the company met state and federal standards regarding water and air cleanliness. During this transition, a new sewage facility, called a bug plant, captured emissions and treated wastewater produced in the coke plant.

Throughout the 1960s, CF&I management dedicated itself to expanding the company's product base and improving the Pueblo plant site in an effort to remain competitive with other steel manufacturers. Ismel Medina (left), William Selvage (center), John Latka Jr. (right), and Robert Milisavlijevich (kneeling) pose with the five-millionth ton of coiled rods produced.

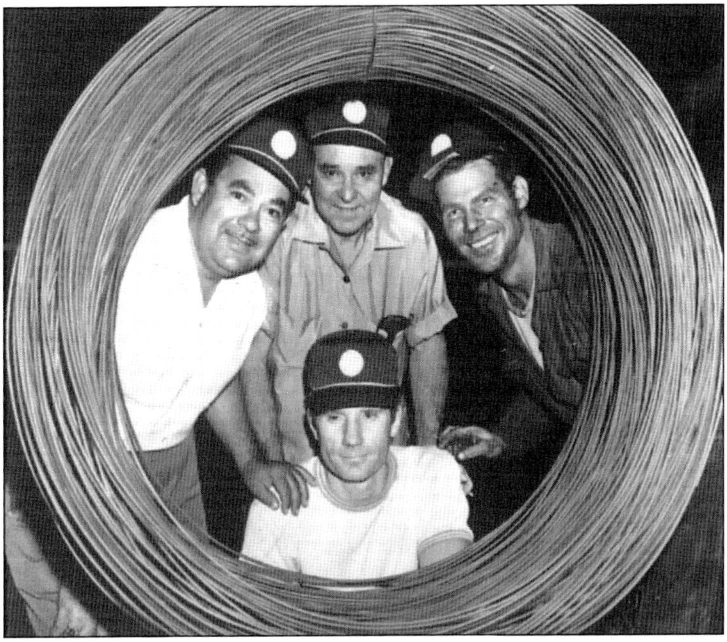

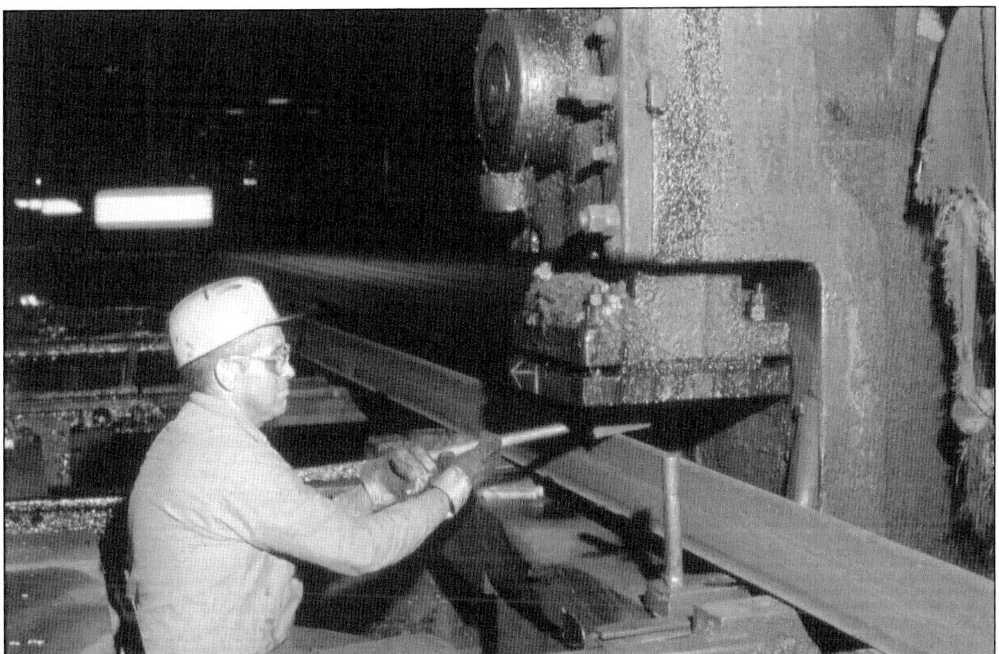

Despite the massive layoffs throughout the steel industry as a whole, CF&I in 1981 remained the largest private employer, responsible for 11 percent of the workforce and about 33 percent of the payroll of Southern Colorado. In Pueblo County, its employees numbered 5,520 that year.

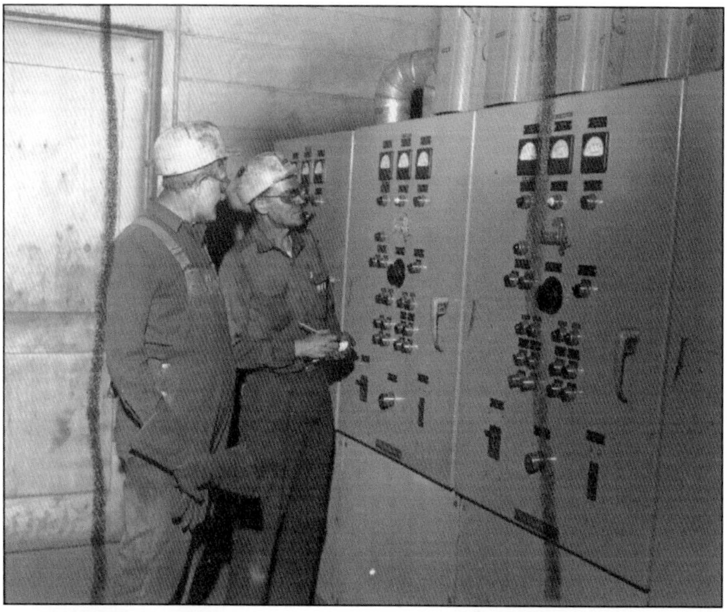

In 1987, teams of employees known as Quality Circles were encouraged to look for cost savings measures in their departments. The next year, concessions were given by both union and nonunion employees that included no wage increases for three years, an across-the-board wage reduction, and a new schedule of health benefits. In exchange, the employees shared in an employee stock option plan.

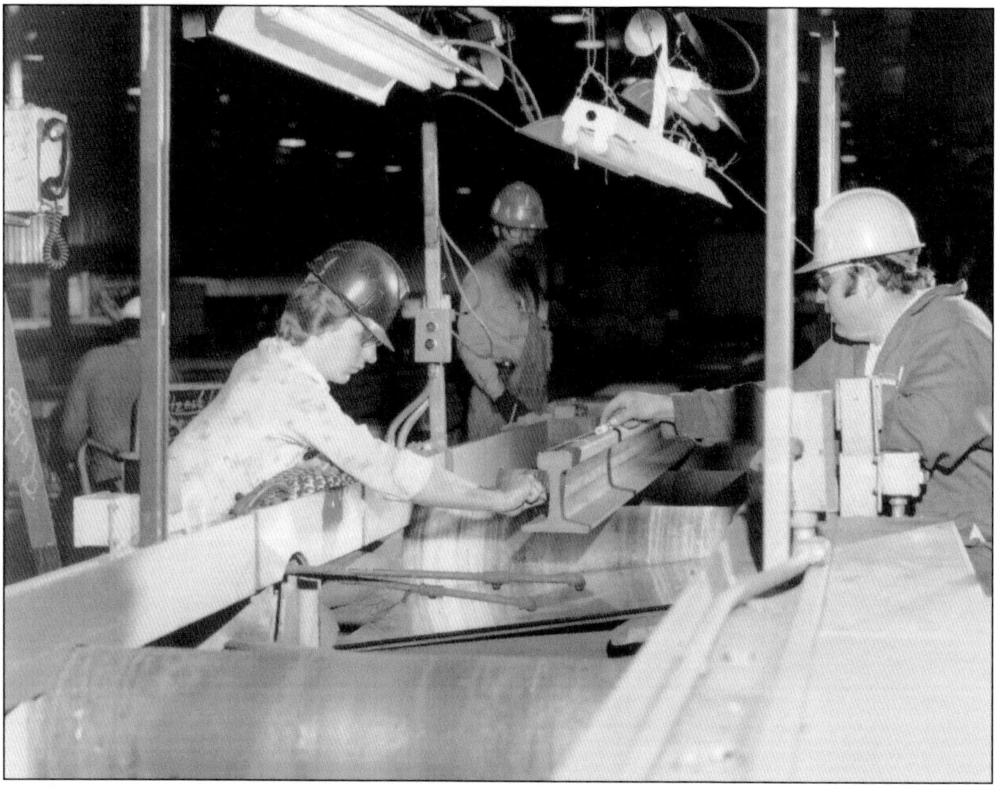

Quality is important when manufacturing steel products, and customers expect perfection. If this rail did not meet strict standards for straightness, it would be squeezed in a machine using high pressure to correct any imperfections. In rare cases, the rail would be sent back to the scrapyard, where the melting and forming process would start again. Here, inspectors give the final approval to rails in 1978.

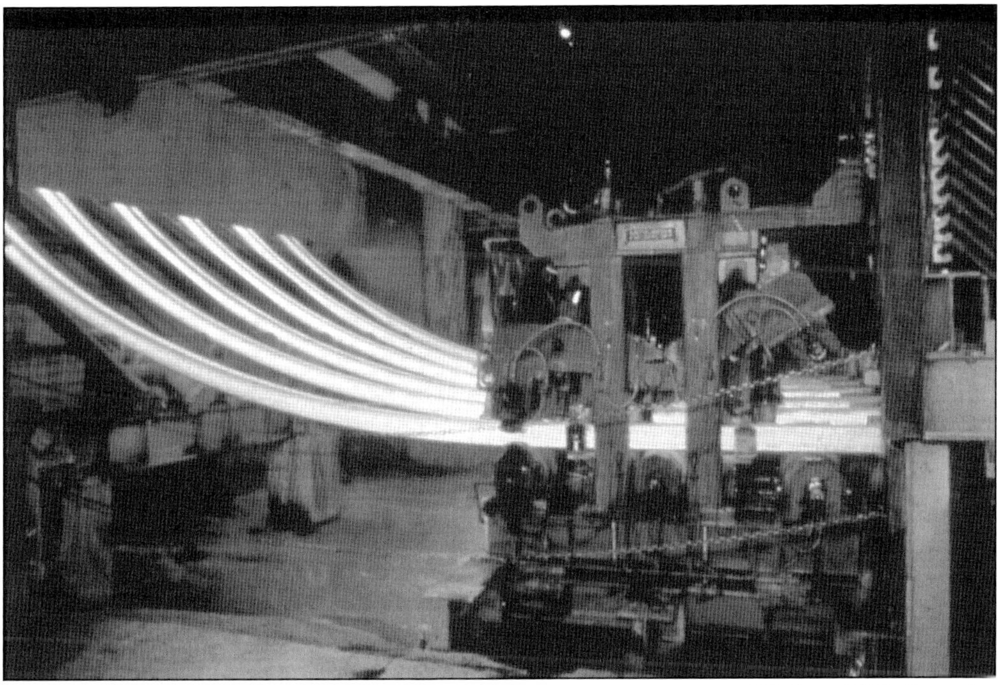

The continuous billet caster, a six-strand machine, began operation at CF&I in 1976. Over the next decade, it produced over 12 million tons of billets. A continuous caster converts steel from its liquid state directly into various smaller steel shapes without further processing. Prior to the continuous caster, all steel was poured into ingot molds and then rolled into billets.

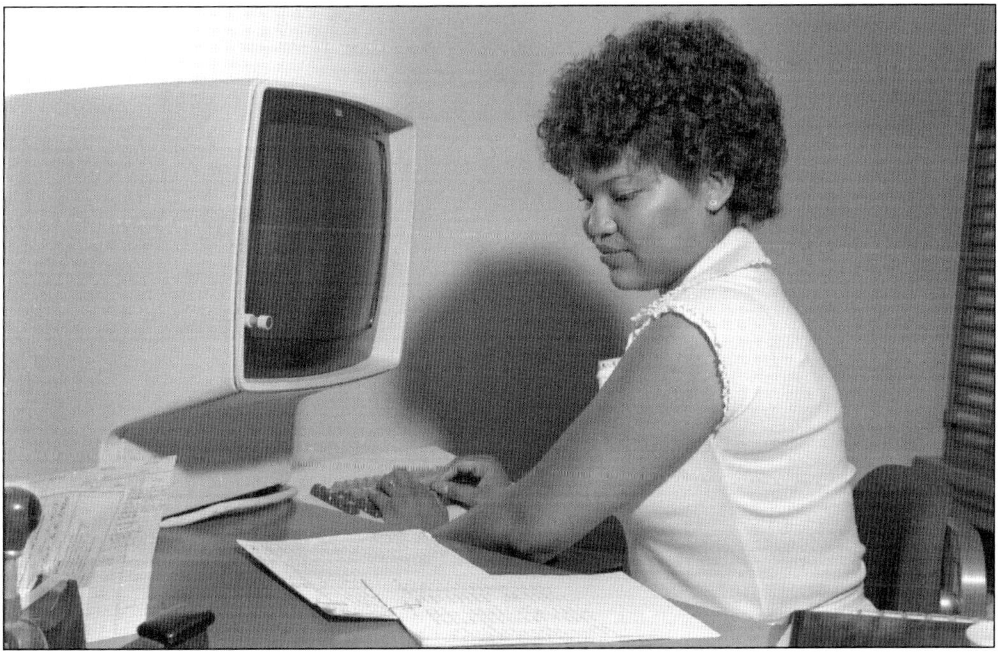

Moving away from a handwritten employment card system to computers in the late 1970s, data entry operators such as Helen Sandoval were able to quickly retrieve basic employment data about the thousands of workers at the Pueblo mill. She enters names into a database in 1978.

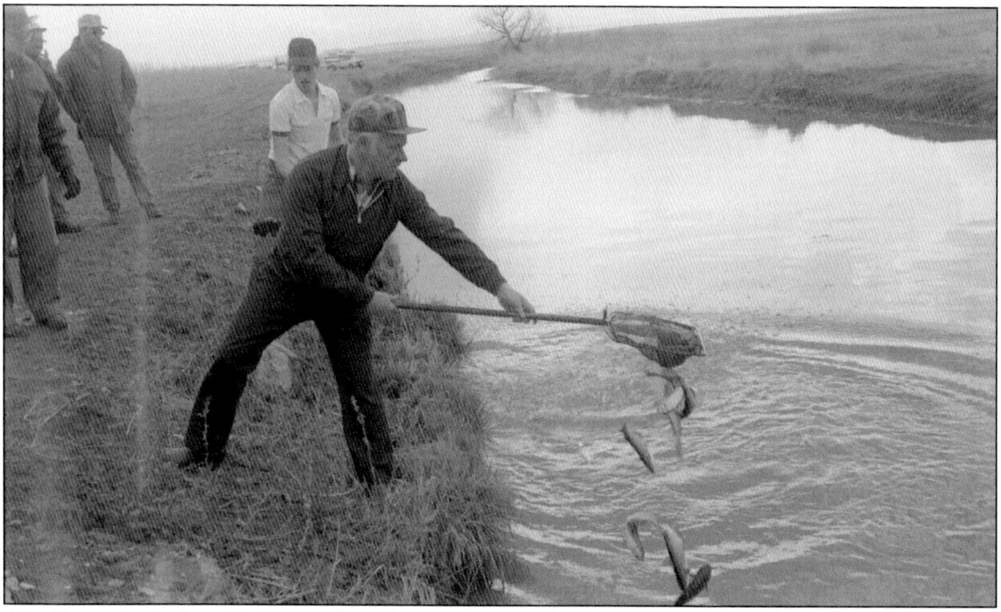

The Fin and Feather Club, an off-site hunting and fishing club, was a respite south of the mill for employees and their families. Opened in 1917, the club remained a staple of outdoor recreational life until it closed in 1974. Here, a man stocks the inlets with fish at one of the reservoirs in the early 1970s.

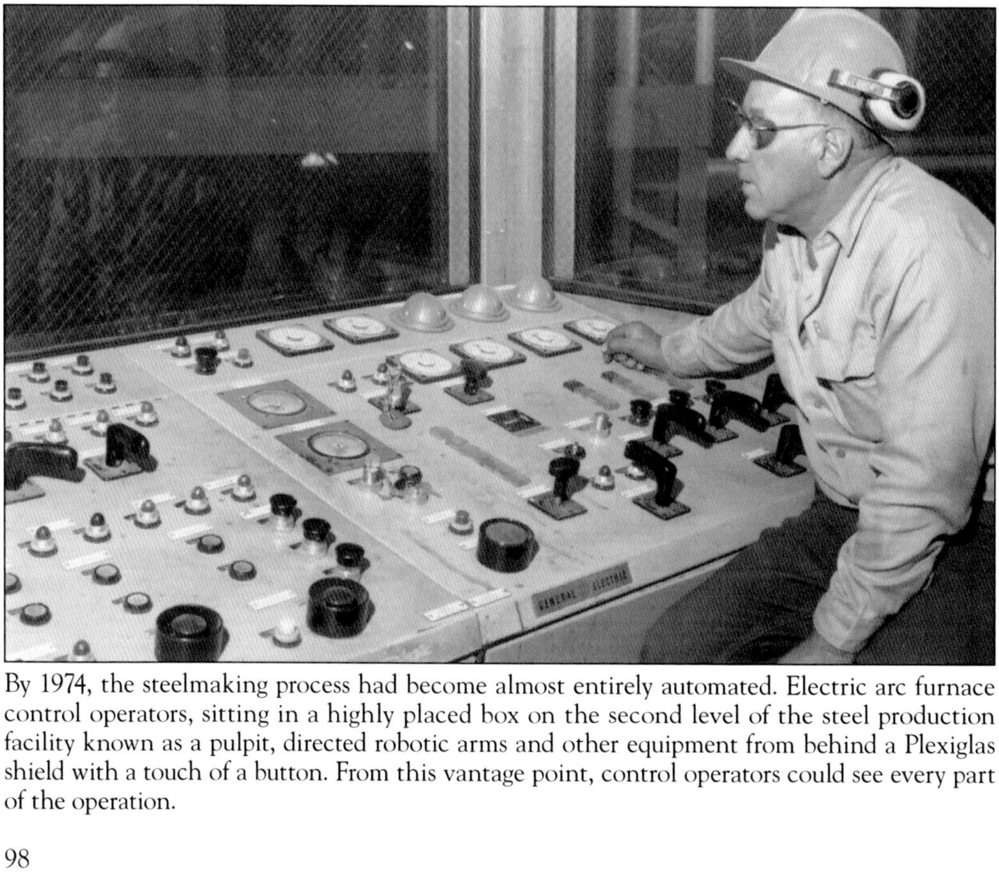

By 1974, the steelmaking process had become almost entirely automated. Electric arc furnace control operators, sitting in a highly placed box on the second level of the steel production facility known as a pulpit, directed robotic arms and other equipment from behind a Plexiglas shield with a touch of a button. From this vantage point, control operators could see every part of the operation.

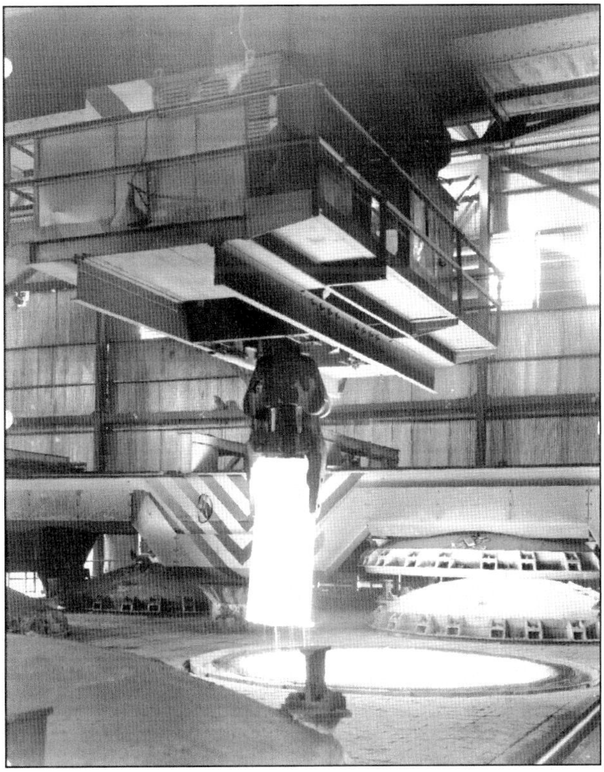

Ingots, large blocks of steel, weigh several hundred tons each. To shape them into a final product, the ingots were reheated in a gas- or electric-powered heating vessel known as a soaking pit until they reached a uniform temperature around 2,800 degrees Fahrenheit. They were then picked out of the soaking pit using cranes and robotic arms. As many as 12 ingots could be reheated in one soaking pit at one time. Skilled crane operators were able to remove ingots one at a time from the soaking pit and place them gently on a conveyor belt. From there, the ingot was rolled, squeezed, and shaped into a final product.

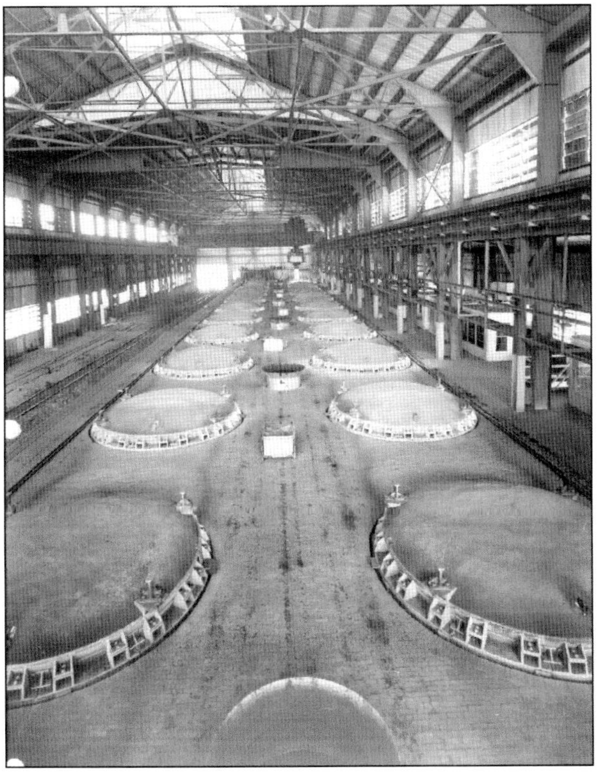

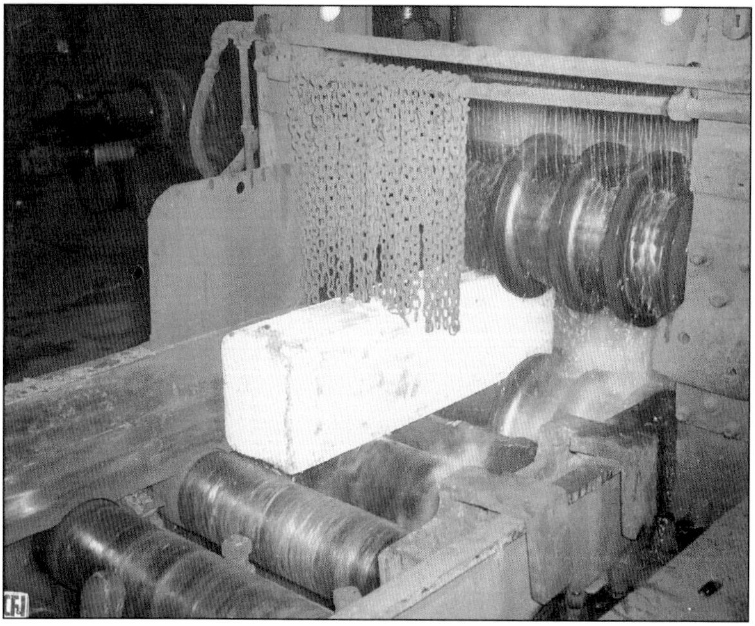

When it is time to shape a block of steel into various shapes for a final product, it is reheated, making it soft and malleable, and enters a machine of large rollers known as a rolling mill. The rollers press and squeeze the steel. The intense pressure elongates the steel, quadrupling its original length. In the 1970s, blocks of steel could be passed through rolling mills as many as 28 times.

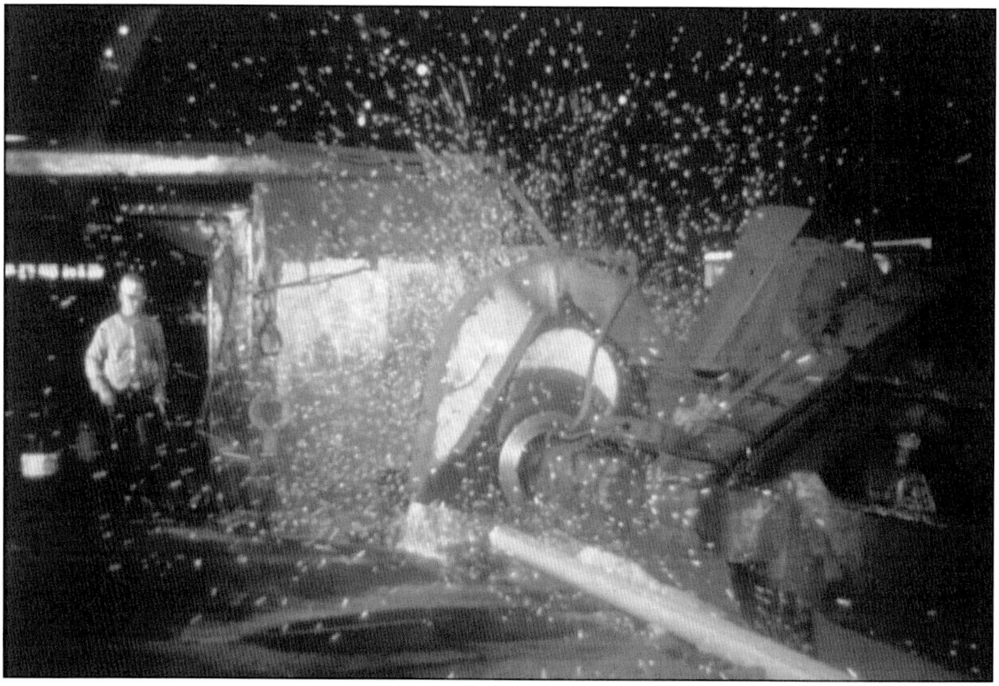

When the ingot is squeezed into a smaller, more manageable block for final shaping, it is known as a billet. In the rolling process, as much as 11 inches on either end of the billet may become distorted during the rolling process. The ends are cut off and are returned to the scrapyard to be recycled into future products.

Scarfing is one of the final steps before the finished product is shipped to the customer. In the scarfing yard, blowtorches known as scarfing torches are used to smooth any rough edges, scratches, or other imperfections in the products before it is shipped to the customer.

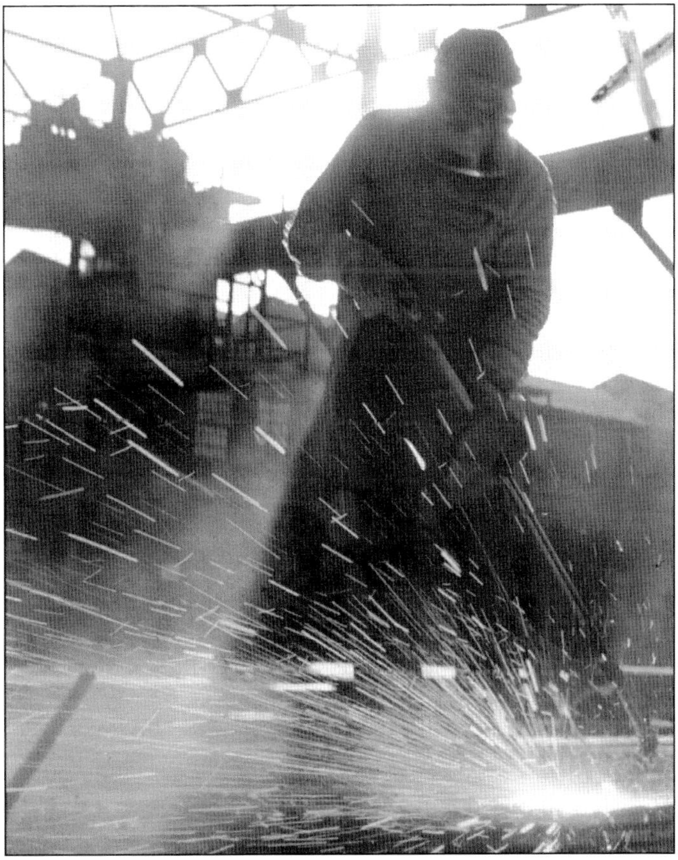

Modernization of the 25-inch mill in the 1970s allowed CF&I to manufacture wide-flange beam sections. Ranging in size from 6 by 6 inches to 16 by 8½ inches, these beams provided more strength than other beams. Because the flanges were not tapered, the surfaces of the wide-flange beam sections made for simpler structural connections with rivets, bolts, or welding.

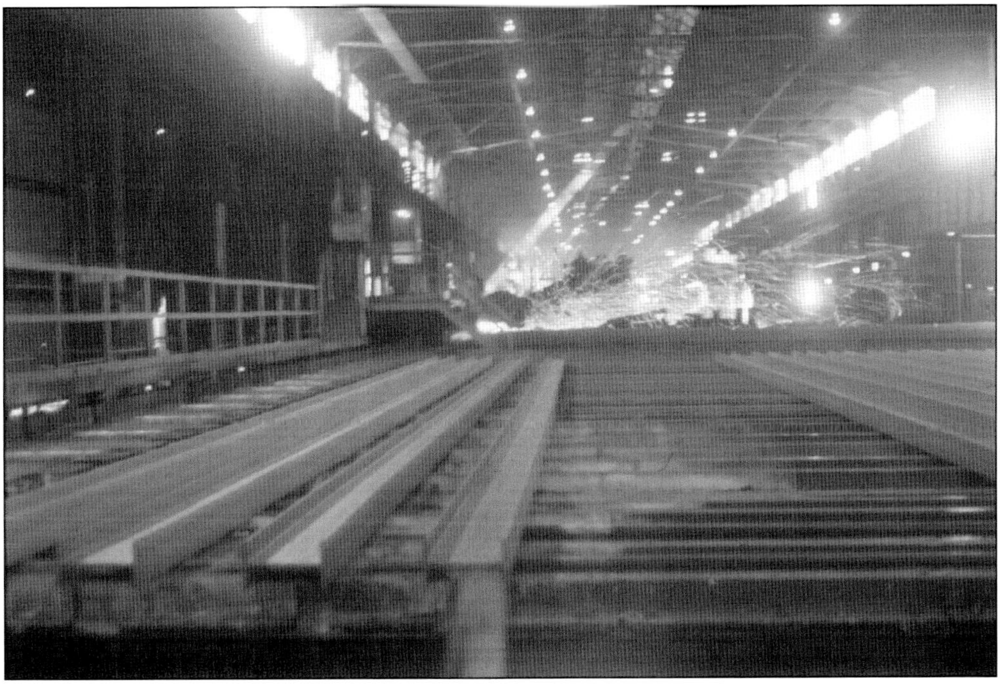

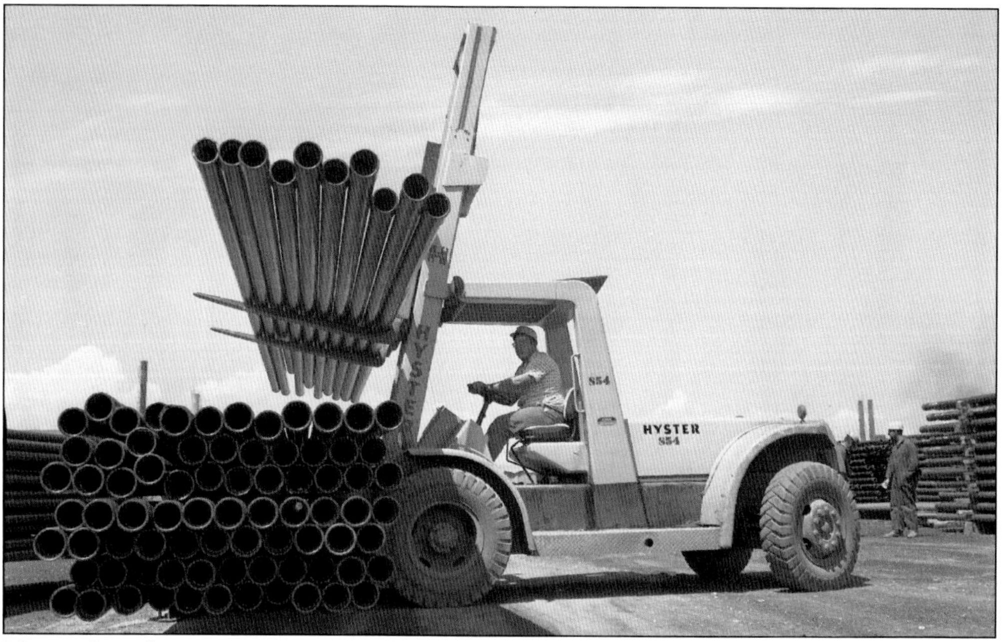

The trucking department was responsible for providing service to departments throughout the mill using forklifts, hydraulic platform transporters, front-end loaders, and various types of trucks to ship products to customers. This operator lifts a load of seamless tubes with a Hyster lift truck.

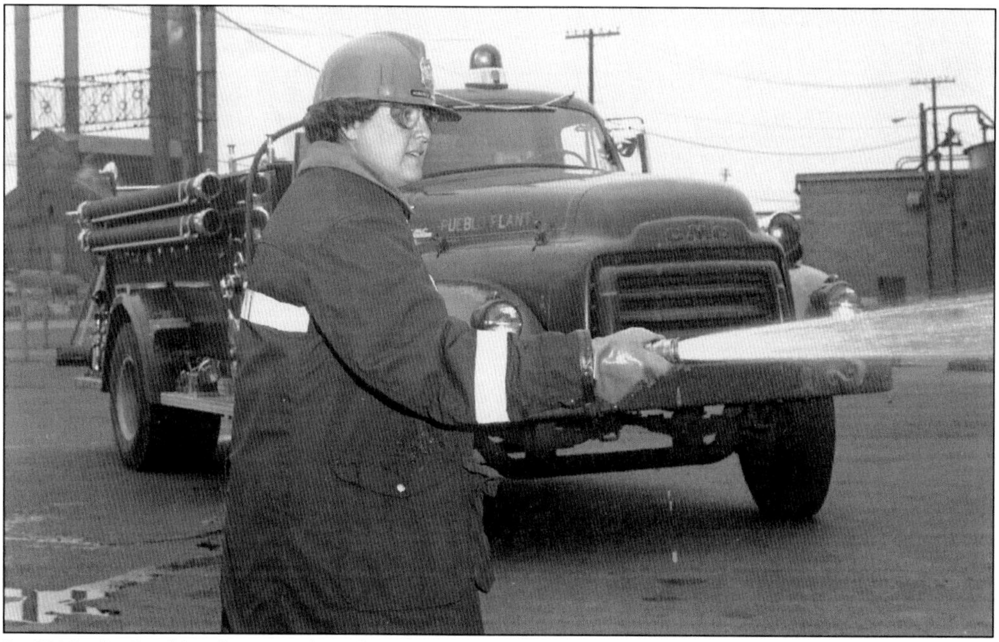

In 1990, the Pueblo plant employed 17 security guards and two supervisors to assist with securing the buildings and their contents and to provide fire and emergency medical services to 1,900 employees. Roberta Johnston, one of the security guards, works a fire training hose during a drill in 1982. The fire truck carried 750 gallons of water and could also hook into one of several fire hydrants on the mill property. The plant encompassed more than 850 acres at the time, and first responders on-site could respond quickly to an emergency.

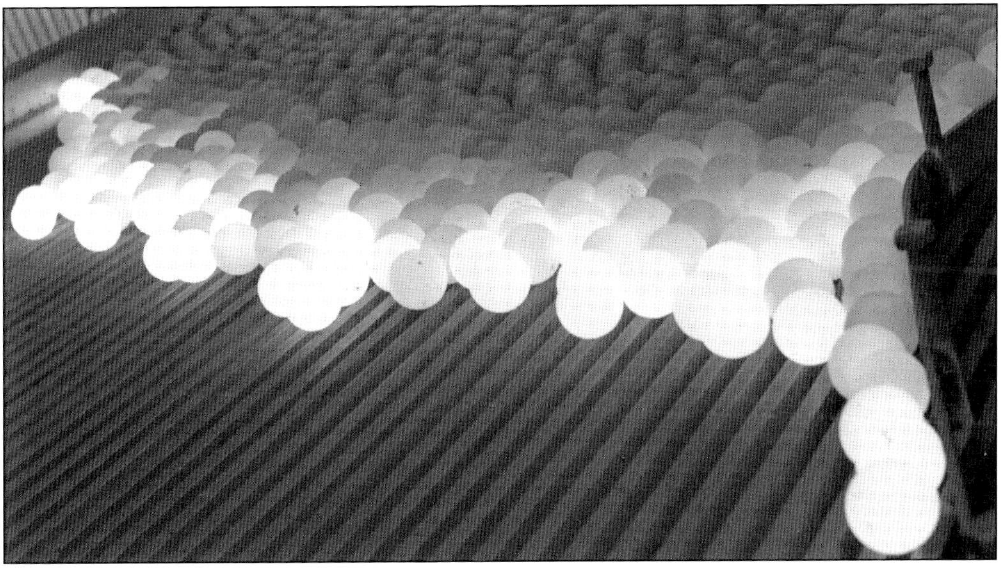

Grinding balls are manufactured in a wide variety of sizes from three quarters of an inch to five inches in diameter and are used for pulverizing ore, grinding cement, and many other essential jobs in the American milling and mining industries. Starting from round bars fed into a ball machine, the red-hot steel balls are dropped into a rotating spool whirling at 800 revolutions per minute, where they are smoothed into spheres.

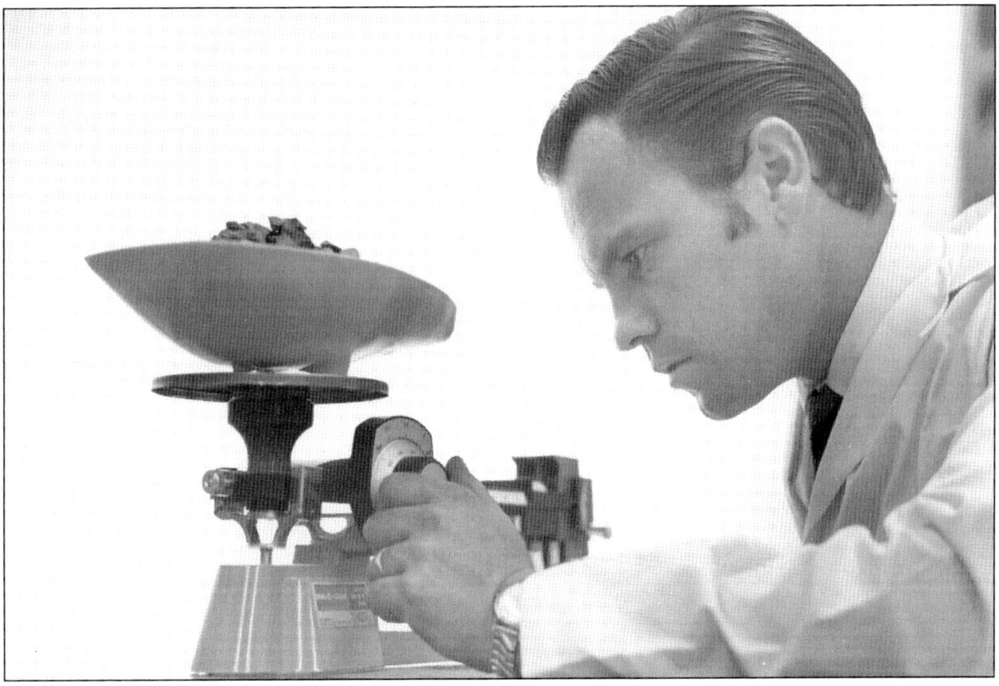

Throughout the life of the company, CF&I maintained its own chemical, metallurgical, and mining laboratories. Engineers assigned to these departments examined and tested the quality of minerals and series throughout the steelmaking process. Without proper quality control, there would be a drastic increase in products or parts needing to be scrapped, reworked, or completely reordered. Chemist Frank May examines a small sample of raw minerals in 1971.

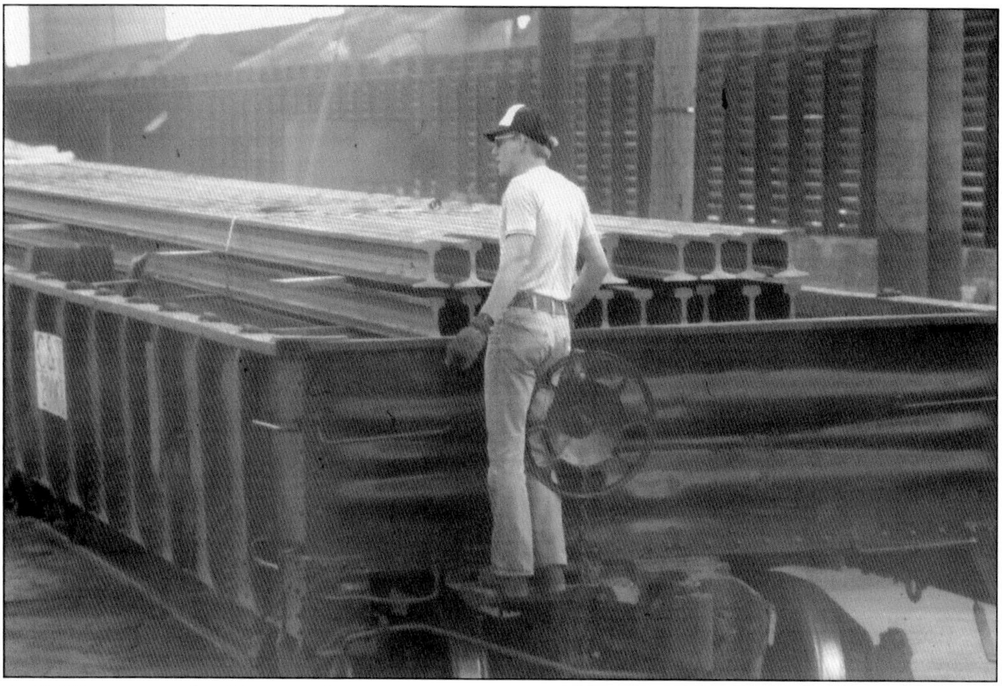

In 1979, a new rail mill opened ushering in a new era of rail products manufactured in Pueblo. By 1985, CF&I served as the largest of three rail producers in the United States, with 550,000 tons produced annually. The rails were sold directly to major railroads, rail contractors, short-line railroads, and transit districts. This worker loads rails into a large vessel known as a gondola to ship to a customer.

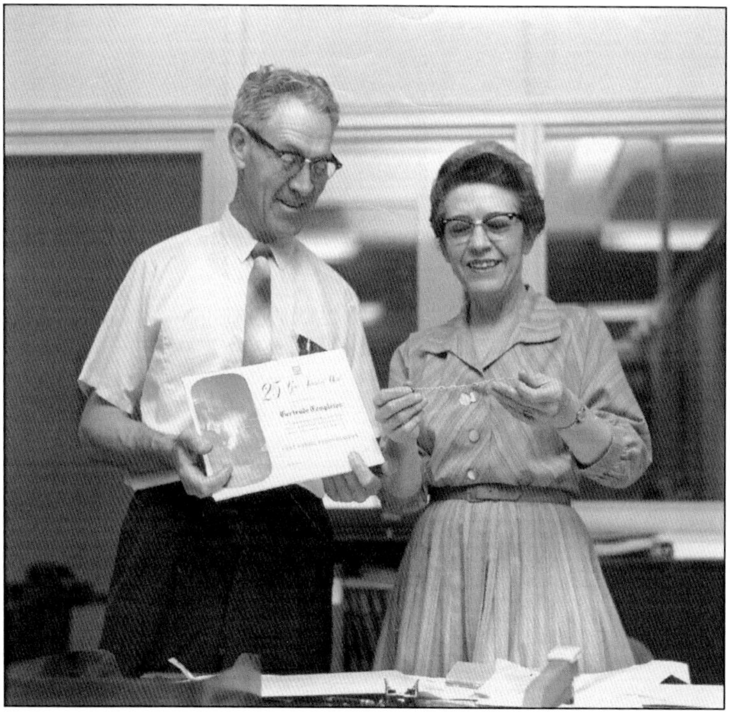

Small milestone incentives were distributed recognizing years spent on the job or hours of safe working conditions. Women received brass charm bracelets and men received tie tacks if they worked for the company for 25 years. Other incentives included belt buckles, jackets, coffee mugs, and screwdriver sets. Gertrude Templeton, an inspector in the quality control department, receives her 25-year bracelet from her supervisor, John Zadra, in 1967.

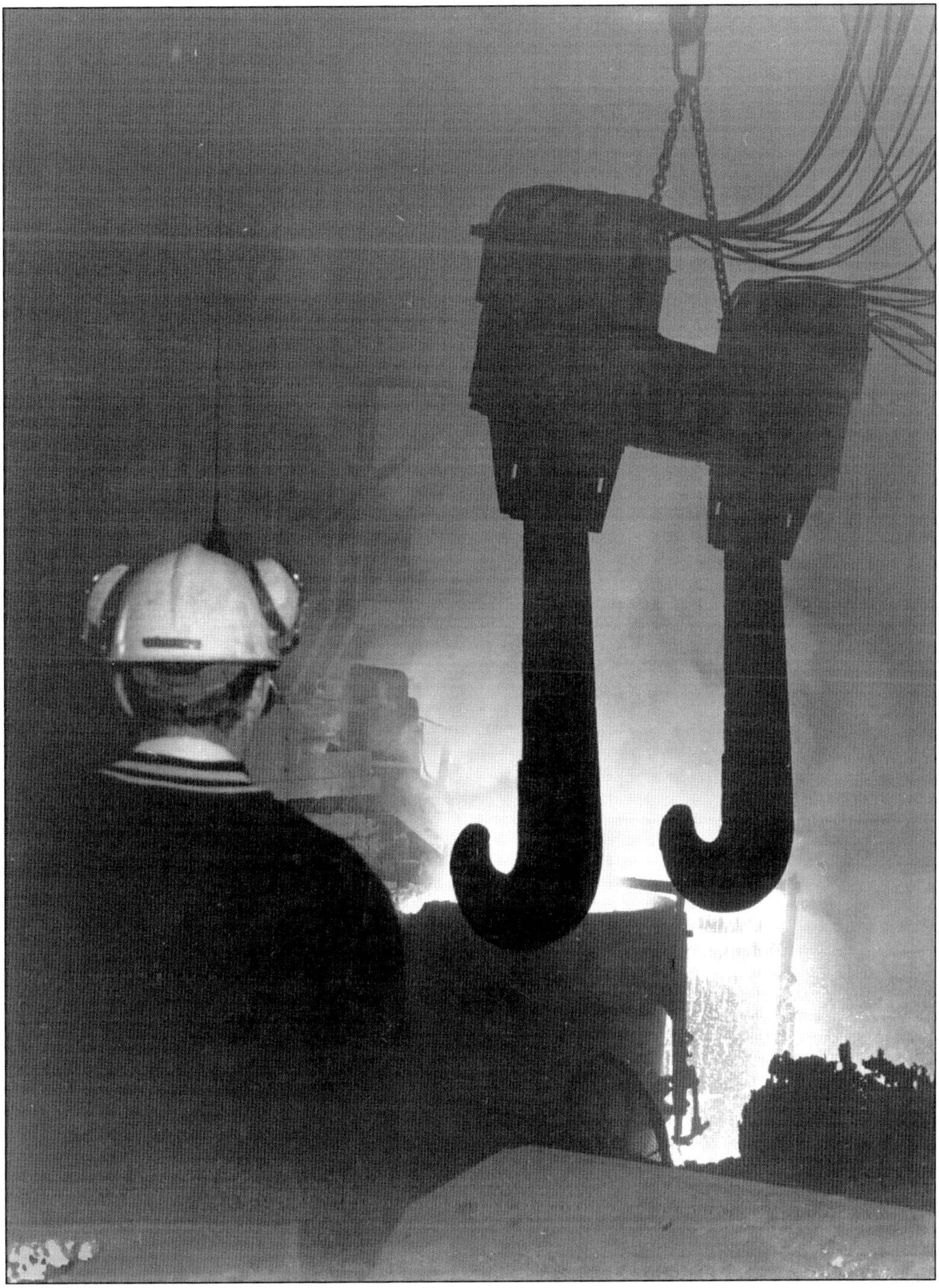

The open hearth furnace at the Pueblo mill poured its last batch of steel on December 12, 1973, bringing to a close an era of steelmaking. The first open hearth furnace was built in 1902. In 1957, when the last furnace was built, there were only 17 open hearth furnaces in operation across the United States. During its 71 years of operations, some 45 million tons of steel were produced at the Pueblo mill using this method before making way for new technology utilizing an electric arc furnace. Shown here is the last pouring of open hearth steel in Pueblo.

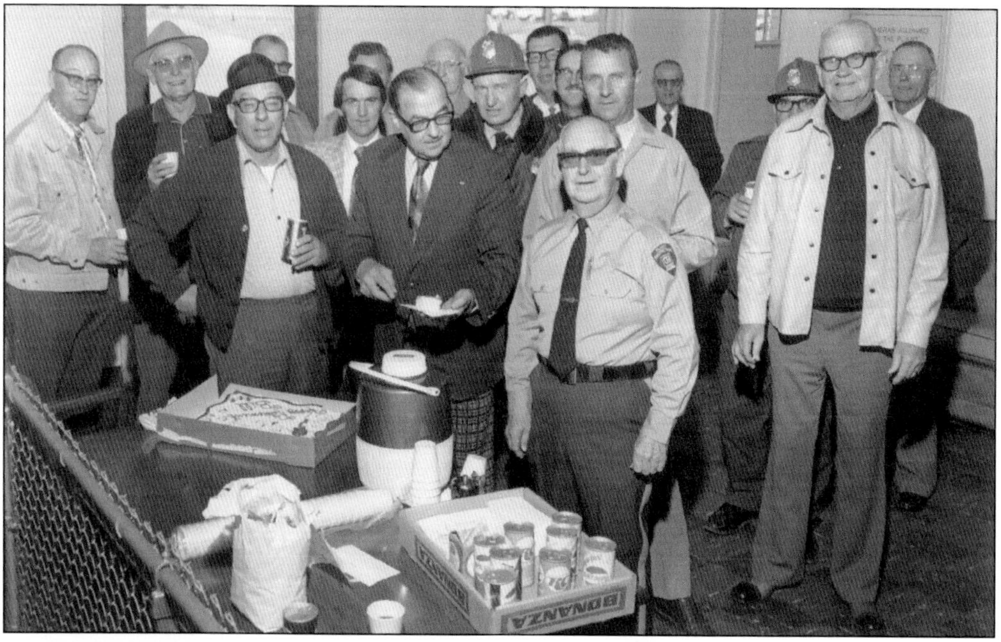

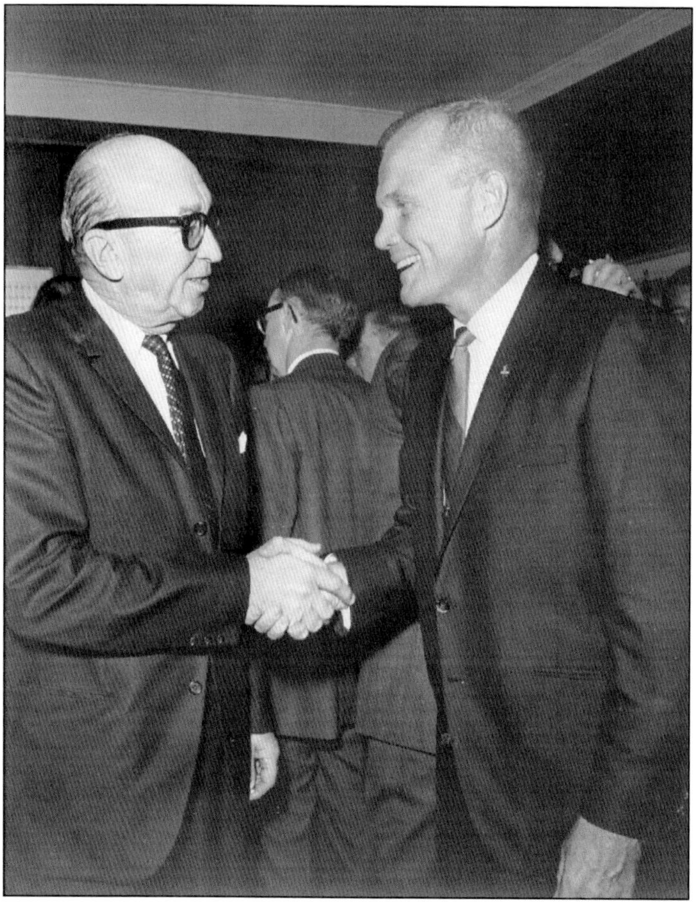

Beginning in the 1960s, as changes in technology were experienced and high competition from foreign steelmakers drove profits down, resulting in financial losses for the company, those on the payroll with multiple years of vested interest began to retire. Hundreds of workers retired quarterly and requested their pensions, resulting in more financial stress for the company. Friends of Bill Smith, employee of CF&I's safety and security department, wish him well in his retirement years. R.L. Hanes (left), vice president of the company's sales department, shakes hands with US astronaut John Glenn at Hanes's retirement party at the company's New York office in 1967.

Seven

The Reach of CF&I

From its first subsidiary company developed in 1888 to the final ones purchased in the 1960s and 1970s, each played a vital role in the development of CF&I as a local, national, and international steelmaker. The first of the company subsidiaries, the Colorado Supply Company Store, opened in 1888. With a few exceptions, the stores in the remote mining communities served as general mercantiles, banks, and post offices. At its peak in the first decade of the 20th century, the Colorado Supply Company employed 135 people with retail outlets spanning more than 600 miles. The chain also had a retail outlet and warehouse in Pueblo.

The 1937 purchase of Buffalo, New York–based Wickwire Spencer Steel Company began the company's acquisition of more than 15 different subsidiary steel-producing companies stretching from coast to coast. Many of these subsidiary companies were noted for their involvement in famous landmarks.

Other subsidiaries included CF&I's own railroad company, the Colorado & Wyoming Railroad, and smaller steel-related support areas such as a gravel pit and internal scrapyard company. With economic constraints placed on company operations in the 1960s and 1970s, CF&I sold many of its subsidiary companies to recoup some of its losses.

Whether affiliated as subsidiaries, customers, or the operators of the Pueblo mill itself, there is no doubt that the reach of CF&I was noted across the region, the country, and eventually, the world.

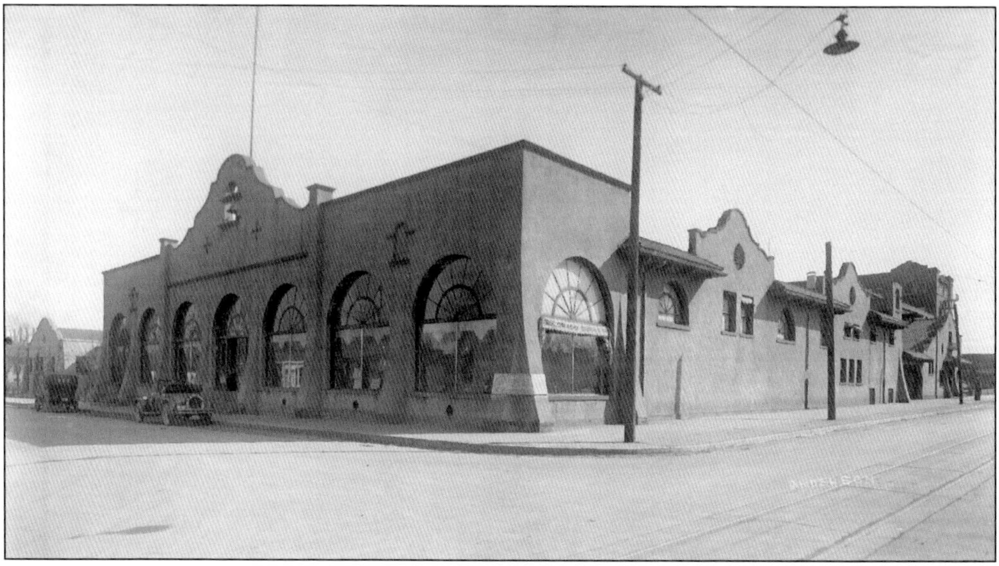

The Pueblo branch of the Colorado Supply Company store opened in 1902, and customers were greeted by mahogany and glass-front display cases, stationary cash registers, a pneumatic tube system, electric lights, central heating, and ceiling fans—all quite novel for the time in a commercial building. Items for sale included clothing, groceries, baked goods, meats, baskets and decorative items, shoes, and toys, and there was a small pharmacy and a newsstand. By 1908, the store, with its wide customer base and 46 retail outlets, recorded $2,762,000 in sales. The Pueblo branch served customer needs until fire engulfed the building in 1953. The building was razed shortly after and never rebuilt.

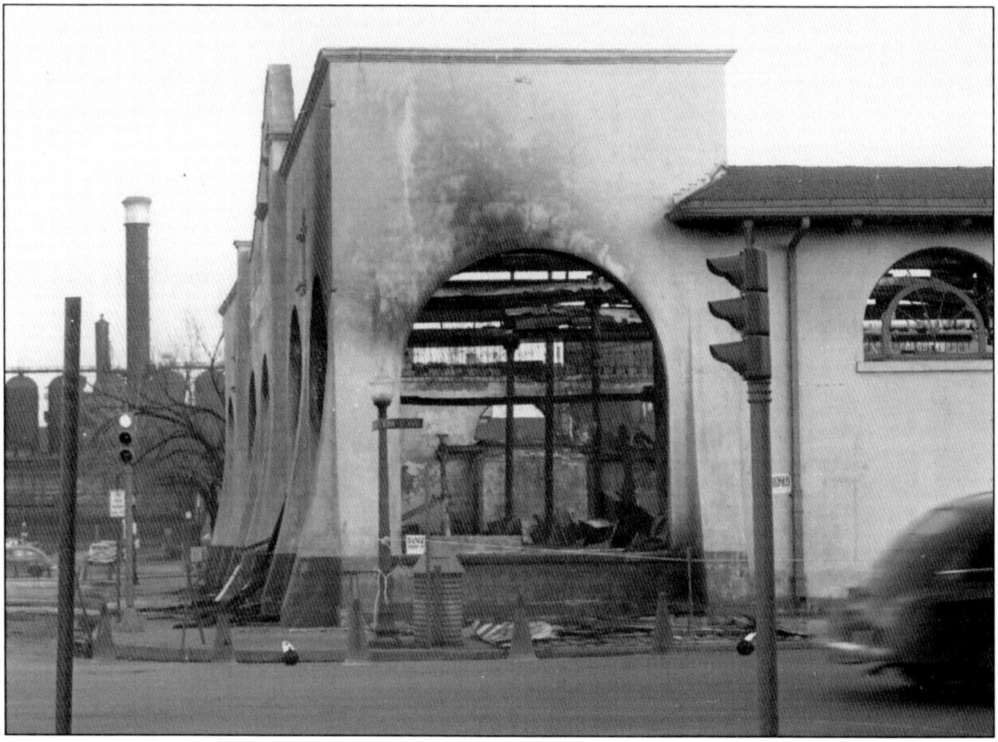

Railroads in the 1930s began to feel competition, with automobiles and buses eroding passenger business and trucks competing with freight revenues. In response, railroads found themselves not needing to purchase new track on lines that were unproductive or to replace worn lines. Thus, the suppliers of these railroads, such as CF&I, also suffered. CF&I's subsidiary, the Colorado & Wyoming Railroad, transported raw minerals and finished products to and from the Minnequa Steelworks in Colorado, New Mexico, and Wyoming. C&W felt the effects of the depressed economy and entered into receivership with its parent company in 1936. Today, the Colorado & Wyoming Railway Company continues to run. The C&W employs 100 people who service several companies in the Minnequa Industrial Complex, including EVRAZ Rocky Mountain Steel Mills, Xcel Energy, Nortrak, Progress Rail Services, and interchanges with both the Union Pacific Railroad and BNSF Railway.

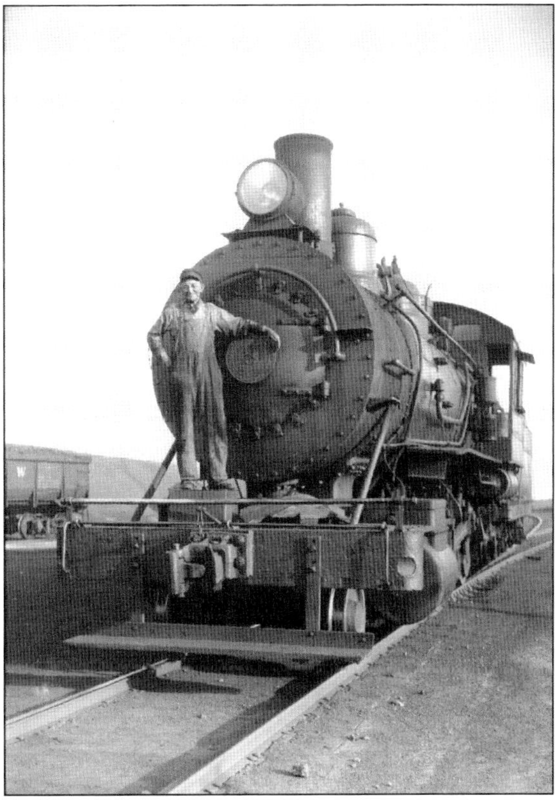

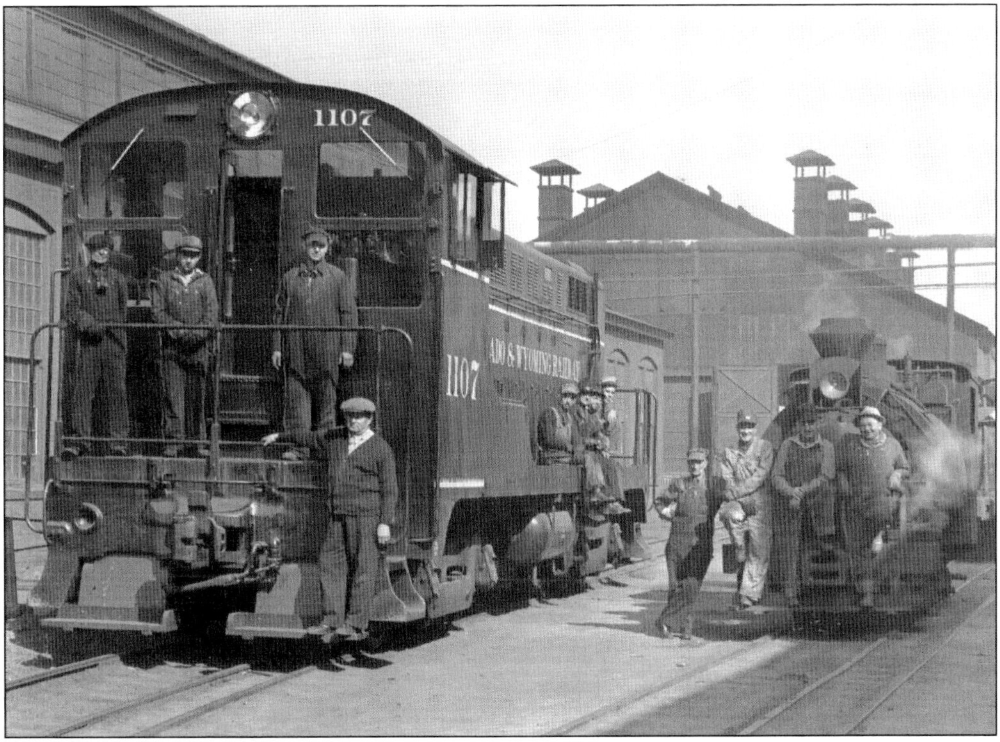

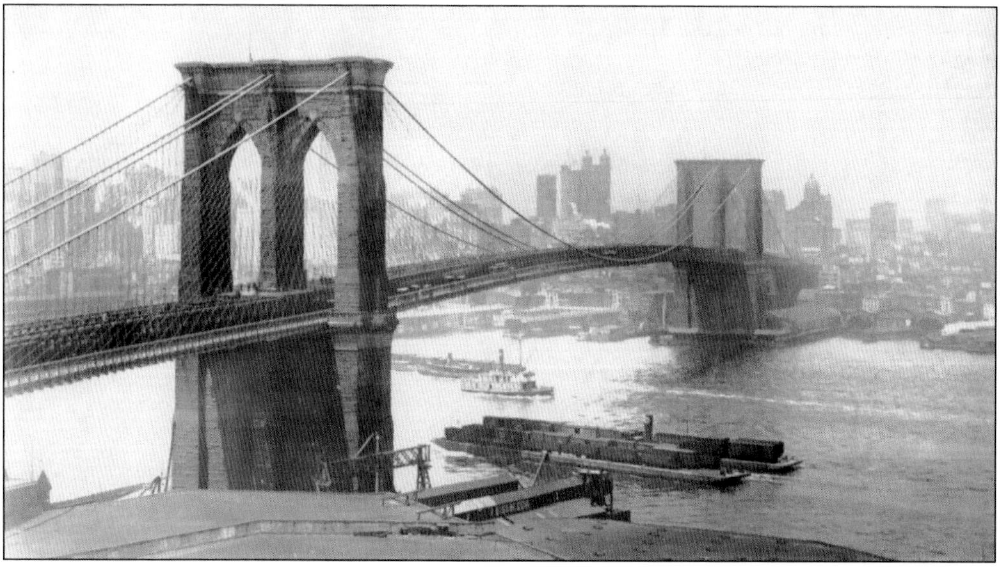

Perhaps the most famous of CF&I's subsidiary companies was J.A. Roebling and Sons, which provided steel for the Brooklyn Bridge, George Washington Bridge, and Golden Gate Bridge. Although these famous landmarks were designed and built long before CF&I purchased the company in 1952, they remained part of the shared legacy of American steelmaking and arguably are some of the most important technological achievements of the industrial era.

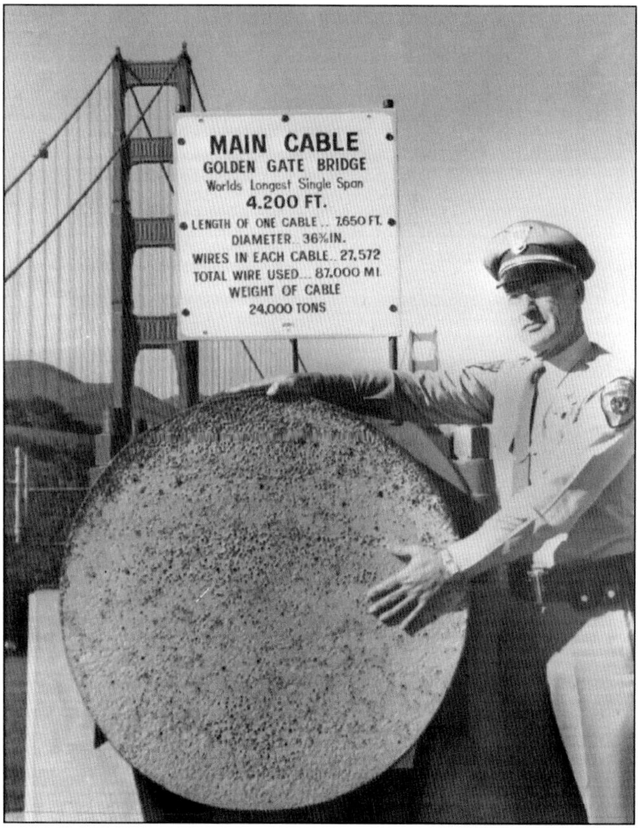

In 1841, John Roebling conceived the idea of making a rope of twisted wires, giving greater strength than the traditional single-strand hemp ropes of the era. Its success launched his wire rope business and brought him commissions to build suspension bridges. A man in uniform poses with an example of the main cable of the Golden Gate Bridge in San Francisco in 1978, showing the strength of the twisted wire.

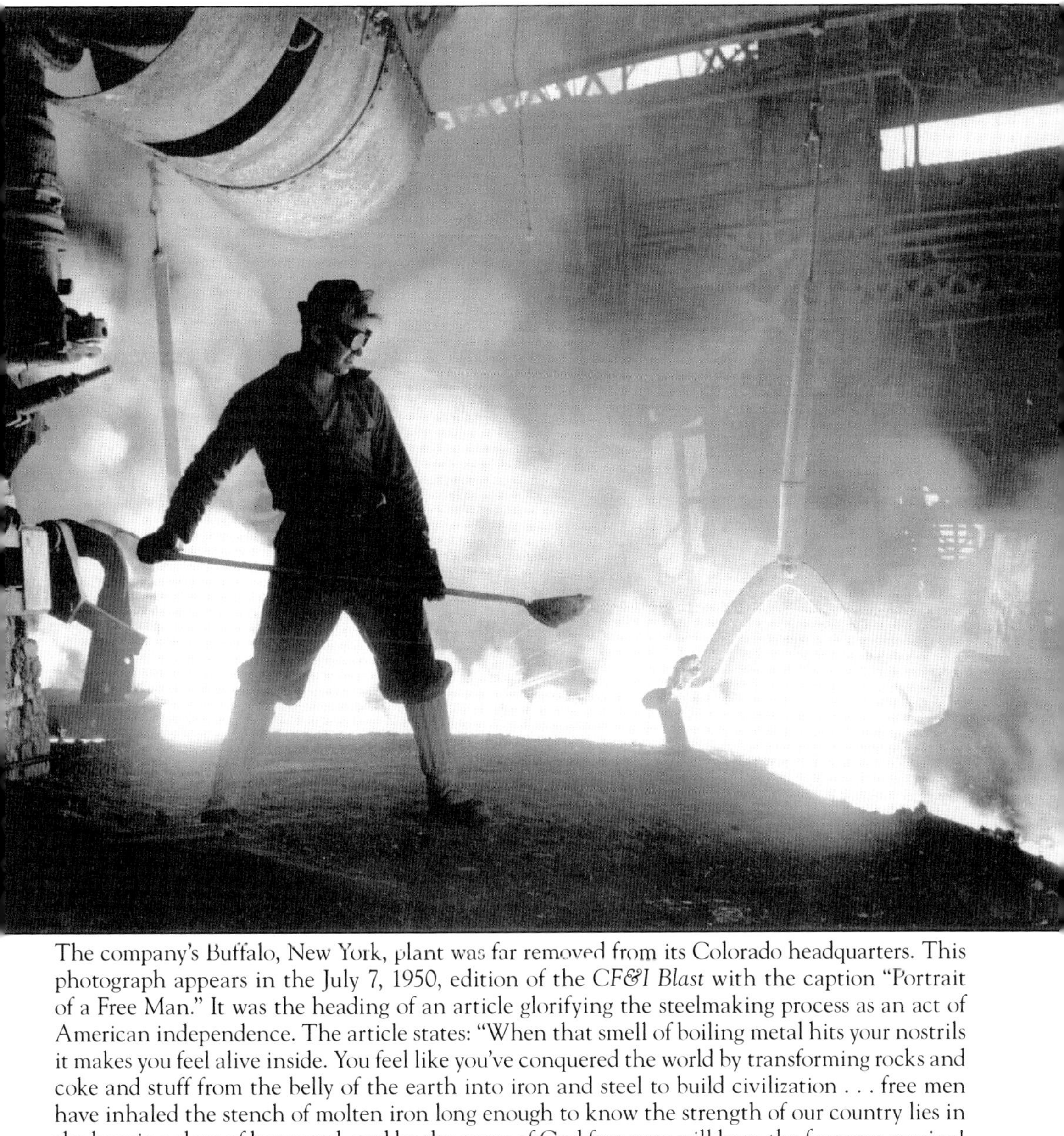

The company's Buffalo, New York, plant was far removed from its Colorado headquarters. This photograph appears in the July 7, 1950, edition of the *CF&I Blast* with the caption "Portrait of a Free Man." It was the heading of an article glorifying the steelmaking process as an act of American independence. The article states: "When that smell of boiling metal hits your nostrils it makes you feel alive inside. You feel like you've conquered the world by transforming rocks and coke and stuff from the belly of the earth into iron and steel to build civilization . . . free men have inhaled the stench of molten iron long enough to know the strength of our country lies in the burning glory of hot metal, and by the grace of God free men will keep the furnaces roaring! Freedom is everybody's job!"

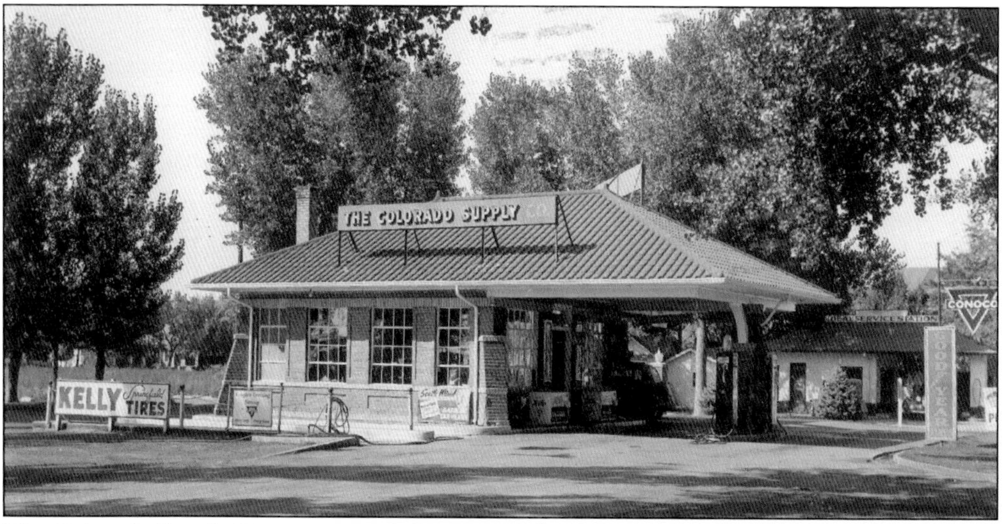

The Colorado Supply Company retail chain opened service stations in the most remote mining communities in the late 1920s and a complete service station in Pueblo in 1930. The station sold gasoline and various brands of tires, offered car washes, and provided small auto repairs. This photograph features the service station at the corner of Lake and Lakeview Avenues, about mile west of the mill's main gate.

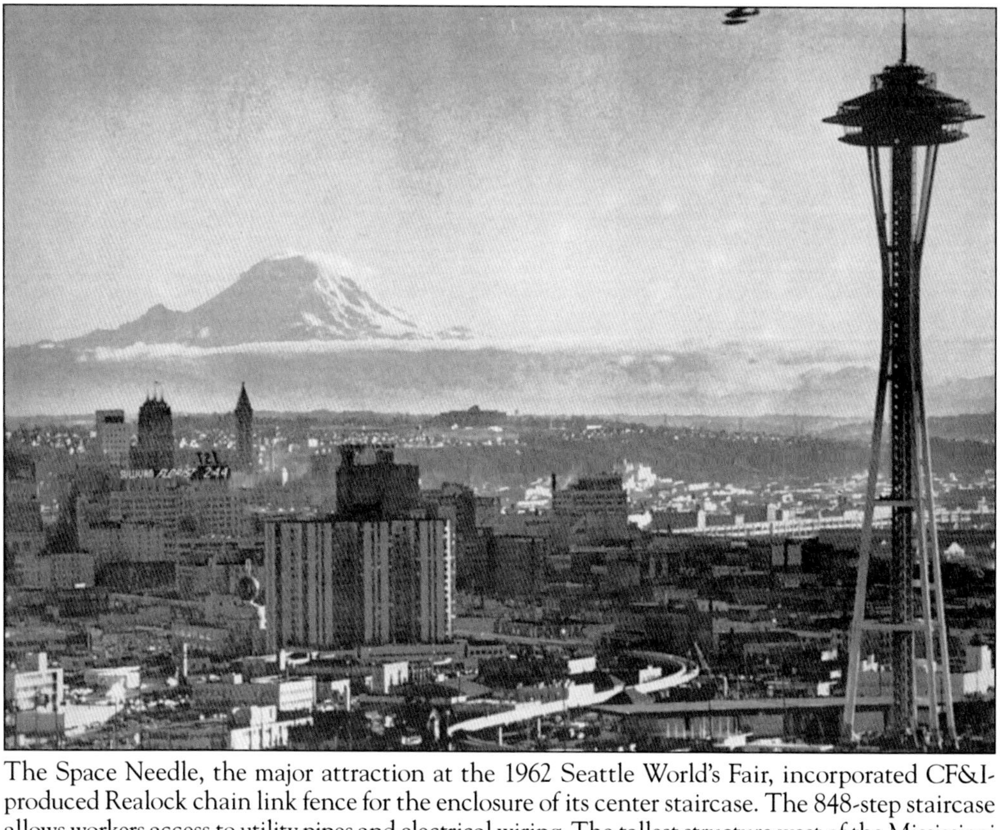

The Space Needle, the major attraction at the 1962 Seattle World's Fair, incorporated CF&I-produced Realock chain link fence for the enclosure of its center staircase. The 848-step staircase allows workers access to utility pipes and electrical wiring. The tallest structure west of the Mississippi River at the time, the Space Needle stands 605 feet tall and cost $3.5 million to build.

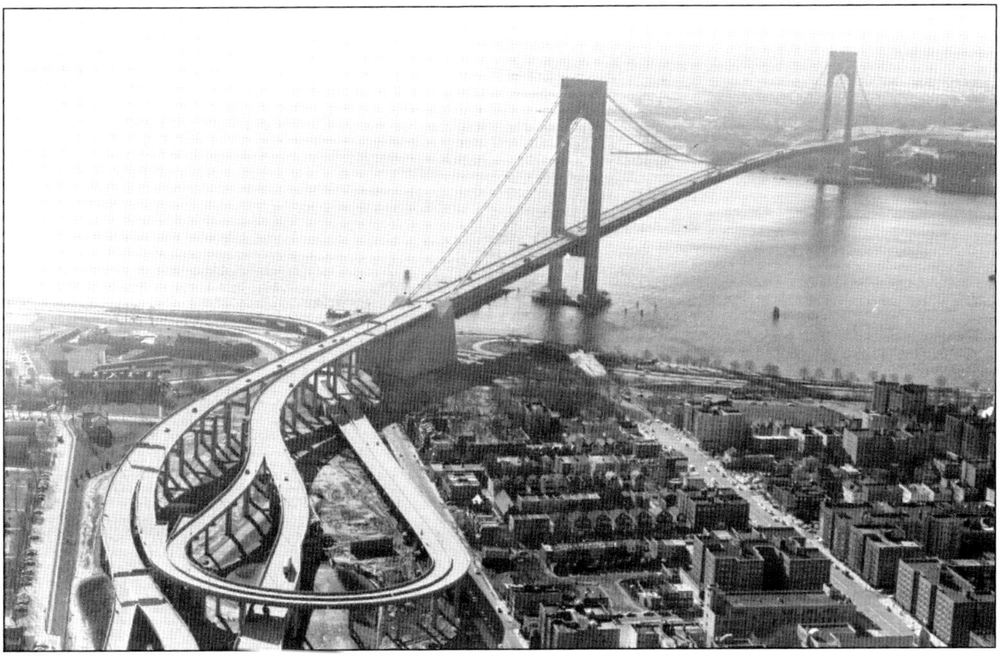

The Verrazano-Narrows Bridge connects Staten Island to Brooklyn, New York, and incorporates steel ropes manufactured at the Roebling mill. Roebling and Sons was owned by CF&I at the time of the bridge's construction. It was designated the longest suspension bridge in the world at its opening in 1964. The bridge's four main cables measure 7,205 feet. The cables were completed at a cost of $57 million.

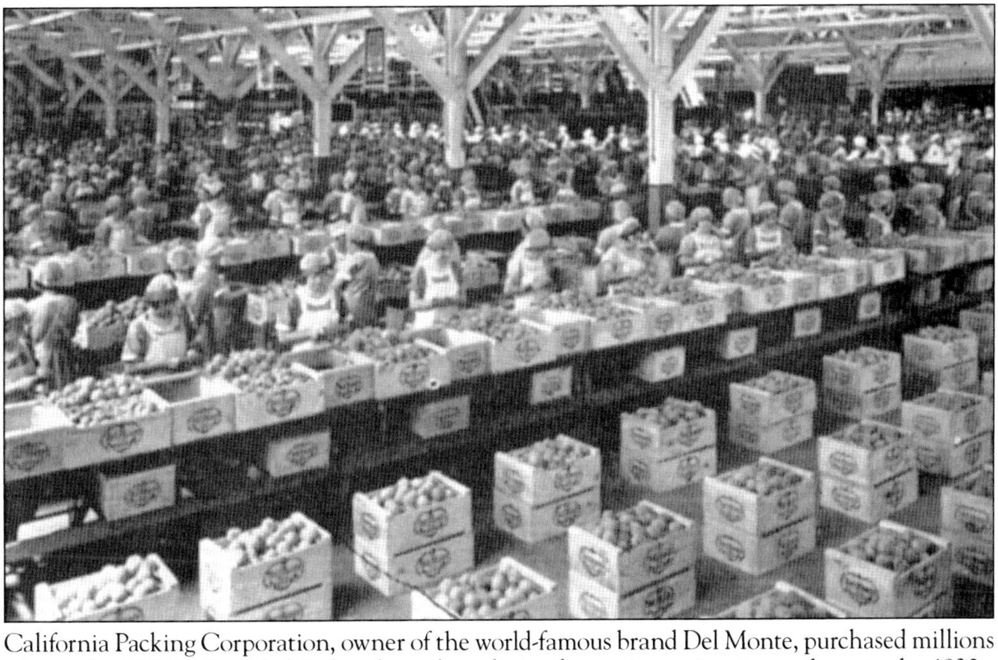

California Packing Corporation, owner of the world-famous brand Del Monte, purchased millions of pounds of CF&I-branded Colorado nails and wire for use in crating its products in the 1930s. Here, women at the California Packing Corporation's processing plant work with crates of produce that will be shipped to grocers around the country.

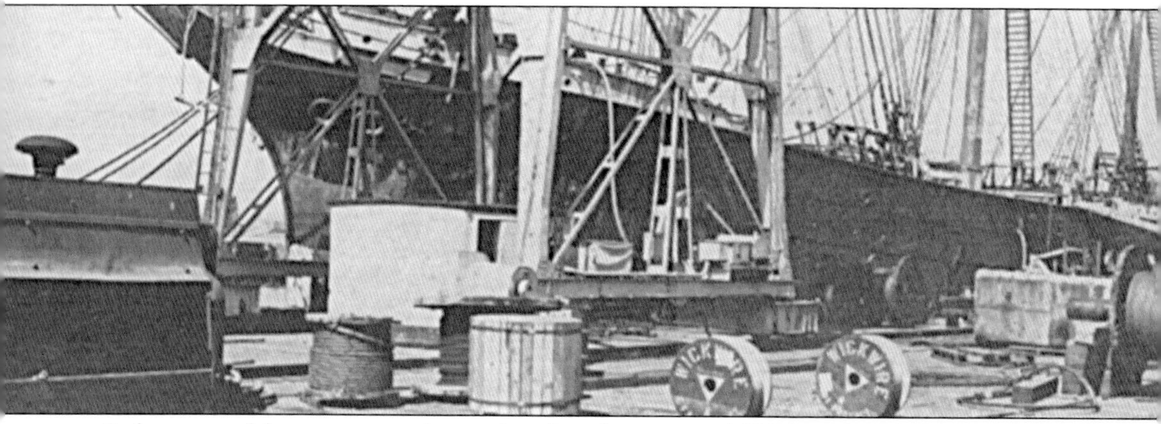

Perhaps one of the more unusual uses of steel products was in 1,900 feet of Wickwire Spencer Steel cables and flats to restore the hull and masts of the trade ship *Pacific Queen*. Originally built in 1886, it was one of the earliest produced steel ships, using rigging rope made of wire rather than the traditional hemp. The ship was also used to deliver lumber and salmon through the early 20th century. A CF&I newspaper printed in 1960 notes that while sailing the Pacific Ocean, the *Pacific Queen* was "the last vessel to fly the flag of the Hawaiian kingdom before statehood in 1959." Before retirement, the ship appeared in the 1935 motion picture *Mutiny on the Bounty*, starring Clark Gable.

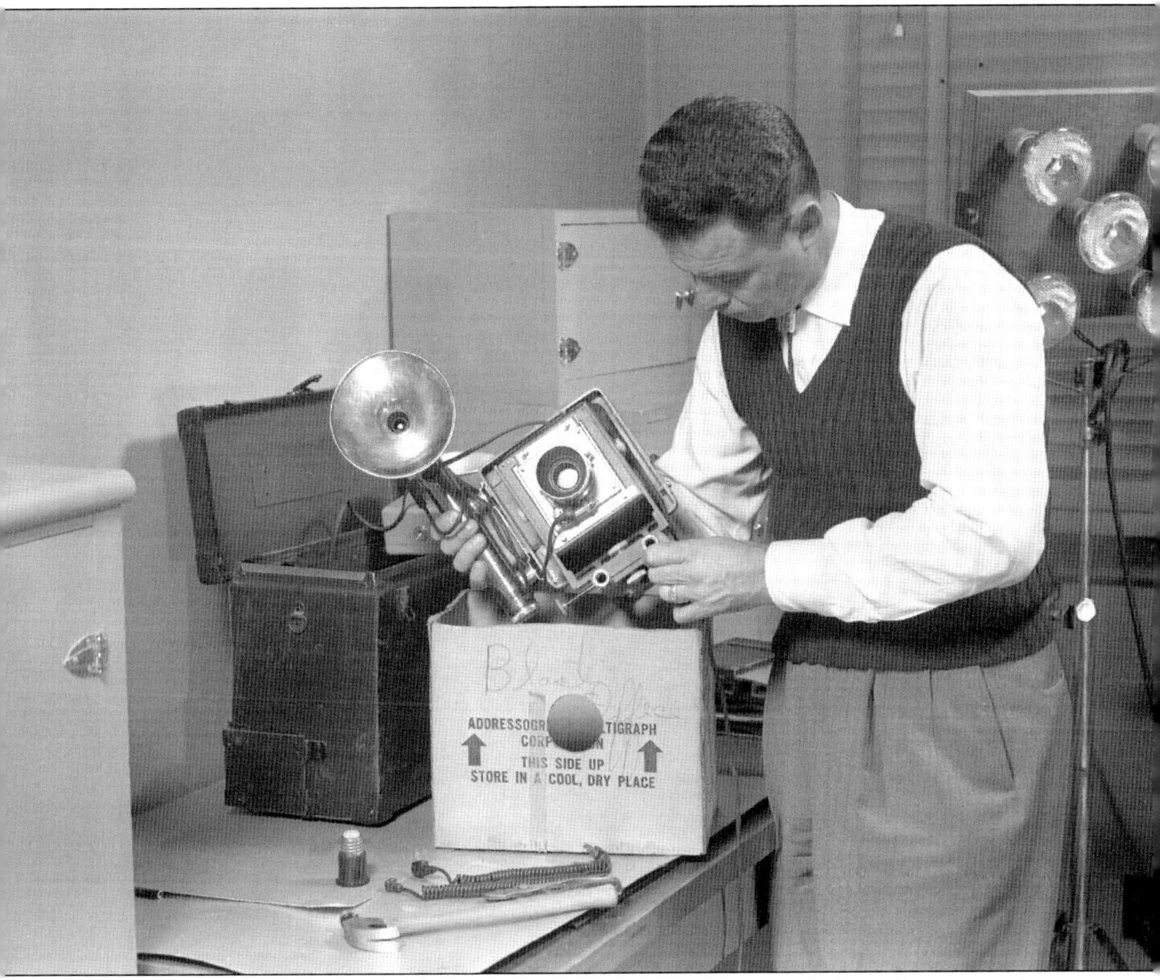

Photographic documentation at a company as large as CF&I was critical. Over the course of its 121-year history, CF&I photographers like Frank Sluder took tens of thousands of photographs that documented life in company towns, construction projects at the steel mill and CF&I subsidiaries, and even staff portraits. Images for other publications such as annual reports and sales brochures were also the responsibility of the photography department. The company also documented the civilian side of its operations, as photographs of workers and their families were taken for company publications such as the *CF&I Blast*. CF&I developed all of its own photographs on-site. CF&I also maintained its own film production crew and produced several company movies highlighting CF&I products and how they were made. These photographs are housed in the Steelworks Center's collection today, proving to be an invaluable asset in documenting the history of the company.

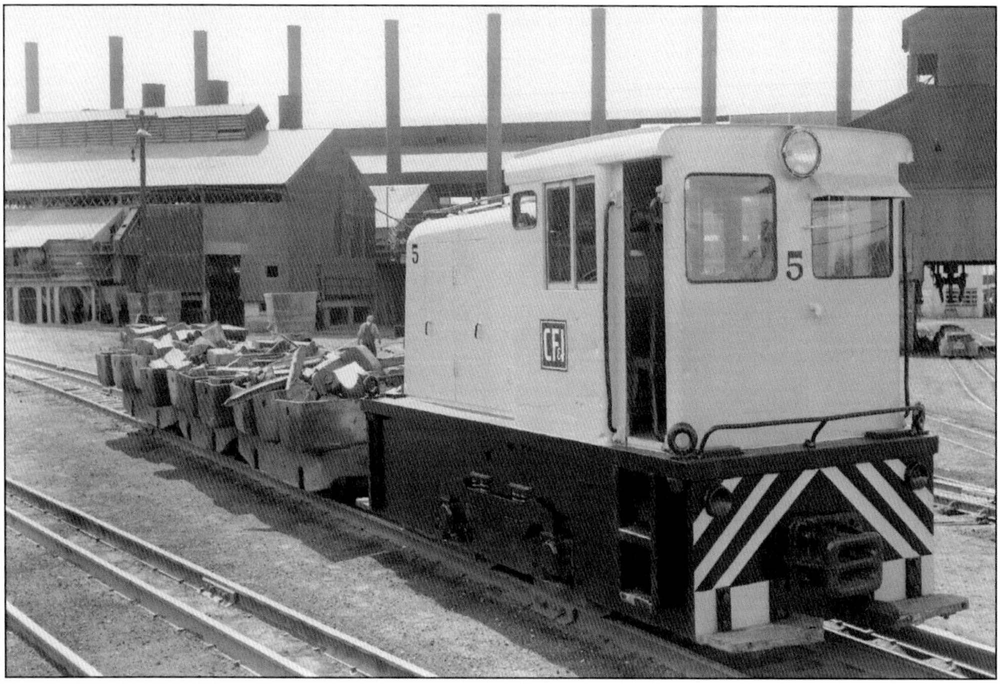

With the advent of the electric arc method of steelmaking, utilizing recycled metal to create new products, many of the subsidiary companies acquired in the 1960s and 1970s were purchased because of their ability to obtain scrap metal for the process. A dinky, or small engine, of the Colorado & Wyoming Railroad moves scrap metal from the scrapyard to the furnaces.

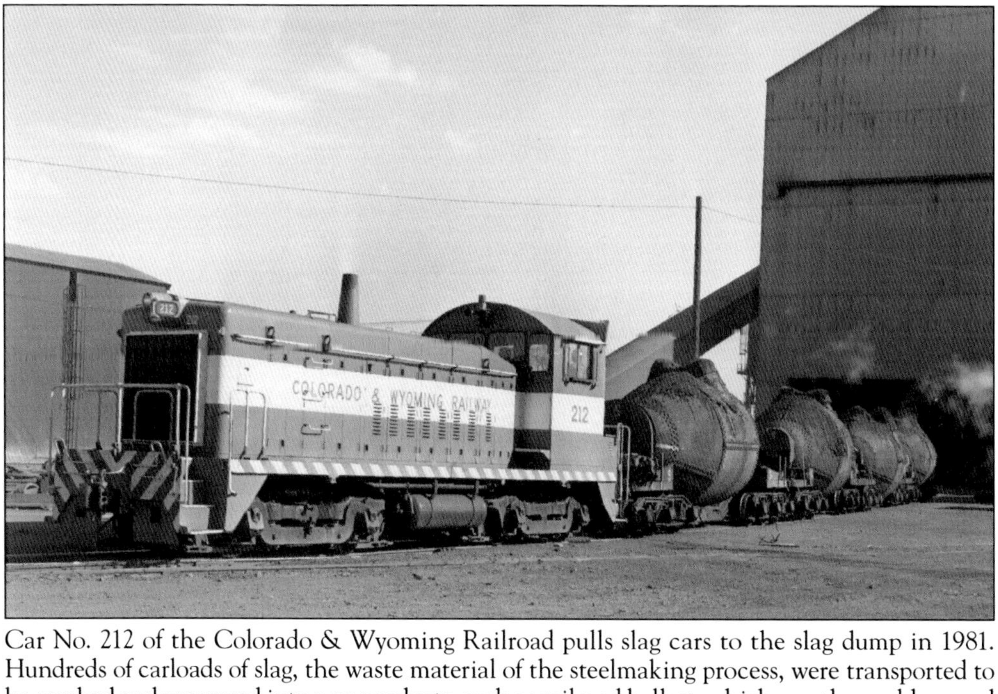

Car No. 212 of the Colorado & Wyoming Railroad pulls slag cars to the slag dump in 1981. Hundreds of carloads of slag, the waste material of the steelmaking process, were transported to be crushed and processed into new products, such as railroad ballast, which was then sold around the country.

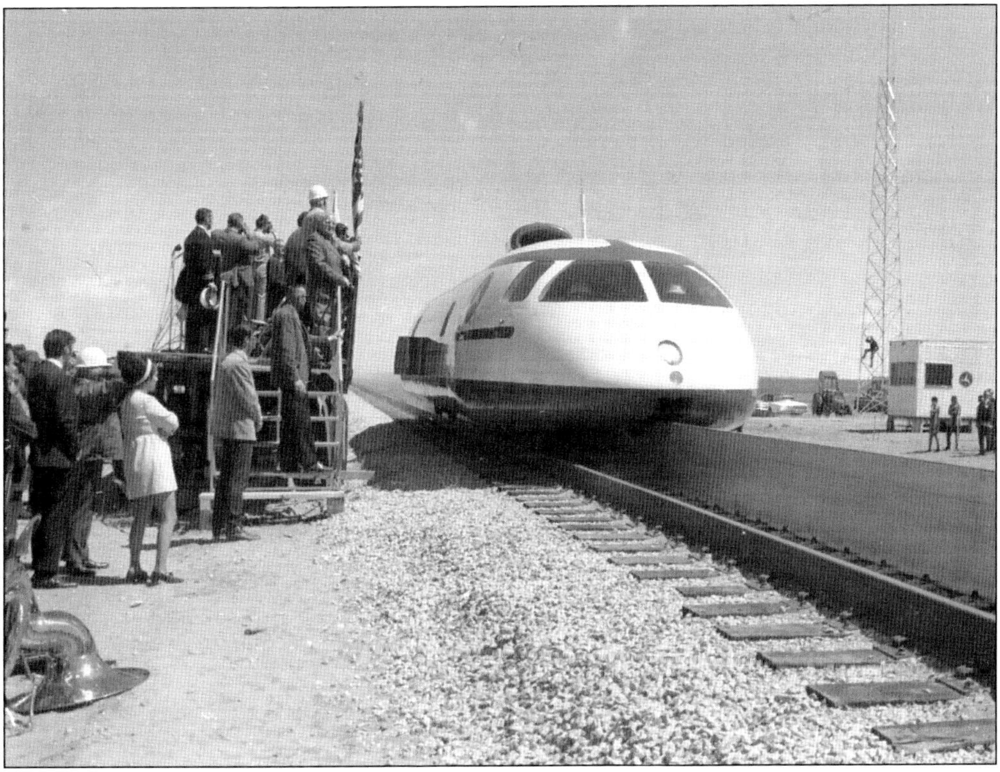

Since the 1970s, the Transportation Technology Center (TTC) in Pueblo has served as the site of transportation research and testing to serve America's railroad industry. Currently, the TTC conducts tests for all categories of freight and passenger rolling stock, vehicle and track components, and safety. This image shows the linear induction motor prototype vehicle in 1971. The vehicle rides on an aluminum fin between the rails made at CF&I's Pueblo mill.

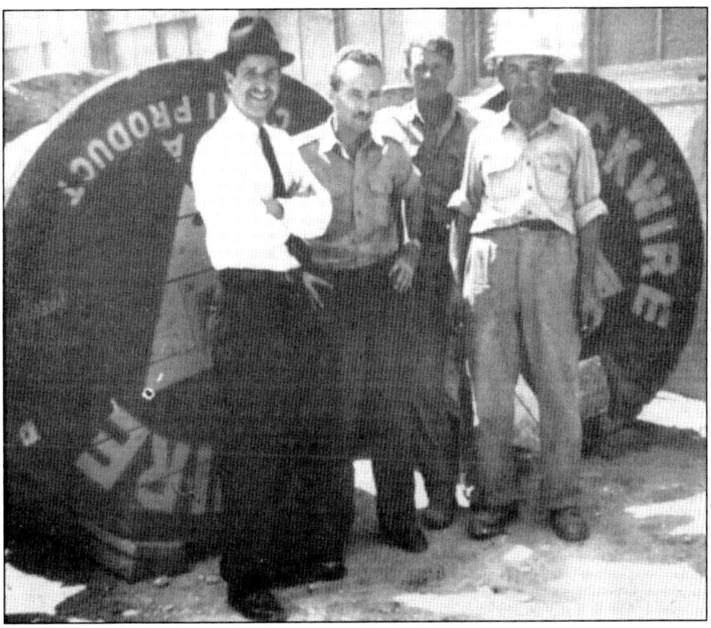

Steelmakers began to see customers with addresses around the world by the middle of the 20th century. From left to right, CF&I customers Raphael Ben Yosef (wearing necktie) and Abraham Padai (with hands on hips), along with two unidentified Israeli oil workers, pose with reels of wire rope manufactured at the Wickwire mill. Matzada Lapidot Drilling Company used the rope in drilling rigs, supplying about 10 percent of Israel's oil needs in 1958.

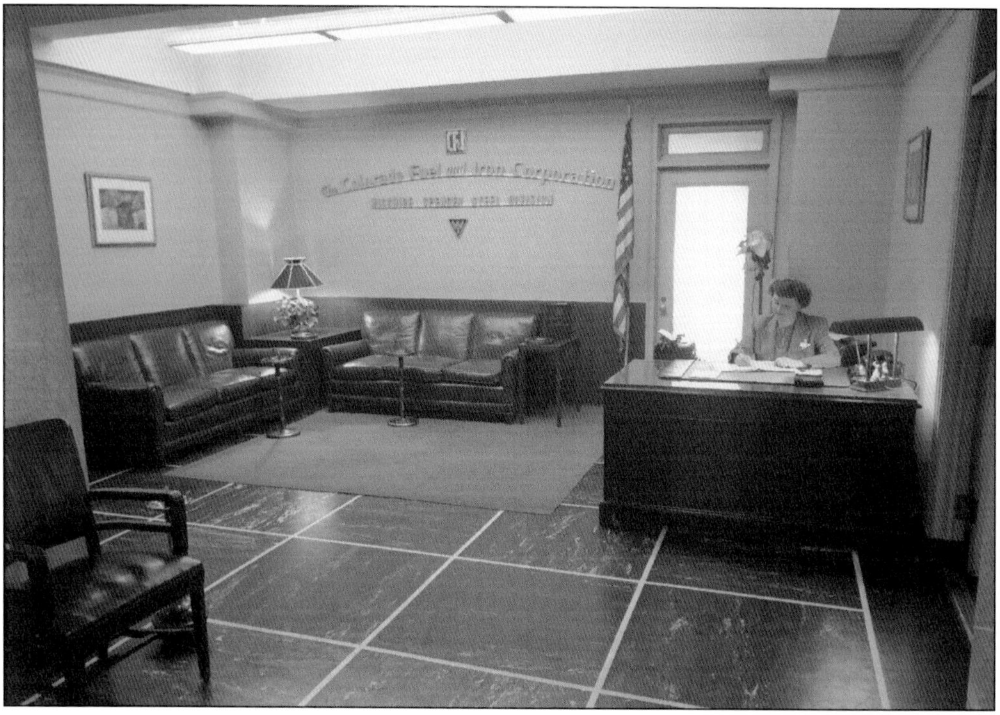

Through an exchange of stock, CF&I acquired Wickwire Spencer Steel's production facilities, including the furnaces and rolling mills in Buffalo, New York; wire mills in Clinton, Palmer, and Worcester, Massachusetts; and the American Wire Fabrics Corporation in Mount Wolf, Pennsylvania, in 1946. The merger of these subsidiaries and the Pueblo mill was timed to diversify the Pueblo mill's sales catalog, meeting the postwar demand for light-metal products. Publicity photographs show the interior of reception office and the exterior of the office around the time of the merger. With the company's diversified product base and greater reach to customers, the net income of CF&I increased by 12 percent in the first year of operation following the acquisition. CF&I operated Wickwire Spencer Steel until the early 1970s.

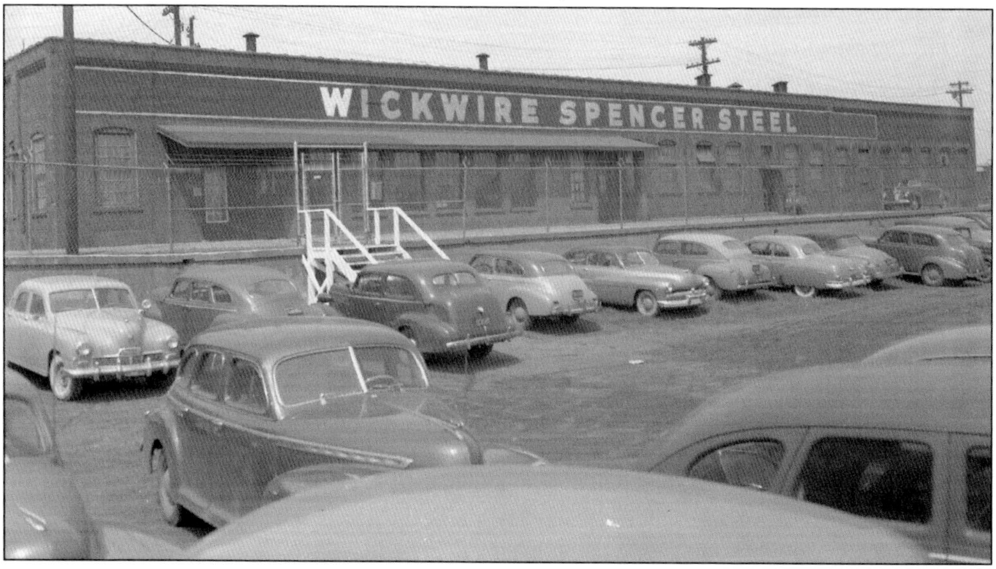

Eight

The Mill Today

Today, the steel mill in Pueblo is owned and operated by EVRAZ Rocky Mountain Steel, a subsidiary of one of the largest vertically integrated steel and mining companies in the world. EVRAZ is a leading producer of engineered steel products for rail, energy, and industrial enterprises. Using an electric arc furnace to melt scrap metal in one of the largest recycling operations in Colorado, the Pueblo plant produces around one million tons of rails, seamless pipe, rods, and bars annually. Though the mill is now only a fraction of the economic force that it once was, it is still an important and active participant in Pueblo's economy, employing around 1,000 people locally. EVRAZ and its employees are also important supporters of humanitarian and children's charities, museums, arts, and educational programs in the Pueblo area.

The current production buildings at the Pueblo plant utilize some of the most high-tech, state-of-the-art equipment in the industry. On the grounds outside of this modern facility, however, are the scattered remnants of forgotten buildings that CF&I once operated, some of which are now more than a hundred years old. Decades of neglect have left many of them in disrepair, while time, weather, and other factors have left others almost completely destroyed.

The authors wish to express their thanks to EVRAZ for allowing them to photograph a few select buildings that are no longer in use. The mill is designated as private property, and photography is normally prohibited, with strict regulations and tight security controlling access to the grounds.

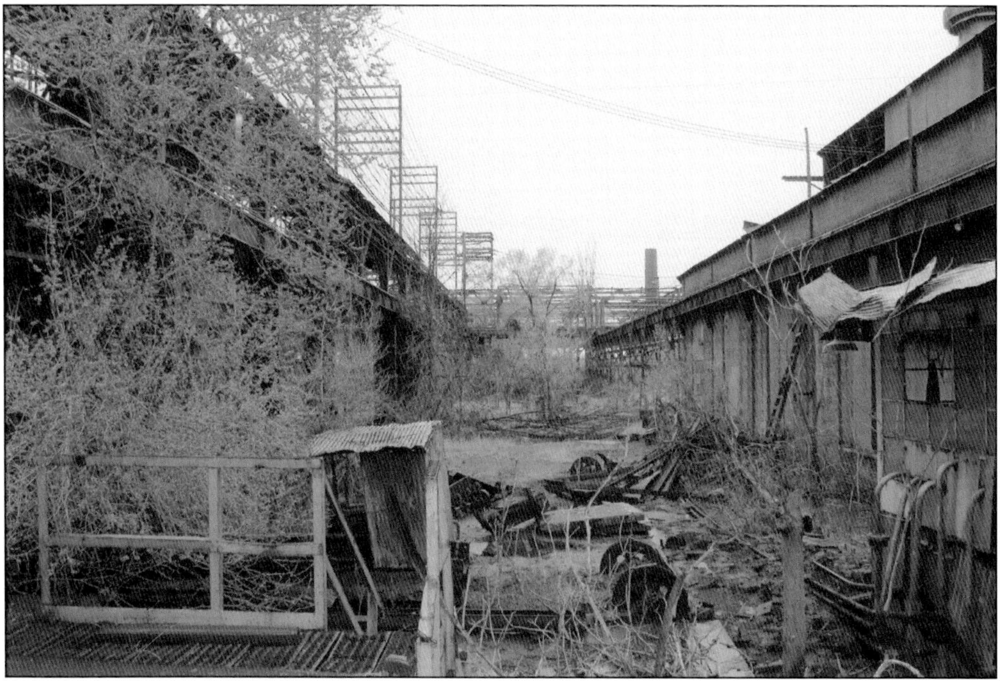

Time and weather are not the only forces affecting former CF&I buildings. There is also the reemergence of plants and animals that inhabited the region long before the arrival of industry. Trees, shrubs, and wildflowers are reclaiming the landscape, overcoming the steel buildings and equipment that people tend to think of as permanent. Many larger buildings are covered in plant life, and some even contain a small number of trees and shrubs growing inside of them, which are fed sunlight through holes in the buildings' partially collapsed ceilings. Antelope, raccoons, and deer are among the animals spotted on the grounds of the mill in recent years.

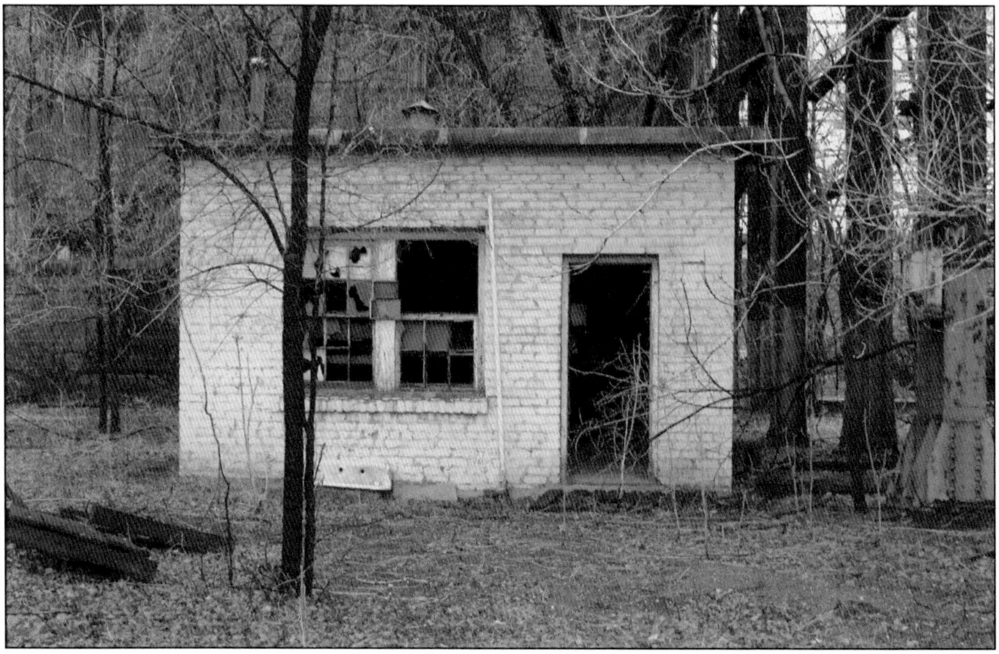

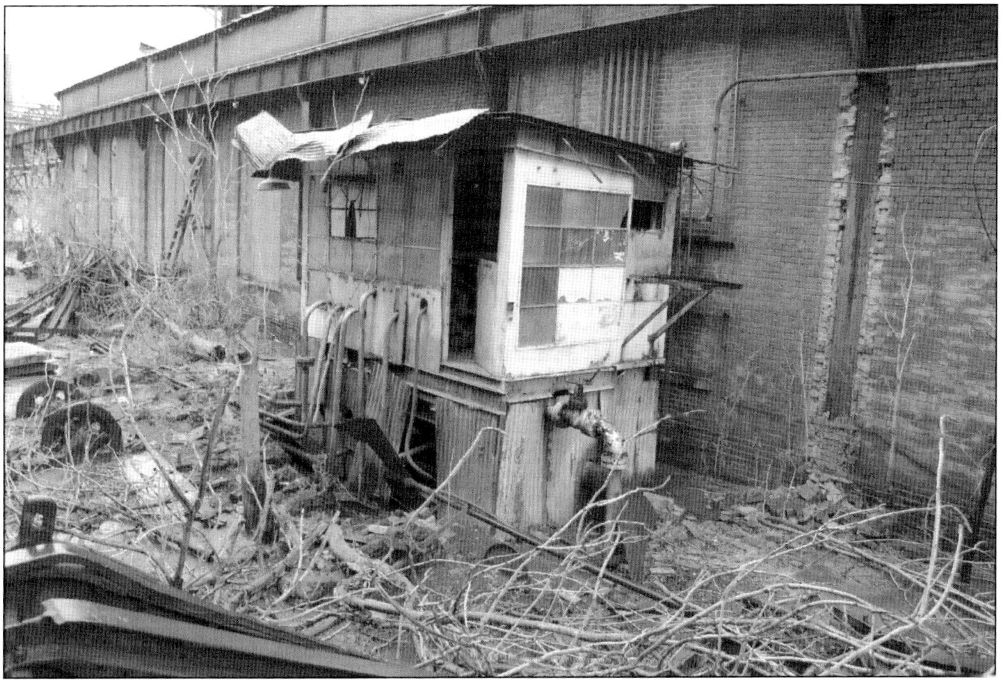

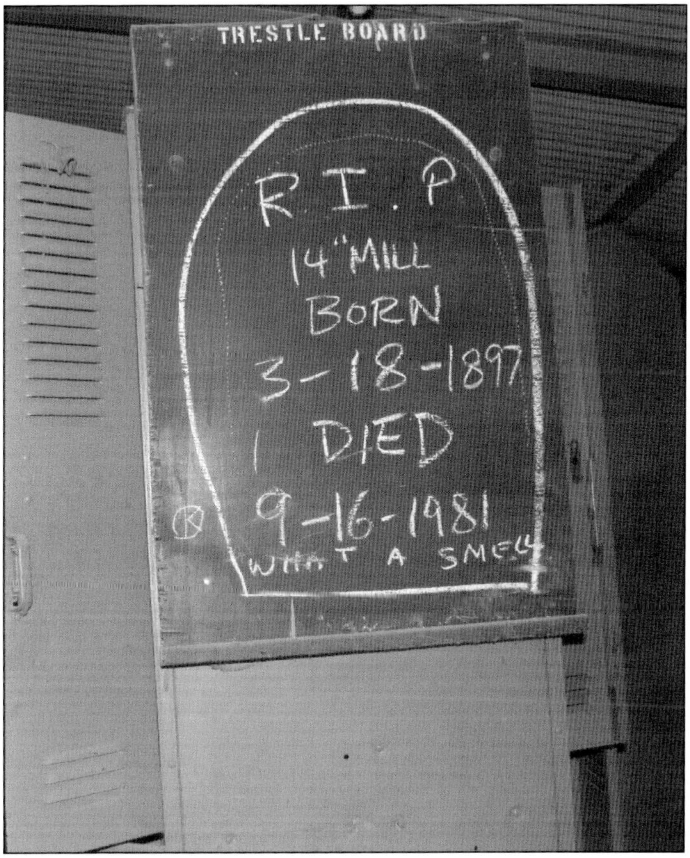

These photographs were taken in 2017 at the 14-inch and 25-inch mills, neither of which have been in operation since the 1980s. In addition to equipment needed to process solid steel billets, which would then be transferred to other departments for further processing, they also contained lunchrooms, changing rooms, and showers. Many of the mill's employees worked side by side in these buildings for decades and considered their workplace a home away from home. The pride employees took in their work and the bonds they created with each other within those walls were so meaningful that, when these buildings finally ceased production, workers often felt an extreme personal loss.

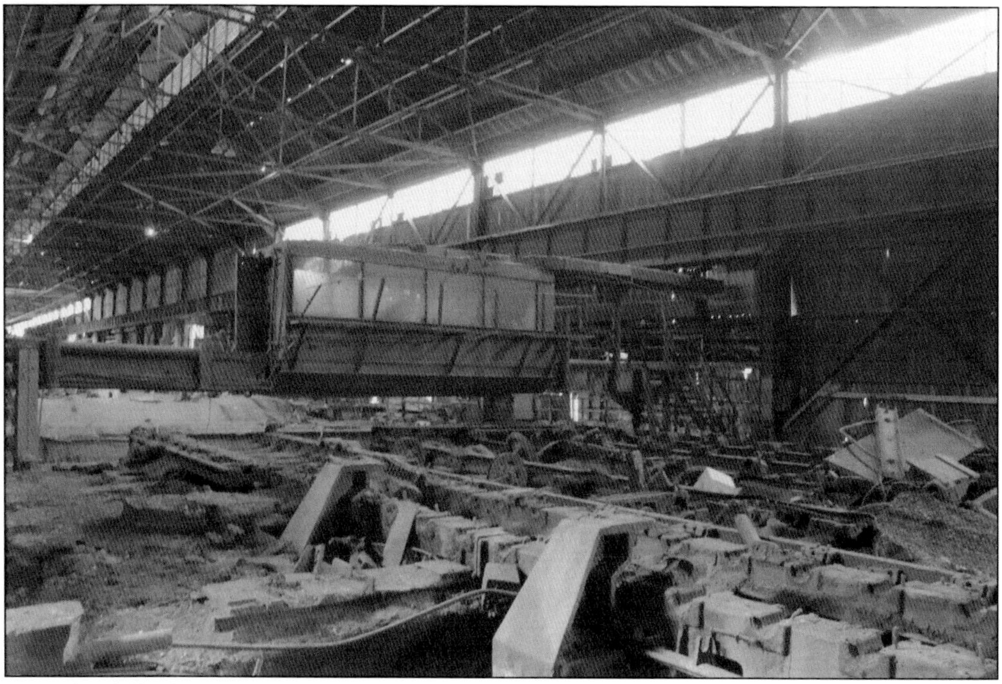

It can be difficult to comprehend what it was like working in some of these buildings simply by viewing them as they are today. Much of the machinery has been removed and reduced to scrap metal, while other equipment has crumbled into unidentifiable piles of twisted metal and bricks. The preservation of photographs from CF&I's past helps researchers understand the processes, conditions, and details of industrial work of the 19th and 20th centuries. These buildings, some of which measured in acres rather than square feet, actually contained smaller buildings inside of them, one of which can be seen here.

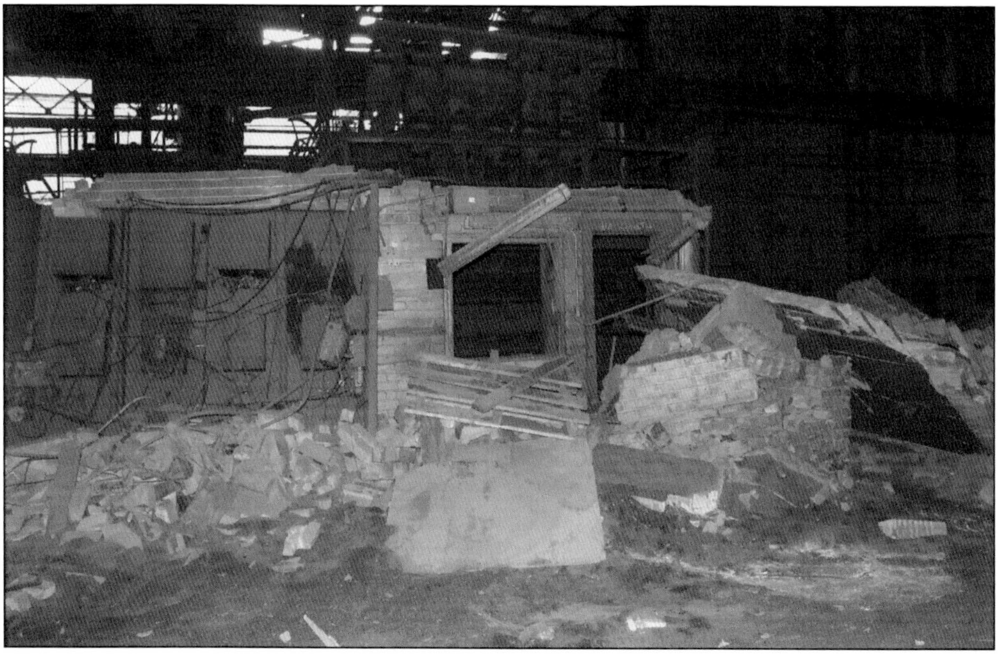

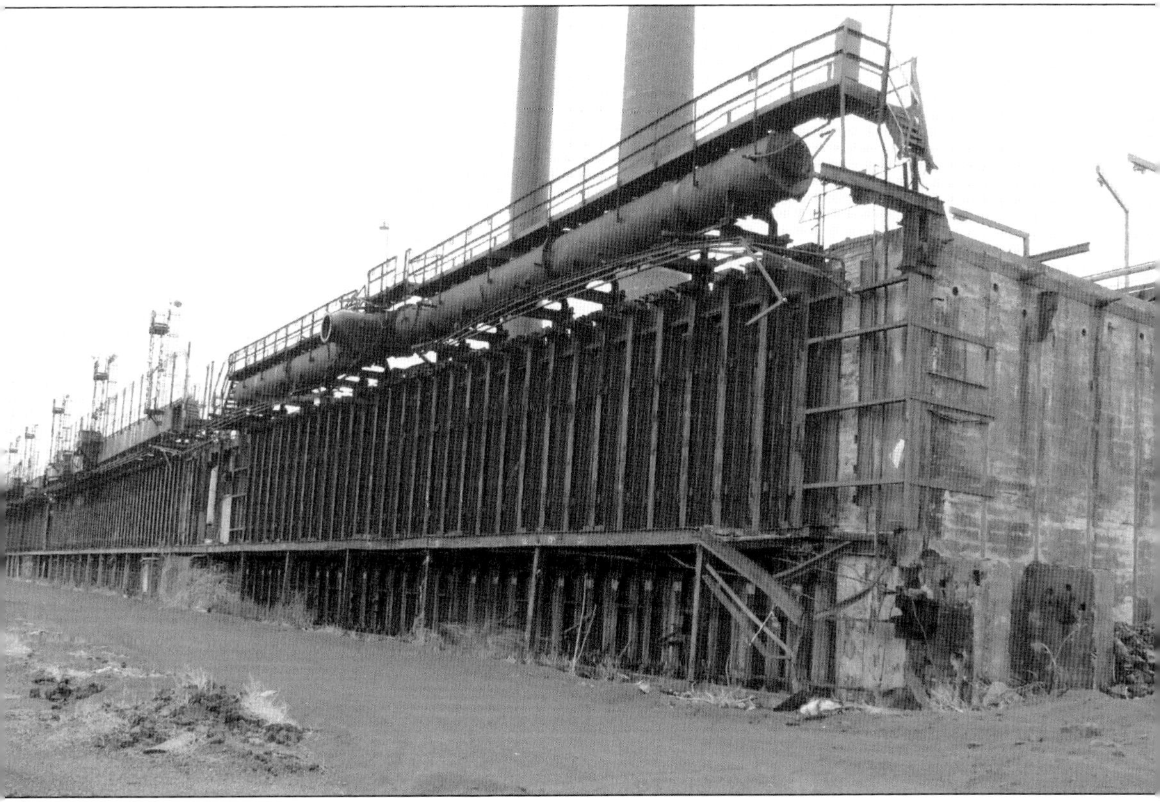

Due to environmental concerns, the former coke plant is currently in the process of a multiyear demolition program. Harmful particles of asbestos and lead, along with a variety of toxic chemicals, have built up in the plant's ovens, heating flues, and chambers over time, so the process of tearing it down is challenging and requires a great deal of preparation and care. Photographs contained in the Steelworks Center's archives show the construction of the coke plant nearly 100 years ago, so having the opportunity to take photographs of this and other structures at the mill coming down is both remarkable and bittersweet. Unlike for many historic buildings across the country, preserving those at the mill is nearly impossible due to environmental concerns and the presence of hazardous materials. Though some of these structures may not be considered visually appealing, they are a testament to the region's rich industrial history.

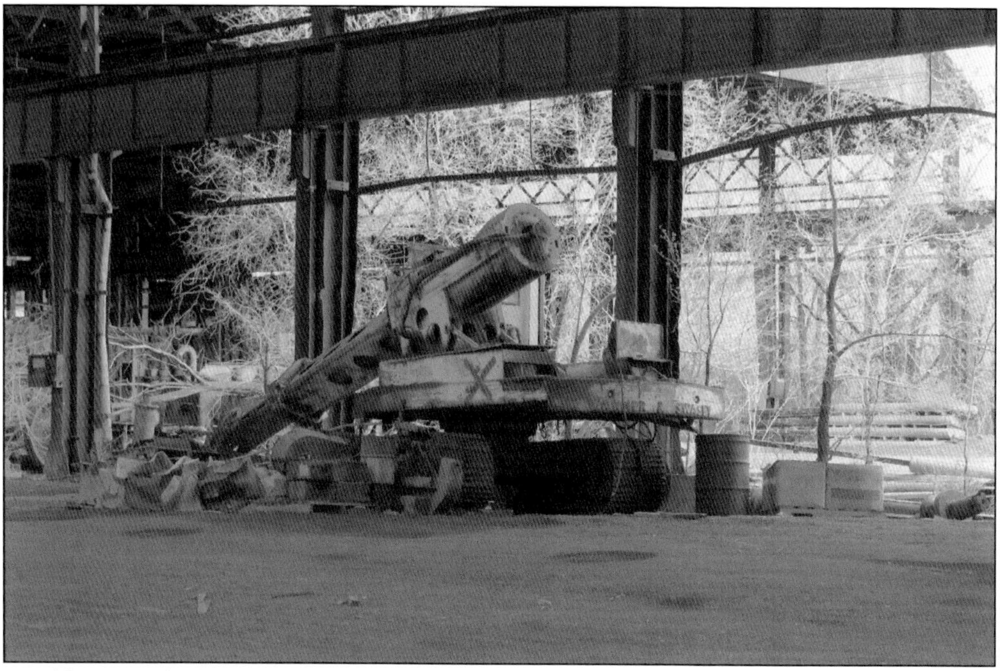

In addition to the historic buildings that remain on the property of the mill, there is also a lot of historic equipment. The crane pictured above, produced by Warner and Swasey in Cleveland, was discovered among a pile of rubble at the 25-inch mill. As a standard telescopic crane, it was likely used for a variety of purposes, but it now appears to be destined for the scrapyard. Davenport locomotives, like the one pictured below, were known as dinkies to mill and mine workers. These small diesel engines were used to haul loads of equipment, supplies, and materials short distances around the mill in Pueblo and at the coal and iron mines throughout the region. Like the Warner and Swasey crane, this dinky's days are probably numbered.

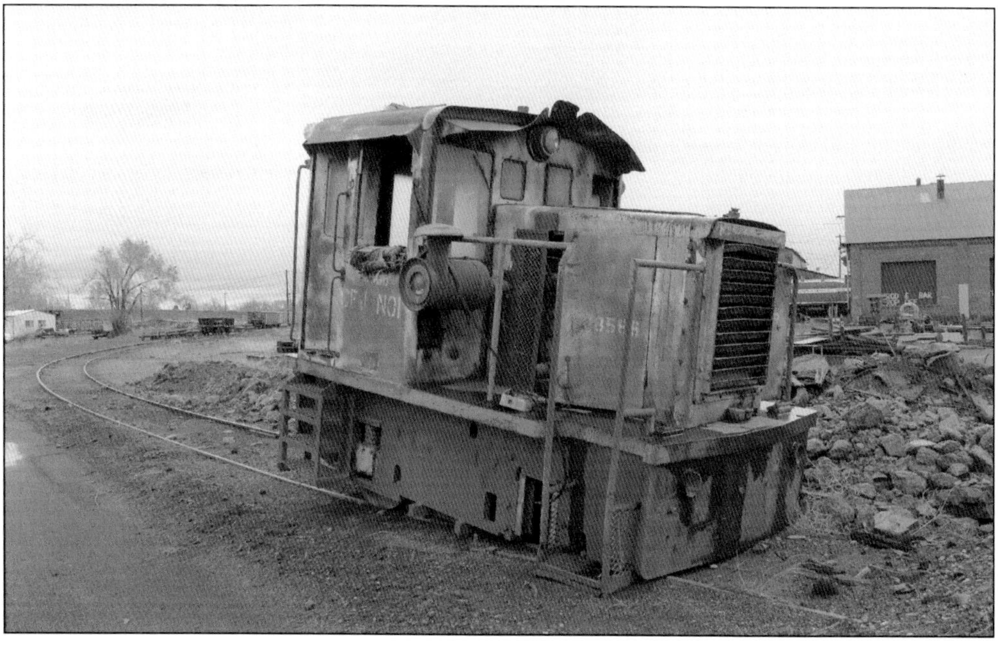

Though nature has reclaimed many of the production buildings on the grounds of the mill, operations continue uninterrupted in others. The 1970s saw the end of the basic oxygen furnace and the introduction of the electric arc furnace, which is still an important part of the process used for steel production at the Pueblo plant today. EVRAZ's electric arc furnace melts more than one million tons of scrap metal per year to meet orders in the rail, rod, and seamless tube mills. Production of rails for railroads continues after 140 years of operation. Construction of highways, bridges, and building foundations uses reinforcing bar products, and the oil and gas industry utilizes seamless tubing at wells all around the world. Due to security and safety regulations, these images of the electric arc furnace are from the 1980s.

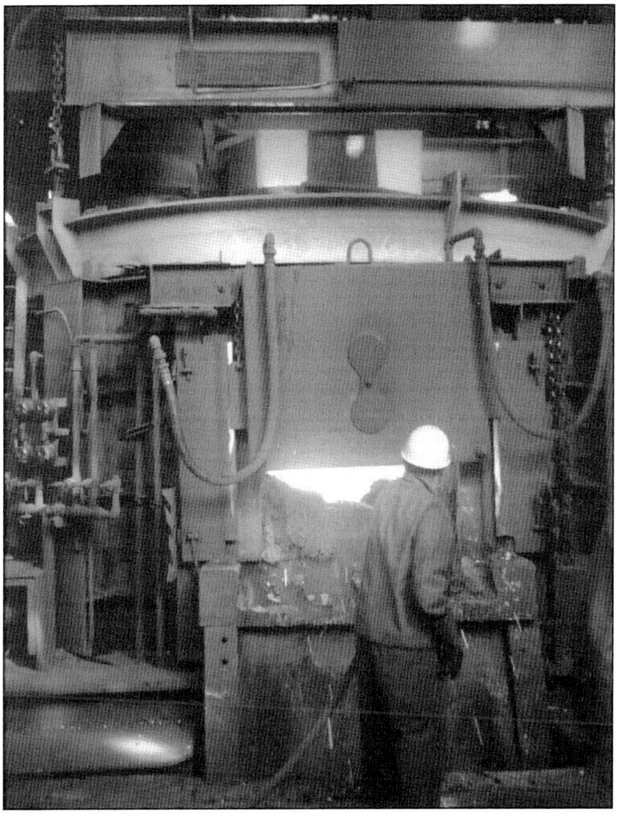

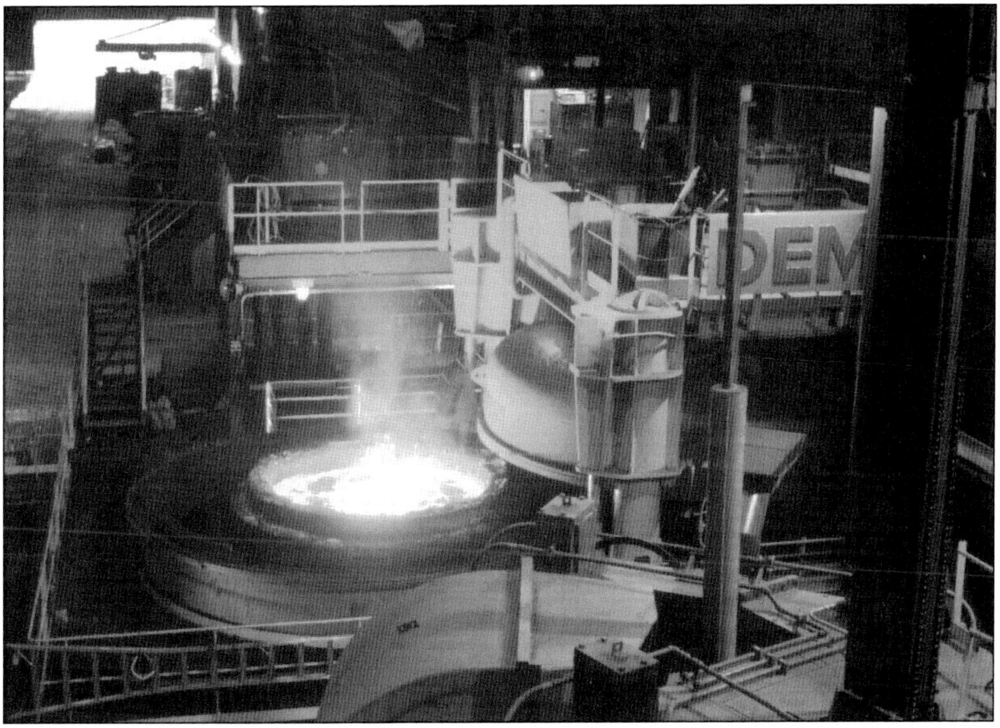

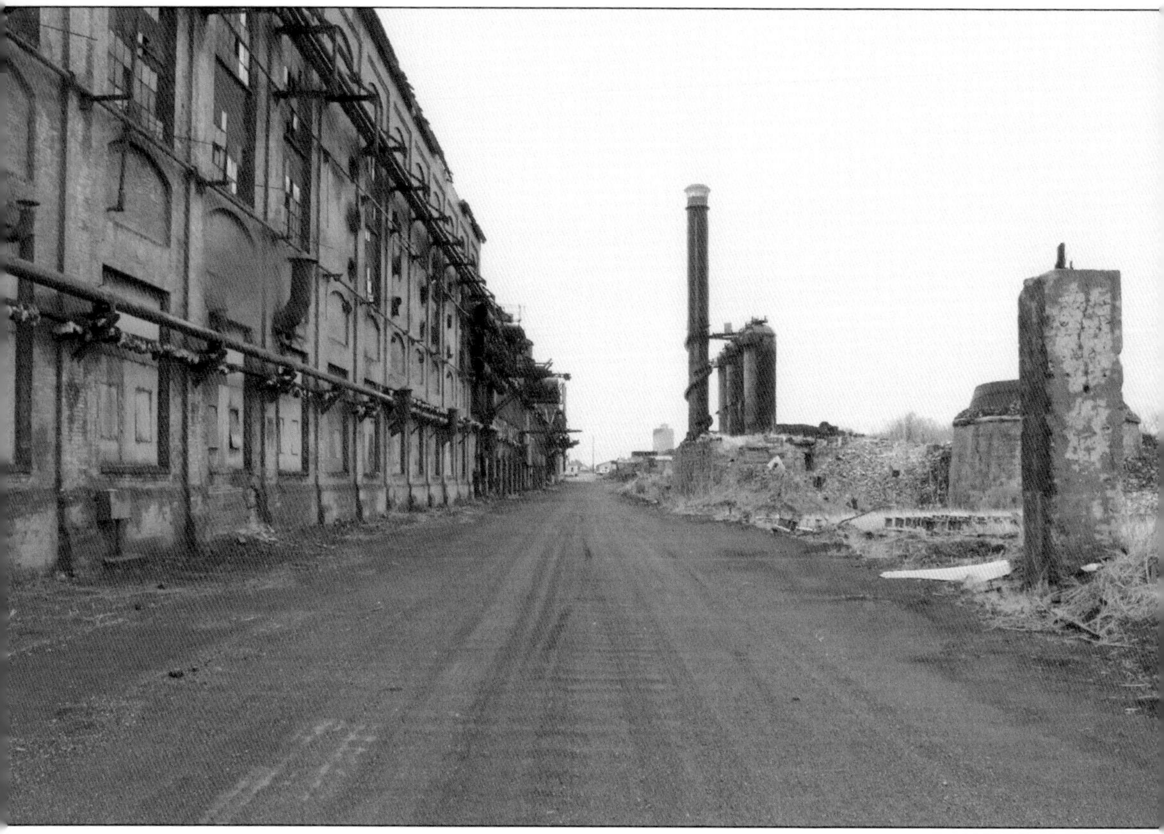

The Colorado Fuel and Iron Company once served as the largest employer and private landowner in Colorado and was a driving force in the industrialization of the entire western United States. The mill itself employed as much as 20 percent of Pueblo's workforce, and nearly every other business in the city depended on the company's payroll to survive. Troubles with the steel industry in the 1980s and CF&I's bankruptcy in the 1990s dealt a series of crushing blows to Pueblo's economy and nearly devastated the entire region. Over the past 30 years, however, Puebloans have managed to overcome these struggles by diversifying their economy, investing in tourism, the arts, and other cultural projects, and by expanding educational opportunities for their citizens. While Pueblo may not be the steel town it once was, it will never forget the incredible impact that the mill and its employees had on the town's unique history.

About the Steelworks Center of the West

In 2000, the Bessemer Historical Society was formed as a 501(c)(3) nonprofit organization by a group of Pueblo's concerned citizens. Its mission is to provide continuing education to the public through the preservation of the historic archives, artifacts, and buildings of the Colorado Fuel and Iron Company and related activities leading to the industrialization of the entire western United States. The organization began conducting business as the Steelworks Center of the West in 2014.

Corporate records, films, photographs, artifacts, maps, and drawings from the collection are housed in the historic main office building of the Colorado Fuel and Iron Company. This vast collection offers a wealth of information relating to labor history, the history of industry, mining, land and water resources, railroads, and corporate history. The collection also includes records of general historical interest and of personal employee history. It traces the history of the huge enterprise that was CF&I, which, in turn, is the history of Southern Colorado.

With generous funding from the National Endowment for the Humanities and many others, the organization is preserving these records, making them accessible to researchers and interpreting them in exhibits at the Steelworks Museum. This archive is one of a handful of such collections in the United States.

Future plans include an expanded museum and a state-of-the-art research center to serve scholars, students, family historians, and lifelong learners. To learn more about the Steelworks Center of the West, or for online access to selections from the collection, please visit our website at www.steelworks.us.

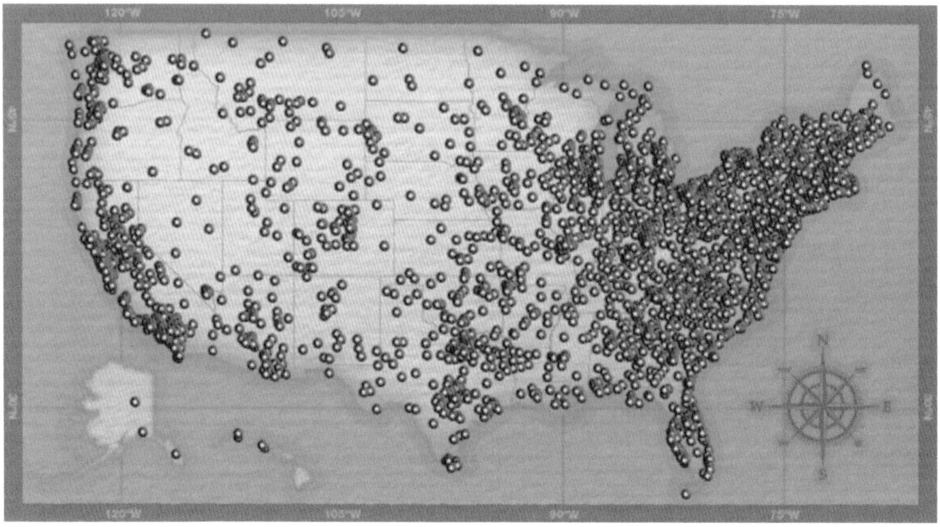